UNDERSTANDING
EDUCATION POLICY

UNDERSTANDING
EDUCATION POLICY

CHRIS ROLPH

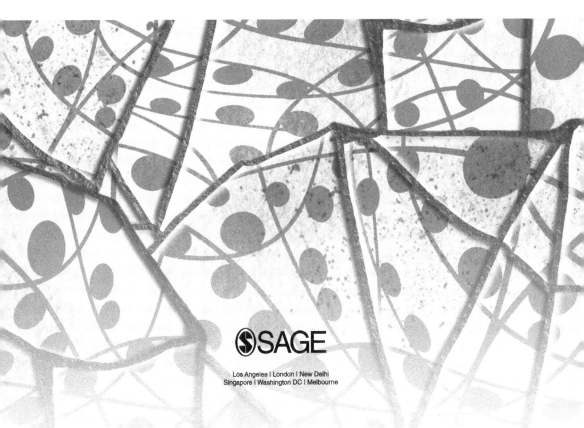

![SAGE]

Los Angeles | London | New Delhi
Singapore | Washington DC | Melbourne

Los Angeles I London I New Delhi
Singapore I Washington DC I Melbourne

SAGE Publications Ltd
1 Oliver's Yard
55 City Road
London EC1Y 1SP

SAGE Publications Inc.
2455 Teller Road
Thousand Oaks, California 91320

SAGE Publications India Pvt Ltd
B 1/I 1 Mohan Cooperative Industrial Area
Mathura Road
New Delhi 110 044

SAGE Publications Asia-Pacific Pte Ltd
3 Church Street
#10-04 Samsung Hub
Singapore 049483

Library of Congress Control Number: 2022944445

British Library Cataloguing in Publication data

A catalogue record for this book is available from the British Library

Editor: James Clark
Editorial assistant: Diana Alves
Production editor: Victoria Nicholas
Marketing manager: Lorna Patkai
Cover design: Naomi Robinson
Typeset by: TNQ Technologies
Printed in the UK

ISBN 978-1-5297-5774-3
ISBN 978-1-5297-5773-6 (pbk)

At SAGE we take sustainability seriously. Most of our products are printed in the UK using responsibly sourced papers and boards. When we print overseas we ensure sustainable papers are used as measured by the PREPS grading system. We undertake an annual audit to monitor our sustainability.

For Catherine, Rachel and Alice, who have given me a better education than I could ever have imagined.

CONTENTS

ABOUT THE AUTHOR

Chris Rolph is the Director of Nottingham Institute of Education at Nottingham Trent University. It has a long history of training school teachers, and is a recognized centre for the study of education. Chris has taught on a range of undergraduate and postgraduate courses, usually contributing to modules on education policy and practice. He supervises a number of doctoral candidates and is an active researcher, with interests in accountability and performativity, and the outworking of education policy into practice.

Before joining Nottingham Trent Chris spent more than 20 years teaching physics in secondary schools. He was a subject leader and Advanced Skills Teacher before becoming a headteacher; he then led three schools over the next 13 years. During this time, he carried out small research projects and published several papers relating to educational policy.

ACKNOWLEDGEMENTS

I would like to thank my colleagues and friends at Nottingham Trent University, whose insights, comments and criticisms have helped to crystallize my own thinking and shape some of the content of this book. My understanding of educational policy has been informed by three decades working in the sector, and I am hugely grateful to the many teachers and leaders who have helped me to grasp the principles of policy and reflect them in practice. As a leader myself it was important to hear the voices of those who have been affected by my own policies, and I am indebted to them for their candour which has illuminated the realities of policy enactment.

I am grateful to those who have provided information for the case studies in this book. Space permits only a tiny glimpse of the work in which they have been and continue to be immersed, but I hope I have provided a small window into their worlds. I am immensely appreciative of the helpful and constructive comments of Diana, my editor, and the support from Sage which has helped to make writing an enjoyable and formative process.

Finally, I must thank my family, who have tolerated my being shut away in a darkened room when we could have been having fun together. They have topped up my coffee, proof-read my writing, and rescued me from the cat who always likes to contribute. I hope that I have done justice to everyone's investment.

1

INTRODUCTION

CONTENTS

This chapter includes:

- An introduction to education and politics, and a discussion of why the two are inextricably entwined.
- A brief description of neoliberalism as it will be interpreted throughout this book.
- An examination of what is meant by policy, described through the ideas of policy as principles, power, practice and paperwork.
- A summary of policy enactment: the process of turning policy into behaviours and practices.
- An overview of the remaining chapters of the book.

INTRODUCTION

In the ancient world, Aristotle identifies two distinct spheres of life: the private domain of the household, *oikos*, and the public domain, *polis*. The *oikos* is identified as the place where education begins – where children start to learn about ethics and morality, and the basic necessities of life – but Aristotle locates schools in the domain of the *polis* – in the political sphere. Two millennia later we can still recognise the difference between the foundational learning that occurs in the home and the formal learning that happens in schools (and by extension, universities, colleges and pre-school settings). If we agree that schools and other educational providers exist in Aristotle's public sphere rather than the home, then we are forced to accept that education is, by definition, politics. Plato, Aristotle's teacher and founder of the Athenian Academy in 387 BC, outlined a theoretical and philosophical basis for education, which he saw as the responsibility of the State for the good of society – and therefore inescapably political (Turan, 2011). Whether we approach it from the perspectives of pragmatism or philosophy, it is impossible to deny that the development of education as conceived by Western civilisation has been intractably bound with the politics of the day.

For Aristotle, children of the *oikos are* 'unfinished' in every respect (Tress, 1997), and need the education offered by school to transform them into cultivated participants in the public domain. While some, such as the political philosopher Hannah Arendt, seek to position the school as a necessary intervening transition point between home and the world (1961, p. 188, first published 1954), the undeniable fact that corporate education is organised and arranged by societal structures – thereby inevitably fashioned by the values of society – positions school solidly in the *polis*. That the leaders and representatives of society will shape both the nature and content of schooling further underlines the concept of education as a political construct. This is as true today as it was 2000 years ago, when Aristotle determined that some studies are useful and necessary for adult working life, while others should be provided simply because they are noble and liberal. Controversy over this balance continues, and because society's leaders determine what is of value and what is taught, the debate is political in every sense.

Reflection on the views of the Ancient Greeks is informative because it demonstrates the intimate relationship between education and politics, and the timeless nature of the ensuing debates. It also sets today's tussles in the context of hundreds of years of history: no policy is developed in a vacuum. There is no blank slate on which to write new policy, free from the influence of history and precedent. Even in states such as Estonia, which had the dubious luxury of re-establishing democracy and developing new policy from scratch after regaining independence in 1991, there are echoes of history both ancient and modern in reforms that were evolutionary as much as they were revolutionary (Lees, 2016). In the same way, it is impossible to consider education in isolation from the bigger political and historical picture. Education only exists, and can therefore only be studied, within the temporal and spatial contexts of politics itself.

Altercations over education relate to its purpose as well as how it is done. Opinions on the purpose of education are diverse and rooted in political perspectives, as we shall discover, but there is a theme that appears to be common across the political spectrum: freedom. The notion of freedom is expressed in different ways: the Brazilian sociologist, Paulo Freire, discussed freedom as emancipation from oppression in his foundational text, *Pedagogy of the Oppressed* (2018, originally 1970). Half a globe away and from the other end of the political spectrum, Margaret Thatcher, as leader of the opposition in the British parliament, asserted that 'personal freedom and economic freedom are indivisible' (1976). Thatcher's view of freedom was of individual independence and autonomy, and institutional liberation from state control – a reaction to her perception of British socialism and the very basis of neoliberal education policy for the next four decades.

NEOLIBERALISM: THE ONLY WAY?

For the purposes of this book we will use Stedman Jones's simple definition of neoliberalism:

> transatlantic neoliberalism is … the free market ideology based on individual liberty and limited government that connected human freedom to the actions of the rational, self-interested actor in the competitive marketplace.
>
> (2012, p. 2)

For Margaret Thatcher, the free market reigned supreme, not simply because of promised economic efficiency but also because in her view it supported a moral and just society (Berlinski, 2008, p. 177). Her belief that there was no alternative to regulating through the power of the market was taken up by her immediate successor and reinvigorated in 2013 by David Cameron, though it seems it was adopted in the intervening years by New Labour as well. Tony Blair came to power on a 'third way' promise of lower taxes, fewer people reliant on benefits and a crackdown on young offenders – if not stealing Conservative policy then at least continuing its principles.

This unwavering sense of direction was not unique to the United Kingdom. Daniel Stedman Jones's definition is of a transatlantic philosophy, and in general it would be fair to say that capitalism as expressed through neoliberalism has been the dominant force in the majority of the developed western world. In 2013, 'il n'y a pas d'alternative' was a sentiment shared by the French Prime Minister and the managing director of the International Monetary Fund, supporting similar statements by prominent European leaders (cited in Séville, 2017). As well as driving economic decisions, neoliberalism infiltrated other aspects of society, including education. The effects of neoliberalism have been more subtle than simply the privatisation of services that were previously in the public domain, with the language of target setting and accountability pervading every aspect of life, such that it seems to have become the unquestioned norm. The obsession with quantifying and measuring is ostensibly justified by the need to provide a degree of informed choice for the 'rational actor' in the competitive market, and the pervasive nature of neoliberalism in education is giving rise to a global marketplace for middle class cosmopolitans, particularly in Higher Education (Ball and Nikita, 2014).

There are, of course, dissenters, in the field of education as in other spheres. The educational establishment was highly resistant in the early years of neoliberalism, but to a large degree has now adopted many of its principles. One might argue that this has been driven by necessity rather than choice, but nonetheless educational providers embody commodification and competition to the extent that almost everyone involved – students, teachers, parents – begin to believe that there really is no viable alternative to the neoliberal mainstream (de Lissovoy, 2013).

From 2010 onwards, English neoliberalism in education has been tempered or complemented by the rise of neoconservatism. Apparently at odds with the neoliberal principle of a weak state, neoconservatism relies on a strong state to support the ideals of traditionalism. Policymakers seem content to settle into a form of dynamic equilibrium which allows for choice in the market to be supported by accountability frameworks, while at the same time centralising state control to maintain traditional values. This harking back to better times represents a point of divergence from other nations, though there are signs that some are following where the United Kingdom has blindly led, and while we may be tempted to think that neoliberalism is ubiquitous, it is not impossible to find nations that are successfully demonstrating policy arising from alternative ideologies (Apple, 2006).

EDUCATION POLICY

It should be straightforward to define policy, in particular, as it relates to education. Superficially we might consider policy to be a set of rules or guidelines: *principles* that govern the various agents involved in educational processes. Almost immediately we recognise that even this simple approach introduces complications because those agents are engaged in activity, so policy must also be about their *practice*. Furthermore, if policymakers are defining rules and boundaries for practitioners to follow, then policy inevitably involves the exercise of *power*. And policy is frequently referred to in concrete terms rather than the abstract, usually in the form of a document – so we might think about policy as *paper*.

POLICY AS PRINCIPLES

Political ideologies, which may be relatively vague and even unarticulated by those who espouse them, give rise to frameworks of principles which, if adhered to, would support the ideological ambitions. Critics of those principles might refer to them as dogma, while supporters would distance themselves from this term and argue that their principles are 'evidence-based'. Such assertions are usually contentious, and it can be argued that research might inform policy at best, recognising that principles sit within a contemporary social, political and historical context, and that policymakers are riddled with prejudice, experience, values and ideas (Bridges et al., 2009). Be that as it may, a scaffold of principles serves as policy, since it informs and constrains behaviour and action. In the case of education, the principle of informed choice is a policy lever that drives accountability and supports the neoliberal ideal of the market regulating itself – whether or not education can truly be considered as a marketplace. The principle that choice gives rise to improvement has been described as an 'assumption': there is evidence to suggest that choice is limited to certain social classes, and that parents prefer a school close to home (Burgess et al., 2015), but the principle has stood the test of time and remains a core plank of education policy in the neoliberal age.

POLICY AS POWER

It is perhaps self-evident that the outworking of policy is seen in the exercise of power if it compels individuals to behave in a way which they would not have chosen to do (this does not necessarily imply resistance, merely that at times it is convenient to allow others to do the thinking and decision-making, and then to follow policy). Policy can be used to high-light power relationships, but it can also allow for depersonalisation of power and decision-making: a leader could imply that while they don't really agree with a particular course of action, the policy dictates it and therefore it must be done. In the same way policy can act as the source of authority such that hierarchy is unnecessary: a group of individuals may resort to policy to guide their decision-making when there is no established authority figure to set their direction (Bell and Stevenson, 2006). Ultimately those who define policy exert power over those who follow policy and, in education at least, it is rare that policy is determined collectively: at best, leaders are elected democratically so that they may set policy for the electorate. There is therefore an inevitable reliance on a political elite, and a consequent hierarchy of power. A frequently seen example of policy as power in schools is uniform. It is for the 'governing board' of a school to determine if it has a uniform, and if so what it is, but parents and children have a duty to comply, and school staff have a duty to enforce it. Countless children will have discovered that they cannot appeal to the logic that inadequate uniform does not affect their learning, and nor can they resort to any individual to plead their case, for the power rests within the policy itself: it is sufficient to say that you have to wear school uniform because that is what the policy says.

POLICY AS PRACTICE

We can conceive of policy as practice in two ways: first that behavioural norms can define policy; and second that policy will be practised as people apply its principles to their actions. In the first case it is through custom and practice that policy is constructed – not from ideological principles but simply because 'we always do it like this'. Policy that evolves in this way may go unnoticed and unchallenged until a change of personnel, in particular leadership, causes someone to ask, why? Engrained habits and behaviours that have become institutional policy are no less strong for want of articulation and they may be difficult to challenge, exhibiting their own power over those who might want to change the status quo.

The alternative sense of policy as practice is in the working out of policy in actions, whether by policy enforcers or policy subjects: those whose lives are affected by the policy. An educational example might be a school's homework policy, which has no life of its own and no meaning unless teachers make it happen. It is through the practice of teachers setting and marking homework, and students doing the tasks (perhaps with reinforcement of parents) that the policy has meaning. This practice forms policy whether or not it is written down as a document. Where policy is specifically defined and then turned into action, we will use the term 'policy enactment'.

POLICY AS PAPER

Finally we consider what Ball (1993a) would call policy texts: the encoding of policy in written form. This may be at the highest level, in national legislation, or as simple as a list of classroom rules in a primary schoolroom. In the first instance we might expect policy on paper to be the authoritative source of policy: where it is clearly described and defined, its limits and boundaries established and the extent of its influence made clear, one might think that policy thus delineated might be crystal clear and non-negotiable. Of course this is an overly simplistic interpretation when we recognise that even black and white policy papers sit within the complexity of a social structure. As Ball eloquently points out, policy texts are doubly at risk of misinterpretation and misunderstanding. First, the intents of the authors (and there are often more than one, which adds to the complexity) may not be adequately translated to the text. Construction of policy often involves debate and discussion, and hence compromise, yielding a blurred understanding even at the point of printing. Second, of course, the policy text is interpreted by its readers, those who need to realise it in practice. As we will see, this is rarely straightforward, and the closer the policy comes to having an impact on the lives of individuals, the more important specific words and phrases become.

Policy papers can be rather like pointillist paintings: taken as a whole the overall intention might be clear, demonstrating a unified image textured with light and shade. Under the microscope of a particular encounter between a pupil and a teacher, however, it can be hard to understand how a particular dot of a certain hue contributes or even supports the whole. An example might be a school's attendance policy. Everyone concerned will probably accept that attendance at school is to be encouraged and is in the best interests of a child. The national government defines, through policy texts, the number of days that children must attend, and how this must be recorded, including the fact that if a child arrives after registration has closed, they are to be marked absent. This makes some sense from a statistical perspective, defining what attendance means for numerical purposes, but in the daily routines of schools a fixed time must be given for register closure, specified in the school's attendance policy document. If a child arrives one minute after this they are marked absent – even though they are in school for the rest of the day. It is clear to see that at this very fine point of decision for the teacher an eminently sensible policy holds the potential to become a confusing point of conflict, where common sense appears to go against clear words in the policy paper.

ENACTING EDUCATION POLICY

The preceding hypothetical example illustrates the intricacy of policy enactment – that is the *process* of translating policy into practice. Again we invoke the language of Stephen Ball and his collaborators in rejecting the notion of policy implementation in favour of the idea of policy enactment (Ball et al., 2012). To assume that policy is simply written and then implemented – put into practice – is to trivialise the work that needs to be done to understand principles, generate papers and exercise power by changing practice. The process of policy enactment is rarely time-bound, done once and then completed. In schools, policy enactment is ongoing through daily routines and interactions – this is where policy comes to life. The richness and diversity of educational settings makes for particularly multifaceted policy implementation, which may change over time and from one specific context to another.

The concept of education policy is usually taken to mean the policy direction as set by the government of the day, and indeed, this is often what we mean by education policy in general terms. However, it is important to understand that policy may be established at every level of the system, from Prime Minister and Secretary of State, right down to individual teachers, classroom assistants and, in some cases, pupils. In addition to what is legislated, Westminster government also defines policy through the Department for Education (DfE), both in terms of principles but also, of course, through papers. These might be mandatory, or advisory and non-statutory, and may carry more or less weight depending on their perceived importance as well as the particular predilections of political masters. Policy enactment, through Local Authorities, Multi-Academy Trusts or individual schools, often involves generating new forms of the national policy – local interpretations of what the policy means for them and how it will be effected. At an even more granular level, policy might be further interpreted by classroom routines and practices. Add to this multi-layer interpretation of policy those rules and procedures that leaders at all levels feel is necessary for orderly operation, and it is easy to see that educationalists are immersed in policy that presses on them from all directions – the very atmosphere in which education exists. It is perhaps unsurprising that some school leaders find this oppressive, in particular when much neoliberal policy is closely linked to accountability mechanisms (Pinto, 2015), though they are not simply passive recipients of policy issued from above. There is evidence that successful leaders are those who are able to combine external policy demands with internal developments in line with a clear moral purpose (Gu et al., 2018).

It is in this context that this book seeks to examine the enactment of education policy in England, and in schools in particular. This is approached through a variety of lenses or key themes, all of which will be familiar to those working in or studying education. More than 40 years after the 1988 Education Reform Act, which was the last major directional shift in terms of national policy, and which signalled the advent of neoliberalism in education, we have reached a point where the vast majority of those working in education have never worked in any other political system. In addition, most of them will have only experienced school as pupils in a neoliberal environment as well, so it is timely to reflect and to try to understand why the system looks as it does. The 40 years of policy enactment largely in one direction have created a particular character to our educational structures and behaviours – but that does not mean it has to be this way. There is insufficient space here to examine the approaches that other jurisdictions have taken to education policy over the last half-century, though that would clearly be of interest; suffice here to examine what we see in our schools, and why that is the case.

THEMES OF THE BOOK

We begin with a tour of the historical context that sits behind the development of education and schooling as we see it in today's world. Chapter 2 looks at the gradual coalescence of primary education from a disparate collection of providers in the late 19th century. Here we find the DNA of today's schools; the origins of some of the characteristics of the 21st-century system can be traced back 150 years. The 20th century included two world wars, each of which influenced the development of education policy, and by the 1950s schooling had settled into the primary/secondary/tertiary structure that has continued to the present day. Chapter 2 concludes with the progressive approaches of the 1960s, whose memory still disturbs and influences the neoconservatives of the 2020s.

Chapter 3 charts the rise of neoliberalism and the marketisation of schools. The landscape of choice, performance measures and accountability, and professed freedom of individuals and schools, can only be understood by reference to mid-century values and prejudices. Thatcher's rejection of socialism, which has persisted for half a century, brought with it an adoption of capitalist values which influenced educational developments as much as it directed economic policy. The chronological approach of this chapter enables key Acts and policy developments to be seen in historical context; these are revisited as they pertain to the themes of the subsequent chapters.

The first theme to be examined in Chapter 4 is that of accountability: the overriding presence that for 40 years has sought ever-more sophisticated ways to measure the effectiveness of education. Accountability measures themselves are not a neoliberal ideal, but the argument is that they provide market intelligence for parents and families so that they can exercise choice as quasi-consumers. Accountability metrics also drive the behaviour of those working in education, so we see performativity in action. Neatly summarised by the phrase 'teaching to the test', performative practices can permeate every aspect of school life, and where behaviour feels inauthentic this generates pressures which go beyond those of basic workload.

The task of managing change and enacting policy falls first to those in leadership, which is the theme taken up in Chapter 5. This looks not just at those who have formal leadership roles but also at the way leadership can be distributed throughout an organisation. Surrounding this is the legal responsibility for schools and other providers which sits within governance. For many the realities of governance can seem latent and obscure, particularly since the advent of academies and Multi-Academy Trusts which began to take on the mantle of system leadership, once the sole preserve of Local Authorities.

Leaders and governors are responsible for good management of all of the resources which fall within their control – both physical assets and human capital, and more besides as Chapter 6 illustrates. This may lead to people requiring skills for which they had never been trained, though professional development activities are gradually catching up with the new models of educational leadership. Education is so much more than teaching, and the multifaceted non-teaching workforce is discussed under the umbrella term paraprofessionals.

The curriculum can be thought of as a resource which must be managed well by educational leaders, but it is so significant that it merits its own chapter. Chapter 7 examines the way in which ownership of the curriculum has moved from teachers and school leaders to central government, and how apparently unrelated policies may shape the curriculum that is presented to learners. The hidden curriculum covers the many other aspects of learning which are not included in planned subject-based lessons.

The theory, practice – and indeed art – of teaching is pedagogy: the mechanism through which learning is planned and the subject of Chapter 8. It would be naïve to think that the activity of individual teachers in their classrooms would not be tainted by national policy, and it is here and through the curriculum that we see the stirrings of neoconservatism. The pragmatism of a bricolage 'horses for courses' approach is in danger of being hijacked by a polarised dogmatic debate that loses sight of real learning; some pedagogical fashions are considered, along with digital learning which was given fresh vitality through the COVID-19 crisis.

Chapter 9 visits a more overarching theme: that of inclusion. The English system has arguably become more inclusive over the last 40 years, though this progress has been in parallel with neoliberal changes rather than because of them, as a short history of inclusion shows. The Special Educational Needs Co-ordinator is one of the few roles which schools must have, and the responsibilities and tensions entailed are discussed. Where inclusion in mainstream either fails or is not deemed appropriate, alternatives are available, and Special Schools and Alternative Provision are therefore included in this chapter.

The idea that some children cannot be accommodated by mainstream provision raises questions of fairness, and these are examined through the lens of social justice, in Chapter 10. Along with an exploration of the meaning of social justice, the chapter also investigates some of the dividing characteristics which may lead to injustice. These include wealth and socio-economic status, race and ethnicity, gender and sexuality, religion and faith, and the vagaries of geography. The reality is that all individuals will have different combinations of these characteristics, so compounding either advantage or disadvantage, and this is discussed through a section on intersectionality.

In Chapter 11, we turn our attention to education which sits outside of the compulsory school years. This includes the grey area of sixth form study, as well as Early Years education for children younger than five, Higher Education, primarily at university, and all other adult education which we embrace with the catch-all label of lifelong learning. These sectors have not featured in the spotlight of Westminster policymakers as frequently as schools, but they are not untouched and they bear the recognisable fingerprints of neoliberalism.

Finally, Chapter 12 attempts to draw together what we have learnt through this exploration of what I have called the policy-practice interface. The pessimism of those opposed to neoliberalism is challenged by an optimism that arises from the humanity found within all educational institutions and structures. There is no doubt that the system is fragmented, but we might question whether or not this is a new phenomenon, and whether this necessarily means it is broken or ineffective. The metaphor of *kintsugi* is used to illustrate these arguments.

Each chapter is followed by a case study drawn from contemporary practice – often in the form of a policy document. Suggested study questions are provided to prompt thinking, either individually or as the basis of a class discussion, and a further text is recommended for more detailed analysis of the chapter's theme.

SUMMARY

This chapter has demonstrated the inevitable link between education and politics, and introduced neoliberalism as the dominant political force in England over the last 40 years. The concept of policy has been explored by considering it as principles, power, practice and paperwork; and the process of policy enactment has been described in order to rebut a simplistic understanding of policy implementation. This has laid the basis for subsequent chapters, which have been briefly summarised.

FURTHER READING

Robin Alexander's *Education in Spite of Policy* (Routledge, 2022) comprises a diverse collection of articles and papers that examine the relationships between education, policy and evidence. These can be read independently or as a coherent whole to gain an insight into 15 years of policy from the perspective of one who has been on both inside and outside. Alexander describes policy as an umbrella term which 'covers the process, context and politics of policy as well as its content; and the transmission, reception and translation of policy as well as its creation'.

2

EDUCATION: THE FATE OF THE COUNTRY - THE DEVELOPMENT OF EDUCATION POLICY

CONTENTS

This chapter includes:

- The development of education policy in Britain, from the mid-19th century to the 1960s, with a brief description of the disparate nature of education in the 19th century before early attempts to rationalise the system in the early 20th century.
- A description of the systematisation of elementary education between the wars.
- An explanation of the development of the nationwide system of secondary education that was introduced after World War II.
- A discussion of the complex secondary picture, and progressivism in primary teaching, that would ultimately lead to the marketisation of education in the 1980s.

INTRODUCTION

This chapter takes its title from a comment made in the House of Commons by Disraeli in 1874: 'upon the education of the people of this country the fate of this country depends' (HC Deb 15 June 1874, 1618). A similar sentiment has been expressed by political leaders time and again in the years between the late 19th and the early 21st centuries. Sometimes this has been acknowledged in a direct quotation, for example above the introduction to the 1943 government white paper *Educational Reconstruction*, but frequently we hear the same philosophy paraphrased more pithily, a notable example being Tony Blair's 'education, education, education' in his 1996 pre-election speech. The point is that politicians of all colours have identified a quality education system as being fundamental to the nation's prosperity and success, and determined that it is the role and duty of policy-makers at the highest level to achieve this.

Some knowledge of history is important if the developments that lead to policy change and implementation are to be fully understood. Politicians and other significant actors on the educational stage react and respond to their own experiences and knowledge, all of which is informed by and embedded in a historical context, not to mention political ideology. The following sections briefly outline policy developments from the mid-19th to the mid-20th century. These created and shaped the system of schools and colleges, nurseries and universities, which we see today. This chapter includes developments after World War II, which provided the arena and created the conditions – and some might say the need – for the dramatic intervention that was the 1988 Education Reform Act.

19TH-CENTURY EDUCATION

During the latter part of the 19th century a pattern began to emerge from an array of relatively unrelated and discrete schooling activities. It was not until the dawn of the 20th century that a recognisable system began to be established. By 1900 there was a mixture of different types of school educating 5- to 12-year-olds. These included orphanages, church schools, poor schools and Board Schools. While the terms may seem archaic, over 100 years later we can still trace the DNA of some of these early ancestors in our present-day organs of education.

Across the country we are familiar with schools that are supported by mainstream Christian churches. This is evidenced through their names: our Lady's Catholic Primary School; St Augustine's Church of England (VA) Junior School; St Mary's Church of England Voluntary Controlled School. While the technicalities of the names, which relate to the governance structures, may elude people, it is clear that a significant minority of our schools have some form of church oversight. Much of this is historical in origin, though numbers have increased in recent years as new faith schools have been opened. At the end of the 19th century, the majority of schools were church schools.

The 19th-century church school movement grew from a sermon preached by Herbert Marsh, a Cambridge Professor of Divinity, in 1811. Marsh's call for the Church of England to establish its own schools in order to instruct children in 'the way they should go' became an unlikely rallying cry, taken up by Joshua Watson, a wealthy and influential philanthropist, and resulted in the National Society which, with the Archbishop of Canterbury as its chair, rapidly established a national network of 17,000 Church schools by the time of the 1851 census (and even today, some are still called National schools). The Roman Catholic Church, which had established a small number of cathedral and monastic schools from the 6th century onwards, also entered the arena of mass education in the mid-19th century, through an 1847 agreement with the government which eventually led to the introduction of Catholic poor schools during the later decades of the century. The initial aims of the established churches were to build schools for the poorest in society; as well as instructing children in the articles of their faith, they would also school them in the necessary skills to live and thrive in the new industrial society. While the philanthropic nature of these developments, and their contributions to supporting the humanitarian needs of society's poorest members, is usually recognised, there is a counter-argument that these schools provided a mechanism of control, designed to preserve the hierarchy of society and keep the proletariat masses in their designated stations in life (Smelser, 1991, pp. 11–14). And while the churches had deep pockets, parents nonetheless had to pay, contributing the 'school's pence', less to fund the running of the school and more to counteract the fear that parents would undervalue education if it were offered free of charge to their children (Louden, 2012).

The growth of the church schools coincided with the demise of so-called monitorial schools – a self-proclaimed 'experiment' in education on an industrial scale, by Andrew Bell and Joseph Lancaster. These schools educated the children (mostly boys) of factory workers, using the factories' principles of division of labour, which, according to Lancaster, allowed for one master alone to:

> educate one thousand boys, in Reading, Writing and Arithmetic, as effectually, and with as little Trouble, as Twenty or Thirty have ever been instructed by the usual modes of Tuition.
>
> (Lancaster, 1806, p. 23)

This feat was achieved by means of a single instructor providing the teaching in one large room, with 'monitors' employed to provide additional instruction and keep order, supported with a system of rewards and punishments. Though the experiment was short-lived, by 1830 there were over 3,500 monitorial schools in England (Hager, 1959), and importantly, we can still see some principles of such schools at work in today's society.

While factory workers enjoyed a stable income and an education for their children, there remained a large underclass of families whose existence was quite literally hand to mouth, and for whom there was little prospect of any meaningful education. The 'ragged schools' movement grew to accommodate these families, and their numbers appeared to increase in line with the rapid expansion of the country's cities. Ragged schools educated:

> the children of costermonger pig-feeders, rag dealers, part-time dock workers, in fact of all those whose work was menial, irregular and ill-paid. Also included in this category were the offspring of these who laid claim to no job whatsoever, the lowest mendicants and tramps, and persons who get their living by theft, who altogether neglect their children; the children of hawkers, pigeon-dealers, dog-fanciers and other men of that class. A great proportion of the children are those of worthless and drunken parents, and many others are the children of parents, who, from their poverty, are too poor to pay even a penny a week for schooling.
>
> (Schupf, 1972, p. 162)

Note that this did not quite represent the lowest strata of society – reformatory schools were introduced to cater for the children of 'perishing and dangerous classes, and juvenile offenders' (Carpenter, 1851).

The ragged schools movement developed along similar but independent lines in England and Scotland, and attracted some well-known public figures of the time who supported the schools both financially and politically. Charles Dickens was one of them; he wrote *A Christmas Carol* after visiting a ragged school and set some of *Oliver Twist*'s scenes in its vicinity. In an 1846 letter to the Daily News, he complained of the frightful neglect of the State in educating its children, calling for this to be brought to the attention of the government, and for others to join him in finding funds for a secular education of the working classes (Dickens, 1846, p. 4).

By 1870, there was sufficient political will to introduce the country's first Education Act, bringing education, and particularly schools, onto the national political agenda. The 1870 Elementary Education Act committed the State to providing education on a country-wide scale, specifically targeting areas where no schools existed and creating non-denominational 'Board Schools' to serve their children. Board Schools were named after local boards of elected community representatives, who built and managed the schools, which were funded by local taxation. A similar development in Scotland through an 1872 Act ensured a parity of provision across the border, and so began the familiar model of state-funded schools with local governance arrangements. The Board Schools did not replace the church schools but sat alongside them, generating a persistent, uneasy tension within the system. An indication of how the concept of the Board Schools permeated the public consciousness is seen in Conan Doyle's writing for the Strand magazine in 1893, where Sherlock Holmes described them as 'beacons of the future' out of which would spring a wiser, better England (in Doyle, 2000, p. 229).

Subsequent years saw a series of parliamentary Acts which addressed two particular concerns: the desire to make elementary education compulsory up to a certain age, and the need to make education free of charge to parents. These two imperatives are by necessity interlinked: if all parents have to send their children to school then there must be a mechanism in place to provide the poorest families with the means to do this. Through today's eyes this may seem non-controversial, but it was the subject of much heated debate, as childless couples resented the idea that their taxes might be used to educate other people's children, and there were wider concerns about the burden on public funds. The time taken to resolve this issue indicates the difficulty of the problem: by 1880 education was compulsory for 5- to 10-year olds, but it was 1891 before the Assisted Education Act introduced capitation grants to schools. These were calculated on the basis of pupil numbers. Initially schools could still charge more than this basic allowance if they so wished, but this Act essentially signalled free education for all. By 1902, while the taxpayer funded compulsory education for children up to the age of 12, the proliferation of Board Schools and voluntary schools prompted future Prime Minister Arthur Balfour to introduce the unifying Education (England and Wales) Act.

Balfour's 1902 Act has been described as political rather than educational (Rogers, 1959; Taylor, 1994), and it was controversial, not least in that it supported government funding for church schools for the first time. In return, the church authorities had to submit to the curriculum demands of the newly formed Local Education Authorities (LEAs). These were based on county or borough councils, and they replaced school boards to provide a comprehensive and uniform governance structure for elementary schools. They also reduced the administrative burden for the government, which now only had to work with a few hundred LEAs, rather than thousands of individual school boards. The Act supported the principle of secondary education for older or more advanced children, but it did not mandate this, so education remained compulsory only up to the age of 12. Developments in Scotland proceeded along similar lines, with school boards being replaced by county authorities in 1918.

Up to this point in the nation's history what we now understand as secondary education – for children above the age of about 11 – had been the sole preserve of the wealthy. Grammar schools had been established in towns across the country since Tudor times. Many of these were short lived: they were established as commercial organisations, and if parents' fees did not cover costs, the schools soon became unsustainable. Surviving grammar schools sat alongside Public Schools, which were fee-paying schools for the very wealthy, taking their rather confusing name from the Public Schools Act of 1868. According to Sydney Smith (1810), they catered for the educational needs of the 'sons of gentlemen', public in the sense that they were open to all who had the means to pay, whatever their family status, background or profession. Although the 1902 Act encouraged LEAs to support 'education other than elementary', the country would suffer two world wars before beginning to shape a modern, if not universal, system of secondary education.

EDUCATION BETWEEN THE WARS

At the beginning of the 20th century the time was ripe for social change, and there might have been a hope that education would be an integral part of societal developments, though not that it would be a driver of social change as some might expect today. Politically, the Labour party's formation began to challenge the bipolar Liberal/Conservative axis. Awareness of a need to support the most disadvantaged was recognised in provisions for maternity payments and old age pensions; unemployment and health benefits were introduced through a new National Insurance scheme (Thane, 2011). Progress was being made towards universal suffrage, and indeed some have argued that this itself stimulates the development of a mass education system which moulds citizens so that they can vote, pay taxes and go to war (Boli et al., 1985).

The number of schools 'other than elementary' began to grow after the 1902 Act. Grammar schools received grants to support their finances from the LEAs, and municipal schools, which were funded entirely from taxation, began to be developed. These schools had curricula which varied from technical skills through to a more academic replication of the grammar schools' provision. The Government's Board of Education moved to raise the school leaving age, but the reality for most children was that unless their families were middle class or well-to-do, there was little opportunity for them to continue in full-time education beyond the age of 14 – and in truth many would leave at the age of 12.

It should also be remembered that the age ranges of these schools overlapped with elementary schools: children would seek entry to a grammar or municipal school from the age of about 11. Entrance was predominantly by way of examination, and there was no sense of direct progression from elementary schools to secondary schools at any age. This rather disjointed approach to education persisted through the First World War, which slowed the pace rather than changing the direction of developments. By the end of the war the 1918 Education Act introduced some commitments to nursery, special and part-time continuation schools, but in many respects it reinforced the class basis of English education (as described by a Liberal politician of the time, J. H. Whitehouse, cited in Sherington, 1976). Education to the age of 14 was to become compulsory, but for the vast majority this simply meant continuing in their elementary school until they could leave and find work.

Although the term 'secondary school' had been used before the war, understanding of the phrase differed widely, sometimes according to the politics of the commentator. In 1922, a Labour Party publication edited by the academic R. H. Tawney described the untidy division between elementary and secondary education as 'educationally unsound and socially obnoxious' (Tawney, 1922, p. 11). He introduced a proposal for an educational system with which we are familiar today:

i.   *Primary*, for all children up to eleven to twelve.
     Subdivided into:
     a)   Nursery and Infant schools for all children up to the age of seven.
     b)   Preparatory schools, for all children between ages of seven and twelve.
          [we would now call these Junior schools]
ii. *Secondary*, for boys and girls between the age of twelve and sixteen–eighteen.
iii. *Higher*, providing education of a University type.

This was supported by a comment that all children should remain in education, progressing through this system, to the age of 16.

With the benefit of hindsight, and the knowledge that it would be a further 22 years before the country was to see compulsory secondary education for all, Tawney might be seen as visionary or prophetic. There was some political consensus on the need to develop a more comprehensive pattern of secondary education: the Manchester Guardian declared that public education had moved beyond political controversy (in Doherty, 1966, p. 54). The scale of the problem was clear in the figures Tawney quoted, suggesting that in 1919 in England and Wales fewer than 15% of children progressed from elementary schools to some form of secondary education (Tawney, 1922, p. 153).

The post-war economic depression limited not only new developments on an educational front, but implementation of the 1918 Act itself: some of its provisions, including the compulsory school leaving age of 14, were postponed or suspended. The collapse of the Liberal Government, a 2-year spell for the Conservatives, and then the first, short-lived Labour administration all conspired to thwart any real progress. Despite the political frustrations, there was ongoing work which would underpin the hugely important 1944 Education Act. William Hadow was commissioned to chair a committee to investigate and write a series of reports on the state of the nation's education system, work that continued for 10 years to 1933. Of the six reports that were published, the third (titled *The Education of the Adolescent* – a phrase borrowed from Tawney) was probably the most influential. It cemented the idea of a primary/secondary transition at the age of 11, but allowed for different types of school for older children, to recognise their different interests and aptitudes. This latter point remains controversial to this day: commentators on the original report (e.g., Selleck, 1972) point out the inconsistency between selecting for children's interests and aptitudes on the basis of a written test of ability at the age of 11.

The provision of secondary education by the mid-1920s was described in parliament as 'dark and dismal' (HC Deb 16 February 1927). The Hadow reports aimed to lift some of the darkness, though it could be argued that the report on psychological tests of ability was insufficiently strong, leading it to cast a long shadow over post-war developments. After Hadow, politicians turned to Spens, whose 1938 committee recommended dividing secondary-aged children into three groups – those likely to go to university, those with practical aptitude, and the rest. These could be educated in secondary schools designed to meet their respective needs: grammar schools, technical schools and 'modern' schools. At the time of the report less than 10% of 11-year-old children were selected to go to secondary schools, with the rest remaining in elementary schools (Spens, 1938, p. 88). The position had changed little since the 1902 Act, but the intervening decades of inaction and debate had contributed to a mindset that was ubiquitous enough to lead to surprising political consensus as the second war in Europe drew to a close.

THE POST-WAR CONSENSUS

At the time war broke out in 1939 the nationwide provision of elementary education had been consolidated, but for children above the age of 11 the system, such as it was, remained in disarray. Fighting a war on a number of fronts drained the country's resources, but at the same time it engendered a spirit of unity that increasingly sought to ensure that once conflict was over the country would not just be worth dying for but also worth living in – for all citizens, not just a wealthy elite (Simon, 1991, p. 35). In one of his wartime speeches the coalition leader, Winston Churchill, referenced the privileges of private education and outlined his ambitions for these to be shared by 'the youth of the nation as a whole' (Churchill, 1942). This attitude applied beyond the world of education to the whole of the national social order (Barber, 1994), so while war raged political progress was made through a series of reports commissioned by Churchill's coalition government.

In 1941, Herwald Ramsbotham, who was at the time President of the Board of Education, published a 'Green Book' which effectively served as a discussion document (though there were attempts to keep its contents secret), responding to the many calls for greater coherence in education once the war was over. Committees were established to examine secondary education, teachers and their training, and public schools, and their reports were published by Norwood, McNair and Fleming respectively. The first of these spurred R.A. 'Rab' Butler, Ramsbotham's successor at the Board of Education, to develop an Education Bill entitled *Educational Reconstruction* (1943). In less than a year this became the 1944 Education Act, which embodied in England and Wales many of the principles that had been seen in the Green Book, and before this in the Hadow and Tawney reports. In other parts of Britain similar desires for a more 'democratic' system of education were addressed (Jones, 2016, p. 12), though with somewhat different solutions, and these were embodied into law with acts covering Scotland and Northern Ireland in 1945 and 1947 respectively.

The 1944 Act had huge significance, not just at the time but on the principles of education which are both embodied and debated to this day. Its key provisions were as follows:

- A Ministry of Education, with accompanying staff and advisory councils to support the Minister;
- Local Education Authorities (LEAs) based on county or borough divisions, with responsibility for providing education for the children living within their bounds;
- Three stages of education: primary, secondary and further education, supported by nursery schools for under 5 year olds, and special schools for children suffering from 'any disability';
- Compulsory religious education and daily collective worship - other than this the content of the curriculum was to be determined locally;
- Compulsory attendance between the ages of 5 and 15, with powers to compel parents to comply.

The 1944 Act was clear that the education provided by its provisions was to be free of charge. However, the Act allowed for independent fee-paying schools to continue to operate alongside the State supported system. The messy compromise which kept church schools within the State system was maintained, with two distinct types of school: county schools, run and operated by the LEA, which was also the employer of the staff; and voluntary schools which pre-existed the LEAs and were owned and run by the churches to a greater or lesser extent.

Where the Act was less clear was on the nature of the secondary schools which would now become a compulsory part of every child's journey through education to the age of 15. In principle the Act could have led to the development of comprehensive (all ability) secondary schools across the country, but in practice there was widespread reversion to the contested ideas of Hadow relating to different schools for different types of children. This resulted in what became known as the tripartite system, with grammar, technical and modern schools to cater for the 'three types of child' (McCulloch, 1994): those interested in learning for its own sake; those with a technical or applied aptitude; and those who were more comfortable with concrete things than with ideas. These categorisations came from the Norwood report, which suggested that selection of the children should be based on teachers' judgements supported by intelligence and performance tests.

The selection issue was further complicated by the fact that not all LEAs adopted the tripartite system, with a small number boldly establishing comprehensive provision, and far more establishing a bipartite system. Technical schools were excluded from bipartite systems either on the basis of principle, or, more commonly, demographics, where there simply were not enough children to sustain three different types of school. Consequently, by 1950 only 4% of the secondary school population was educated in technical schools (McCulloch, 2002).

At the end of the war the newly elected Labour government committed itself to the tripartite system through its first two Ministers for Education, Ellen Wilkinson and George Tomlinson. While the technical schools never took root on a large scale, the vast majority of LEAs developed some form of selection process, with children being allocated to either grammar or secondary modern schools on the basis of a test taken at the age of 11 (the 11+). Labour's implementation of Conservative-led coalition policy was one example of the broader post-war political consensus that characterised the years after the war. While there were dissenting voices, there was genuine agreement around the need to rebuild the country, which included paying attention to education and developing the welfare state, not just hard economics.

Simply passing an Act of Parliament does not, of course, immediately translate into everyday reality for educators and learners, and there was a huge amount of activity within Local Authorities to turn the policy into practice. This was eloquently captured by Martin Wilson, Shropshire's Chief education Officer, who described:

> Piles of paperasserie. A multitude of meetings. A clangour of consultations and claims.
> No hours enough in the seven days.

> (quoted in Simon, 1991, p. 9)

Over a period of three years, the 1944 Act was translated into a nationwide primary/secondary school system, with national pay scales for teachers and a school leaving age of 15 (from 1947). School meals were introduced across the board, and free milk provided in primary schools. Supporting the expansion of secondary education was not straightforward: there were worries about the supply of additional teachers that would be needed, and temporary classrooms had to be constructed to accommodate the additional children.

In addition to organising schools, provision of Further Education colleges was discussed both nationally and regionally, and an expansion of universities was planned. This latter activity was driven not by the Education Act but by the war, which led national leaders to identify a need for increased 'scientific man-power' in order to maintain Britain's position in the world (the Barlow report, 1946).

By the end of the decade there was still much work to do if the 1944 Act was to be implemented in full. Post-war austerity had constrained the abilities of both ministers and Local Authorities to make much progress in terms of school reorganisation. Increasing the pressure, the beginning of a baby boom was adding to the numbers of children that schools would need to accommodate. The commitment to universal free secondary education immediately benefited the pre-existing grammar schools, but it took much longer to establish the other 'modern' schools in the system. The 11+ entry test, based not just on a notion of intelligence but also on language, grammar and logic, favoured children of articulate – and generally well educated – parents, so it can be argued that it contributed to social division and failed to bring about the levelling that was intended (Hart et al., 2017). The sense of elitism was further exacerbated by the introduction of the GCE ordinary and Advanced level (O and A level) examinations. These subject-based tests replaced the existing School Certificate, but because the GCEs had a minimum age limit of 16, they could only be taken by those still in school after the age of 15: those in grammar schools.

Some aspects of the post-war consensus were beginning to crumble – though it has been argued that there was an overriding but unspoken common approach to the economy from all governments between 1944 and 1976 (Marquand, 1988, p. 18). Before the 1944 Act had been fully implemented, it was already being undermined. There were calls within the ruling Labour party for comprehensive schools instead of bi- or tripartite systems (Benn, 1980), and at the same time a pro-selection and unashamedly elitist argument was being articulated: in an influential booklet Eric James, High Master of Manchester Grammar School, spoke of 'the dangers of equalitarianism' (1949, p. 94). The pragmatism of consensus was in danger of becoming an ideological battleground. That the Welsh settled in favour of comprehensive or bipartite schools (containing both grammar and modern steams) and Scotland on 'omnibus' (bipartite) schools, may have more to do with the difficulty of constructing large, self-sustaining schools in rural and sparsely populated regions than it has to political idealism. Although the Scottish Advisory Council on Education recommended a comprehensive system with a core curriculum and common examinations in 1947, it did not come to pass until 18 years later (Bryce and Humes, 2013, p. 51). Across the whole of the United Kingdom, and England in particular, the establishment of universal secondary education was merely scene-setting for the fights to come.

CAPITALISM'S GOLDEN AGE

The quarter-century after World War II has been characterised as capitalism's golden age, though the post-war economic boom was late in coming to the United Kingdom. The western world united against the perceived communist threat, production was high, and the level of employment was unprecedented in peacetime (Denman and McDonald, 1986): this, combined with rising pay levels, contributed to the development of a consumer society. The nature of work changed, with the balance beginning to shift from manufacturing towards service industries, consequently generating a requirement for higher levels of education among increasing numbers of school leavers. In the United Kingdom, 13 years of Conservative government, initially under Winston Churchill, oversaw an expansion of education both because of the burgeoning population and also to accommodate the increasing numbers of children who wanted to stay on beyond the school-leaving age of 15. In crude terms, the emphasis was on quantity rather than quality.

Within government in the early years of the 1950s arguments raged around funding for schools, with a variety of cost-cutting mechanisms suggested to help balance the books – including at one stage *lowering* the school-leaving age. Elsewhere, amongst those responsible for arranging education on a local level, the disagreements were around philosophy: mostly selection at 11+ which was becoming increasingly contentious. Regarding funding, a tipping point came in 1953 when Rab Butler, now Chancellor of the Exchequer, expressed his concern 'whether the size of our educational apparatus is not in excess of our resources' (Dean, 1992, p. 16). The year 1954 saw a new Minister for Education, a renewed drive to implement the 1944 Act more fully, and a commitment to increased spending – which was realised in 1955 after Churchill's resignation and a resounding election victory for the Conservatives. The government took up the battle cry for grammar schools and the 11+ exam, labelling calls for comprehensive secondary education as socialist proposals and confirming its own commitment to grammar schools and secondary moderns. However, its lukewarm support for technical schools, and allowance for comprehensives 'as an experiment' (Simon, 1991, p. 184), ensured a muddled and mixed economy of practice that would fuel the debates for decades to come.

While this activity was playing out, the expansion of Further Education colleges, catering for 16–19-year-olds, progressed by a process of slow evolution rather than via any clearly planned strategy. The number of students in Further Education colleges and adult education centres, both full and part time, doubled between 1939 and 1950 (Bolton, 2012, p. 20). Barlow's earlier identification of the need for more scientific knowledge amongst the workforce was beginning to be realised: the number of university students studying science and technology doubled between 1938 and 1955 (MoE, 1956, p. 4), but there was still a need for more university places and also – because the grammar schools alone could not provide sufficient numbers for these – increased capacity within the Further Education sector. The government published a White Paper called *Technical Education* in 1956 (MoE, 1956); this reaffirmed Disraeli's words that in the worldwide scientific revolution it would be the countries 'with the best systems of education' that will win (p4), noting that at the time, despite the expansion of technical (mostly post-15) education, not enough had been done for Britain to avoid being left behind. The paper made reference to 'spiritual and human values' (p6), and subsequent years saw an expansion of both science-based and liberal studies within the colleges (Lawson and Silver, 1973, p. 424). Over the same period there was a corresponding growth in Higher Education. Student numbers increased, and so did the number of universities: several university colleges and adult education colleges achieved independent university status.

As the state of the country's economy improved, so did the government's ability to spend money to support education. The education budget doubled during the 1950s; a combination of the post-war baby boom was swelling pupil numbers, the outworking of the 1944 Act was keeping older children in secondary schools, and there was a recognition that schools needed some capital investment in order to create appropriate buildings for the national primary/secondary structure. Additional schools needed additional staffing, and the number of teachers increased by 25% over the decade. In order to train them the number of teacher training colleges was increased in commensurate fashion.

Simply providing enough schools and teachers for the population's children is not, of course, the whole story; the real debate was around the nature of secondary education. As the numbers in schools grew, so did the chasm between those who wanted to see comprehensive provision beyond the age of 11, and those who were committed to retaining the selective grammar/modern system. This polarisation became a political argument, with the Conservative Party supporting selection and Labour and other liberals favouring comprehensives. For the pro-selection lobby, the arguments often revolved around maintaining grammar schools – which served about 20% of the local population – rather than the system of selection itself. The fact that most working class children ended up in technical or modern schools (Carter, 2016) fuelled the idea that grammar schools were for the middle classes, and the notion that a grammar school education could lift a hard working child from their lowly station in life proved to be the exception rather than the rule. That the modern schools had no GCE O level examinations contributed to a situation in which three quarters of secondary-aged children were educated in schools which had no clear idea of their purpose, where education was 'pedestrian', offering little hope or challenge to its pupils (McCulloch and Sobell, 1994). The 1943 idea of secondary education with schools 'of diversified types but of equal standing' (BoE, 1943) was very far from the lived reality of England in the 1950s.

In 1963, the Newsom Report was one of several commissioned by the government to report on various aspects of education (CACE (England), 1963). The report's title, *Half our Future*, referred to its investigation of the school experiences of children of average or less than average ability: 50% of the population on whom the future would depend (again referencing Disraeli). The report acknowledged the difficulties in defining average and below average, but nonetheless clearly identified a large proportion of children whose talents were not just unrealised, but thwarted by poor teaching, a weak curriculum, and 'limitations of home background'. In other words, schools of the time would never be able to break cycles of deprivation, and the stratification of society would be preserved. Importantly, the Newsom report made no judgements about the type of schools children attended, yet it still served to undermine support for selection or tripartite systems – not least because it asserted that intelligence is not a fixed quality, and that intelligence tests measure an acquired characteristic.

The Newsom Report made a number of recommendations, including raising the school-leaving age to 16 (which was finally achieved in 1973), linking education with industry and the world of work, introducing a school-leaving certificate for all children, and a commitment to a broad curriculum that included the arts and personal and social development. There was a section dedicated to the training of teachers (up to this point any graduate could teach, without training), and a call for investment in school buildings and technology. The report was based on a detailed survey of schools, and it found that there were specific geographical differences to children's educational experiences that fundamentally boiled down to social status: in poorer (slum) areas the educational provision was weak and teachers didn't stay there long. One recommendation was for enhanced pay for teachers willing to work in these challenging areas (along with the need to deal with the general social problems in these areas).

The year 1964 saw a change of government, and the new Labour party administration continued to increase spending on Education, which rose from 4% to 5% of GDP during the remainder of the decade (Simon, 1991, p. 599). The number of children in the country's schools continued to grow, and the capital investment recommended by Newsom spawned a national series of building projects. The first centrally funded comprehensive schools were built, but although the government expressed support for comprehensive secondary education, it failed to deliver the concrete change in policy for which some had hoped. This may seem surprising, given the ongoing debate around the benefits or otherwise of selection at 11+ which led to a 'clear trend' for Local Authorities, even those under Conservative control, to build experimental comprehensives (Whitty and Power, 2015, p. 13). The government took the view that as LEAs were inclined towards comprehensive education it would be sufficient for this to be the encouraged direction of travel, rather than an imposed policy – a decision that proved disastrous for those who wished to see the outright end of selection. By 1970 the opportunity was lost: the Conservatives returned to power, and given their commitment to traditional values, they were never going to bring forward a bill to outlaw selection. Nonetheless, with no clear policy to set a direction, momentum and inertia ensured that the move towards comprehensivisation continued, and the number of comprehensive schools doubled under the auspices of the new Education Secretary: Margaret Thatcher (National Archives, n.d.).

A new examination was introduced in 1965 for children who did not gain places in Grammar schools. The Certificate of Secondary Education (CSE) was a subject-based examination for 16-year-olds. Tests often included coursework elements and there was a wider range of vocational subjects that were not available in GCE O-level examinations. In terms of standard, the highest CSE grade (grade 1) was set to overlap with the lower pass grades of the O-level. In practice, until the raising of the school leaving age to 16 in 1973, large numbers of secondary modern pupils still left school at 15 with no qualifications.

The 1960s also saw an increased divergence between the United Kingdom's nation states: strong resistance in Northern Ireland confirmed a commitment to 11+ selection which has never been seriously challenged. In Scotland, a clearer articulation of uniform 12–18 education by an administration that was unashamedly centralised developed a coherent policy to abolish selection in 1965 (though it took 10 years to work out in practice). This, along with the introduction of the Scottish Certificate in Education, helped to address the growing demands to stay on at school and gain qualification, challenging the old ideas that academic education and qualifications were the preserve of the elite minority (Anderson, 2013). In Wales, as in England, commitment to the traditions of the grammar school coloured the nature of comprehensive education. Here, selection was abolished, but secondary education was multilateral with tight ability streaming: there was 'no strong comprehensive ethos' (Jones, 2016, p. 80).

Changes to secondary education had a knock-on effect in primary schools, where one of the tasks of teachers was to prepare children for the next steps of their educational journey. When most children had to sit an 11+ test primary schools tended to stream them by ability so that some could be drilled to sit the exam – somewhat ironically when the premise of the 11+ was that it tested innate intelligence. Rigid streaming, and effectively selection before the age of 11, was much less necessary if children were going to a comprehensive or multilateral school, and therefore primary schools found space in the curriculum in which they could innovate and experiment. Schools were influenced by 'progressive' ideas: this loose term has been traced back to the 18th century when traditional orthodoxy was challenged by visionaries and reformers (Reese, 2001) who saw the child as an actor with agency, rather than a passive absorber of education. Progressive primary education became much more mainstream in England in the 1960s, when it emerged as a 'social construction' to characterise and describe observed practice (Brehony, 2001, p. 414). Its values often included child-centred teaching, activity-based learning and a project-based approach to the curriculum.

At a time of 'liberal optimism' (Sugrue, 2010), the government commissioned a report into all aspects of primary education – including a review of curriculum and pedagogy, which hitherto had been left in the hands of professionals in schools. The 500-page Plowden Report was published in 1967, and it came to represent the zenith of progressive education in England's Primary schools, stating uncompromisingly that 'at the heart of the educational process lies the child' (Plowden, 1967, p. 7). The emphasis was on activity and experience rather than acquisition of knowledge, but this did not come without cost: critics of the report suggested that in a climate of permissiveness children were losing the habits of learning and discipline (Gordon et al., 2013). Such criticism came to be embedded in a series of influential reports – the Black Papers – which were published between 1969 and 1977. These contained highly charged essays which passionately and deliberately set out to shock and disrupt the emerging system (Simon, 1991, p. 398): 50 years later the shockwaves continued to ripple through the system.

SUMMARY

This chapter has charted 100 years of development of a nationwide system of education, shaped by government policy and reflecting societal change. In it we can see recognisable features of today's schools, colleges and universities which will be explored in subsequent chapters. The diverse and disparate foundation stones laid in the late 19th century have been described; the consequences of the 1902 Act which incorporated and embedded the fracture lines has been outlined, and inter-war developments explained. The tripartite model which became the basis of the post-war consensus and the familiar tertiary system has been described, leading to muddled secondary provision and progressive primary approaches ripe for challenge from the right.

FURTHER READING

Education Policy in Britain in the Twentieth Century by Gordon et al. (2013) documents policy developments through the 20th century, beginning with the faith- and class-based legacy of the 19th century. The detailed analysis of historical development is followed by thematic discussions, including a chapter on the education of girls, and overviews of the different phases of education, from primary schools through to adult and higher education.

3

TWENTY-FIRST-CENTURY SOLUTIONS: THE MARKETISATION OF EDUCATION

CONTENTS

This chapter includes:

- An outline of the rise of neoliberalism, as a response to progressivism and lack of clear leadership that developed during a period of rapid expansion for education.
- A discussion of the tipping point that was the 1988 Education Reform Act, which cemented the principles of marketisation into education policy.
- A description of developments under John Major's premiership, which included new accountability measures and, importantly, the birth of Ofsted.
- An account of the work done by New Labour to further the principles of accountability and market forces up to 2010.
- A brief explanation of the drift towards neoconservatism through the policies of the coalition and Conservative governments.

INTRODUCTION

The liberal optimism of the 1960s was followed by a bleak period in which the education sector shared the nation's misery as it slid towards the winter of discontent at the end of the decade. Progressives resented the challenge faced by their models of education, while traditionalists bemoaned the dire state of affairs, as they perceived them. The time was ripe for change, and this chapter outlines policy developments over the next 50 years, from the time of Edward Heath's government through to 2020. This period saw the marketisation of education, initially through Conservative policy, but later as an almost ubiquitous mindset influencing the educational policies of all governing parties. As the 21st century progresses, there are signs of tension between market-based neoliberalism and neoconservatism, which seeks to bring the sector closer to 'traditional' values.

THE RISE OF NEOLIBERALISM

Ted Heath's Conservative government of 1970 initially seemed somewhat powerless to resist the ongoing expansion of education: Secretary of State Margaret Thatcher expressed support for selection even while she approved more comprehensive schools, and she achieved notoriety by abolishing free school milk in a futile attempt to reduce the soaring costs of schooling. The focus for school building projects moved from secondary to primary schools, and the raising of the school leaving age to 16 was finally implemented in 1973. Commitment was demonstrated to pre- and post-compulsory school-age education, with developments to nursery provision and expansion of colleges and polytechnics. However, a proposed increase to the number of university students did not materialise: the government was running out of money.

The second half of the 1970s saw Labour in government but without any real appearance of power. The economy had taken a nosedive, and this – combined with difficult relationships with unions inherited from the previous government – conspired to ensure that radical developments on any front were all but impossible. The commitment to comprehensive secondary education continued, but so did the spirit of compromise with which a weak Education Bill compelled LEAs to draw up plans for comprehensivisation, without outlawing selection altogether. Political arguments became increasingly heated, and these were complemented by outlandish stories in the press which captured the imagination and indignation of members of the public who felt that traditional values were being eroded. Employers complained that school leavers lacked the basic skills needed for the world of work, and child-centred teaching allowed an informality which, unless teachers were highly skilled, adversely affected 'performance in the 3 Rs' – this according to the Prime Minister's own advisers (DES, 1976).

In an attempt to bring order to the chaos, Prime Minister James Callaghan prepared a speech which, with hindsight, can be seen as a pivotal moment in educational terms, after which the direct intervention of the State into the daily machinations of educational life started to become the norm. Callaghan made a speech at Ruskin College in October 1976 which, in the eyes of some commentators (e.g., Whitty and Menter, 1989), accepted some of the criticisms made in the Black Papers. In the Ruskin speech Callaghan justified the need for debate, pointing out that the country was spending more than ever before on education (the high point of 6.3% of GDP in 1975–6 has never been repeated). The speech initiated a series of consultative discussions over the course of the following year which became known as the Great Debate. In Callaghan's words, this was to be 'a rational debate based on the facts'. Those facts included a recognition of some parental unease, an understanding of employers' dissatisfaction and a concern that university graduates were still not supplying the technological workforce that the country needed. The speech did not explicitly suggest solutions to problems, but in outlining the perceived problems it inevitably led to a way forward that would be a change of direction for the Labour party. Callaghan identified the key questions as:

> the methods and aims of informal instruction, the strong case for the so-called 'core curriculum' of basic knowledge; next, what is the proper way of monitoring the use of resources in order to maintain a proper national standard of performance; then there is the role of the inspectorate in relation to national standards; and there is the need to improve relations between industry and education. Another problem is the examination system – a contentious issue
>
> (Callaghan, 1976)

Callaghan articulated resistance to some of the 'lurid' notions expressed in the Black Papers, but his speech cracked open the door for those who wanted to see different forms of control, not just in schools but across education as a whole.

In the hands of Shirley Williams, Callaghan's Secretary of State at the Department for Education and Science (DES), the education world saw much debate and consultation, but little in the way of action. With comprehensive education now embedded in law, at least in principle, there were calls for a single 16+ exam to replace the two-tier GCE/CSE examinations. Findings from a major investigation into primary education (as recommended by the Plowden report) were published, recommendations were made regarding the management of Higher Education, and Mary Warnock's committee reported on its 4-year investigation into special educational needs (SEN), all in the same year (1978). Williams's department developed policy at a seemingly snail's pace: first a Green Paper (consultation) on assessment and accountability in 1977, then a White Paper to address a single 16+ exam (1978) – only to see its work lost as the country slid inexorably into the winter of discontent and Labour fell from power.

If Callaghan's government was characterised by dithering and inaction, the opposition had been learning from earlier mistakes and was regrouping prior to taking power in the 1979 election. Its new leader, Margaret Thatcher, was not afraid of confrontation and was prepared to stand on principles which she viewed to be 'right', even if the general populace thought otherwise. The last of the Black Papers was published in 1977; the sense that these were wild ideas espoused from extreme positions was beginning to be undermined. Later it was said that what was once unthinkable was becoming the basis for legislation (Gordon, 1988), and perhaps it was no surprise that Thatcher appointed one of the Black Paper authors, Rhodes Boyson, as Under-Secretary of State for Education when she came to power. The New Right, as it came to be called, encompassed both neoliberal and neoconservative attitudes. These were united in their opposition to welfare support, but diverged in their commitment to individuals and the free market, and to duty, tradition and a strong state respectively (Loxley and Thomas, 2001). When the Conservatives came to power in 1979, the voice of the New Right was loud but not overwhelming; by the time of Thatcher's demise neoliberalism held sway almost without question.

In contrast with the previous administration, the new government brought two education bills to parliament within its first 6 months in office. These removed the requirement for LEAs to plan for comprehensivisation, and developed an assisted places scheme which provided financial assistance for parents of 'bright children from modest backgrounds' so that they could be educated privately (Conservative manifesto, 1979). An important move towards neoliberalism was the inclusion of the duty of LEAs to comply with parental preference, removing the idea of catchment areas and introducing the idea of a market in education, with the parents being the discerning consumers, able to choose which school they would like to send their children to. Parents were also given some influence over how schools were run, with the introduction of elected parent governors to the governing bodies of maintained schools. In order for parents to make informed decisions about which schools to choose for their children, there needed to be an understanding about the quality of education which they offered, and how that could be measured. This ensured that the debate around curriculum that had begun five years earlier continued at the highest level: the government produced a 'flurry' of publications on the matter (Simon, 1991, p. 485). The recommendations of the Warnock report were recognised in a 1981 Act, which gave children with particular educational needs the right to be educated within mainstream schools. This instigated a decades-long move towards inclusion, which is considered in detail in Chapter 9.

By 1981, Margaret Thatcher had reshuffled her cabinet to lose some of the so-called wets, and she surrounded herself with ministers who were more prepared to take a hard line instead of seeking compromise. Sir Keith Joseph, the incoming Secretary of State, set himself against the 'educational establishment' which he saw as woolly and liberal, establishing a right-wing tradition that climaxed 30 years later when Michael Gove took issue with what he disparagingly called 'the Blob'. Joseph suggested that if there were problems with the curriculum in schools then the teachers were to blame – his relationship with the profession only went downhill after this and any hopes for clear and decisive action were dashed. There were perhaps early signs that Joseph's priorities revolved around reshaping the party around the market, and that he had little real interest in education. A series of strikes followed Joseph's moves towards performance-related pay for teachers – though this first skirmish was won by the unions the direction of travel was set, and eventually this particular battle would be won by the neoliberals. Joseph was probably less extreme in his thinking than some of the government's advisers, but for a short period he busied himself with investigating the ultimate in a free market for schools: a voucher system which would allow parents to spend their vouchers at the school of their choice. It was eventually decided that vouchers would, in Thatcher's words, create a colossal administrative burden, and the idea was dropped as being unworkable.

With or without vouchers, the idea of transforming education into a market was not lost, and after the 1983 election, when Thatcher returned to power on the back of the Falklands War victory, the right-wing advisers operating behind the scenes continued to try to steer ministers towards the ideas of the New Right. Direct State intervention was seen in the area of the curriculum, formerly the domain of teachers, LEAs and exam boards. Keith Joseph rejected plans for science syllabuses to include reference to social and economic applications of science; he called for history teaching to hold as its aim the development of pride in British culture; and he introduced the Technical and Vocational Educational Initiative (TVEI) to develop a new technical and vocational curriculum. This latter project was well funded (not from the Education budget), and, combined with the Lower Achieving Pupil Project (LAPP) aimed at the bottom 40% of secondary pupils, was perceived as a manifestation of the tripartite system inside comprehensive schools (Hillier, 1990). Keith Joseph himself described the combination of academic track, TVEI and LAPP as 'differentiation within schools' (1984, cited by Chitty, 1989, p. 159) as he appeared to give up a return to the fight for selection. This was somewhat at odds with more general support for the idea of a single 16+ examination that would soon see fruition.

A White Paper published in 1985 was provocatively entitled Better Schools (DES, 1985). While noting that some schools were performing well, and making polite comments about LEAs, it identified shortcomings and weaknesses, some of them serious, and several times stated that the government has a duty to intervene. The driving force for its proposals was not education per se, but the economic prosperity of the nation. In a now familiar refrain the Paper stated that 'education is an investment in the nation's future'. That education was to be measured through a universal examination at 16+, the GCSE (General Certificate of Secondary Education) which would replace the GCE O levels and CSEs, requiring differentiation within schools in order to meet the needs of all children. Explicit mention of the differences between the 'best schools' and those with substantial weaknesses, similar comments regarding the best and worst teachers, and identification of a lack of challenge by the LEAs all set the tone for the revolution that was to come.

By 1986, Joseph's grasp of Education was loosening whatever grip it had, and ultimately the 1986 Education (No. 2) Act progressed through parliament under his successor.

The Act took power from LEAs and gave it to parents, who would now have more rights to complain, and an even stronger voice on governing bodies. Governors would be required to report to parents and to the government; LEAs had to report on finances and curriculum, to provide governor training, and to consult with governors on staff appointments. Discipline became the responsibility of the headteacher, with governors providing checks and balances. The curriculum content was put into the public domain, with schools required to publish their curriculum, the LEAs having to do the same for 16–19-year-olds, sex education policies introduced, and any political indoctrination outlawed. The 1986 Act may have shaken the world of education and opened it up to public scrutiny, but it was merely a foretaste of what was to come. After Keith Joseph's vacillating period at the DES Margaret Thatcher turned to Kenneth Baker, who (at least retrospectively) claimed to have a clear idea of how to resolve what was commonly agreed to be the mess of education. Baker said:

> When I became Secretary of State for Education in 1986, I was convinced that the key to raising education standards across the country was a national curriculum.
>
> (2013, p. 1)

Baker's statement clearly picks up the theme of the Better Schools White Paper, and he immediately set about making a difference. The New York Times noted his sense of personal responsibility in bringing about a populist consumerism which would continue to take power from the 'producers' (teachers and education administrators) and move it to the hands of parents on the one hand, and central government on the other (MacLure, 1987). Baker's City Technology Colleges (CTCs) exemplify the latter point. These were conceived as independent schools which received their funding directly from central government: independent in this sense relating to freedom from LEA oversight, not in the sense of fee-paying private schools. City Technology Colleges initially received funding from sponsoring industrialists and had to maintain strong links with industry and commerce, manifest in a specialised curriculum. Over the next five years, 15 CTCs were opened, providing a different choice for parents exercising their right to express a preference of secondary schools. Baker's commitment to technical and vocational education continued long after he left office, and into the 2020s he remained actively engaged in finding creative ways of providing a more specialised curriculum offer for some pupils.

The CTCs were to provide a model for Academies – still 10 years in the future – and for Grant Maintained (GM) schools which would soon be introduced through the 1988 Education Reform Act. After the decline in birth rate following the post-war baby boom, Baker looked for a way to avoid having to close good schools whose rolls were falling. In principle, allowing them to opt out of LEA control and to receive funding on the basis of pupil numbers would make the market the arbiter of decisions to close small schools: good schools would recruit well and become financially sustainable, while others might wither on the vine and be forced to close. Baker's plans went further than this, with ideas that all schools could have control over their finances, and that a national curriculum would be precisely defined across a large number of subjects, with an emphasis on traditional values. He negotiated with the treasury for more money for schools and universities, which had suffered at the hands of Keith Joseph who was content to see budgets cut, especially those in Higher Education. Baker's concepts were popular not just with the right-wing supporters of the party, but also in the tabloid press which seemed to delight in pointing out examples of how the educational system was failing the country's children. There were, of course, sensible and well-argued critics from across the political spectrum and at various levels in the hierarchy, but education became a key aspect of the Conservative manifesto for the 1987 election and this saw them returned to power with a large majority. Kenneth Baker felt he had a mandate for reform, and no time was wasted in bringing proposals to parliament.

THE 1988 ERA

It is hard to overestimate the impact of the 1988 Education Reform Act (ERA). Through it, Baker changed the direction of mainstream educational thinking, introducing a new norm, aspects of which are rarely questioned today by those who have known little different. However, the changes were significant and profound, giving rise to controversy and debate which has been as long lasting as the effects of the ERA itself. At the time it was recognised that a new orthodoxy was being introduced, one in which the professional autonomy and expertise of teachers was to be replaced with control by parents and government, in a Bill that was seen to be unavowedly political in its intentions (Deem, 1988).

Just weeks after the election the 'Great Education Reform Bill' was introduced to parliament, colloquially and humorously referred to as the Gerbil, which seemed to belittle and underestimate its importance. The Bill was published in November and by July of the following year had become law. The speed of progress through parliament belies the controversy that was sparked once its contents and their implications became clear. However, the Bill emerged relatively unscathed from extensive external consultation and rigorous examination in the House of Commons, embodying an ideology that was 'overtly that of the market place' (Simon, 1991, p. 538).

The ERA comprised four sections relating to schools, further and higher education, education in inner London, and miscellaneous items respectively. Section 3 seems to strike a somewhat discordant note amongst the national restructuring of education, but dissolution of the Inner London Education Authority (ILEA) to move responsibility to the London boroughs eliminated a strong Labour power base. Described in parliament as an act of political vandalism (HC, 1988), it was ostensibly an attack on low standards and poor value for money.

The first section of the ERA shaped the landscape and vocabulary of today's schools. A National Curriculum was outlined, taking the form of three core subjects (English, mathematics and science) and a further six foundation subjects, all of which would be taught right through primary and secondary schools up to GCSE level. To these were added a modern foreign language (MFL) for secondary pupils, and Religious Education, which, though compulsory, was not part of the National Curriculum but subject to an 'Agreed Syllabus'. The 11 years of compulsory education were broken down into four 'key stages': Key Stage 1, age 5–7; Key Stage 2, 8–11; Key Stage 3, 12–14; and Key Stage 4, 15–16. From these the now familiar National Curriculum years arose: Reception, and Year 1 through to Year 11 (identification of lower and upper sixth forms as Years 12 and 13 was more gradual). The National Curriculum did not just define content but also specified what pupils should have achieved by the end of each key stage through 'attainment targets', and how this would be assessed. While the detail of the National Curriculum was tweaked by subsequent governments, the principle of a nationally prescribed curriculum has remained with us and is explored in more detail in Chapter 7; regular assessment was to form the bedrock of accountability which will be investigated in Chapter 4.

A section on admissions – which reaffirmed the right of parents to express a preference, and prevented schools from rejecting children if they had room to accommodate them – was followed by statutes relating to local management of schools (LMS). LMS represented a 'spectacular reduction in LEA control' (Harris, 1991, p. 170), in which schools would receive funding through a so-called budget share (via a complicated formula, but fundamentally in proportion to the number of children in the school). In effect, the LEA role was merely to passport the money through to the schools, whose leadership could then decide how it would be spent. Governing bodies were also given the responsibility for appointing and dismissing their own staff, though these remained in the employ of the LEA.

For schools that wanted even more autonomy, the ERA included provisions for them to opt out of LEA control altogether and become grant-maintained (GM). The decision to opt out was put in the hands of parents, by ballot, and once GM status was achieved governing bodies would own the assets including buildings and sites, and become the employers of staff. As in the prototypical CTC model, GM schools received their funding directly from Whitehall; LEAs saw a corresponding reduction in their budgets for each school that opted out. The ERA gave the legal basis for the CTCs, some of which opened almost immediately, though there were fewer in total than Baker had originally envisaged.

With regard to universities, the right of tenure for academic staff was removed, to be replaced with something approximating to normal employment rights, though their freedom of speech was explicitly preserved. Universities and polytechnics would be funded directly through a grant mechanism, and FE colleges by an LEA administered formula similar to schools.

The ERA was immense and represented such a tectonic shift of established custom and practice that some opponents felt that its ambitions were unlikely to be realised. There were misgivings within the governing party itself, but these did not prevent rapid progress towards realising the visions within the Act. In terms of a lasting culture shift towards a quasi-market of autonomous educational providers the ERA was undoubtedly successful. As a mechanism to ensure an entitlement to a high-quality educational provision for all (including children with special educational needs), its impact was compromised, as there was an inbuilt tendency for good, successful schools to attract investment at the expense of those that, for whatever reasons, might be struggling. While superficially introducing a universality to challenge the old class-based distinctions, the ERA redefined the system yet still allowed the middle classes to prosper (Gibson and Asthana, 2000). Locally managed schools and potential investment by industry and commerce was still a long way from the privatisation of education which Keith Joseph might have imagined, but the nod in this direction was enough to spark controversy which continues to colour today's debates.

While the ERA was being implemented Margaret Thatcher became a victim of her own self-belief: determination that she was right in the face of widespread opposition led to her downfall as the Conservative party sought a leader that could win the next election. As a parting gift to the educational world she oversaw the passage of a parliamentary bill that allowed for loans to be made to university students: the thin end of the wedge that would ultimately see the removal of student grants altogether.

MINOR CHANGES UNDER MAJOR

Under John Major the course that had been set by the ERA was established, confirmed and consolidated. Derek Gillard aptly summarises his period of tenure as 'more of the same' for education (Gillard, 2018). Schools began teaching the National Curriculum, the first end of key stage tests for seven-year-olds were set in 1991, and a year later the first league tables of schools were published. According to John Major, these provided the information that parents had a 'right to know' in order to make informed decisions about where to send their children. Teachers' pay and conditions were set by a new body answerable to the Prime Minister, and there were renewed attacks on progressive education which still threatened to undermine standards. The defining act of Major's first term of office was the introduction of a new inspectorate: the Office for Standards in Education (Ofsted).

The 1992 Education (Schools) Act provided for an inspection regime which would see all maintained schools and nursery schools inspected and judged on a regular basis, with the head of Ofsted (HMCI: Her Majesty's Chief Inspector) reporting annually on the findings to the Secretary of State. Any sympathy towards the principles of a national inspection framework on the part of teachers was comprehensively undermined by the second and longest serving HMCI, Chris Woodhead, who seemed to take delight in challenging and provoking the teaching workforce. Ofsted became almost universally despised and feared by teachers, but remained, with league tables, one of the key aspects of accountability that the marketisation of education demanded, and which is explored in more detail in Chapter 4.

Two further Acts of Parliament in 1992 sought to bring market principles to bear. In the FE sector, colleges were removed from LEA control and established as independent business. In Higher Education the 'artificial distinction' between universities and polytechnics and colleges was removed. This resulted in England's polytechnics and the larger colleges of London University becoming universities in their own right, with powers to confer degrees. Almost immediately afterwards a general election saw the Conservatives, against expectations, continue in government.

Although the CTC programme had come to a quiet end, Major's government did progress the idea of industry links and school specialisms with the Specialist Schools programme. This allowed for secondary schools to attract additional funding in return for a more specialised curriculum (initially related to technology, but later broadened to cover other curriculum areas) and, importantly, achieving demanding academic targets. Head-teachers, keen to swell their budgets, constructed ambitious plans based around an amended curriculum, and fears that the ability of specialist schools to select children based on their 'aptitude' for given subjects proved to be groundless. Over time the Specialist Schools movement became a significant contributor to the government's raising standards agenda (Levacic and Jenkins, 2006). A significant minority of schools opted out of LEA control to become GM, but not in the numbers that had originally been hoped.

During Major's second term of office, developments within education were consolidatory rather than revolutionary. A number of Acts were passed which tidied up loose ends from the ERA, eliminated most of the remaining vestiges of the 1944 Act, and strengthened the idea of marketisation within education at all levels with the idea of parental choice underpinning policy developments. Vouchers were introduced for nursery schools to allow all families to benefit from a pre-school education if their parents so chose. There was a drive towards greater inclusion in mainstream schools yet at the same time a contradictory growing discourse arose around pupils' individual needs, for which diversity between schools might cater. Boosted by the HMCI's comments, the government felt free to use such terms as 'failing schools', and it appealed to traditionalists by suggesting that successful GM schools might have additional freedoms, one of which could be to convert to grammar school status. The National Curriculum was reviewed and amended (see Chapter 6 for more details), and the wide variety of post-16 qualifications was expertly analysed in some detail – and then largely left alone (the Conservatives' ability to commission reviews and then ignore their findings later became a recurring theme).

Somewhat ironically, for a party whose full name is the Conservative and Unionist Party, policy developments helped to drive a wedge into the crack between the practices in the United Kingdom's four countries (Gillies, 2013, identifies 1980 as the 'departure point' for Scotland). While a modest number of schools opted out of the English LEAs, those taking this option in Wales and Scotland were very small (Jones, 2016). The recession of the 1980s had hit the industrialised areas of Wales and Scotland hard, and neither country was a natural heartland for Conservative voters. There was curriculum reform and some toying with testing of children under the age of 11, but Scotland made a clear move away from England's direction of travel. Northern Ireland clung to a more traditional selective approach to secondary education, and Wales managed a halfway house position in which some, but not all, of England's policies were adopted. Any expectations of realigning the nations were lost when New Labour devolved decision-making powers to a Scottish Parliament and a Welsh Assembly.

NEW LABOUR, NEW MILLENNIUM

By 1997, the Conservative administration was running out of steam, and it was finally swept aside in the election which handed a huge parliamentary majority to Tony Blair. Hope that his New Labour government might turn the educational clock back, or at least change the direction of travel, must have been dashed when the New Labour manifesto was published prior to the election: though there were commitments to nursery education for all, smaller class sizes and increased access to technology, there were also remarkably familiar comments regarding underperformance, low standards and 'failing schools', public/private partnerships, and monolithic comprehensive schools. The manifesto was unashamedly written to secure election victory rather than to explain socialist thinking, and in fact it set children's education above political dogma (20 years later Theresa May was to use a similar phrase to justify selection).

If there was ever a moment in which the effects on education of neoliberalism (and to a lesser degree, neoconservatism) could have been reduced, subdued or even eliminated, it was May 1997. The fact that the Blair government continued with many of the educational policies and principles of the preceding administrations cemented the hold of neoliberalism, and secured its march into the 21st century.

One example of New Labour's commitment to the general direction of travel which exemplifies the actions that some found astonishing, if not shocking, was not just the affirmation of Ofsted, but the retention of the deeply unpopular Chris Woodhead as HMCI. Labour retained the 'standards agenda', and to be fair had always promised to do so in their manifesto. The academic, Michael Barber, was put in charge of standards and effectiveness. Even he, as a Downing Street insider, described New Labour command and control policy as 'shock therapy' (2010, p. 272); one strand of the '21st century solutions' that education needed (the others being quasi-markets, and devolution and transparency). If league tables and inspection were the sticks to beat the donkey, the carrot was funding for high-performing specialist schools; this programme was not just continued but hugely expanded (with the inevitable consequence that the funding received by each school decreased considerably). However, it was clear from the outset that pressure on schools to achieve high standards would be ongoing and unrelenting, and that there would be no real challenge to the somewhat muddled infrastructure that now supported children's learning. An early White Paper used a phrase that was frequently repeated: standards not structure (DfEE, 1997), though the subsequent Act tinkered with structures, as former GM schools became 'foundation' schools rather than the 'community' schools which were still run by the LEAs.

In an effort to show distinctiveness from both the previous Conservative incumbents and the socialist stereotypes, Tony Blair used the expression the 'Third Way' to describe the market and government as equal actors in redistribution of wealth and the pro-motion of social equity. Hall (2003) described this as a hybrid regime: a social demo-cratic form of neoliberalism. Education was seen as the focal point at which these opposing actors seemed to meet. Nor was this effort focused solely on schools: early in his first term of office Blair introduced the Sure Start programme to support under-4s in deprived areas and a national childcare strategy to support childcare outside of school hours and thus enable more parents to access work. New Labour's ambition was for 50% of these children to be able to attend university by 2010 (compared with about 33% when they came to power). In an apparently contradictory move, student loans were expanded, maintenance grants removed and tuition fees introduced for Higher Education. Notwithstanding this contra-indicator, the government sought to consoli-date a coherent approach to Further Education (16–19-year-olds) and made 'lifelong' learning a part of the educational lexicon as it encouraged adult participation in learning activities.

New Labour continued the government's increasing preoccupation not just with cur-riculum content but also with pedagogy – the way in which the curriculum was taught. Literacy and numeracy hours were introduced for all primary schools, to make sure that children learnt the basic skills they would need to access the rest of the curriculum. There were national guidelines on how to teach these lessons, and investment in technology for schools through a National Grid for Learning. This came with bizarre strings attached: NGfL training had to include pedagogy related to numeracy and literacy, but could not include IT skills to help teachers get to grips with unfamiliar equipment and software. Secondary schools were expected to organise teaching groups by ability, and all schools were set challenging targets on the understanding that failure to achieve these could result in closure and a 'fresh start'.

Money was invested in education, mostly from the treasury but also through partner-ships with business and industry. Some of these were more successful and long lasting than others, but all such partnerships were grist to the mill for opponents of the privati-sation of education. To add to these complaints, some of the services that to date had been carried out by LEAs were put into private hands in the name of efficiency and cost effectiveness. Once again, the market was being used as a regulator within the system through Adam Smith's invisible hand.

To the consternation of leaders of struggling schools – often small secondary moderns – in rural towns, much of this new money was directed towards urban areas, through projects like Education action Zones and Excellence in Cities. Further support for these areas was to come through City Academies, which were to follow the model of the Conservatives' CTCs, complete with private sponsors' capital investment complementing direct revenue grants from central government. While there would inevitably be other intrusive factors to deal with, it was clear that new Labour were only going to extend and prolong the age of neoliberalism in education (Smith, 2009).

A second period in office saw the same pattern continuing. Further money was spent on education, notably through the *Building Schools for the Future* programme, though much of this work was carried out through controversial Private Finance Initiatives (PVI – initially launched by John Major in 1992) in which the public sector contracted with private companies to complete significant procurement projects. Specialisms for secondary schools were encouraged, the Academies programme lost the city emphasis and was expanded, and the DES was renamed the Department for Education and Skills (DfES). Education became target-driven, with outcomes at the age of 16 becoming the primary metric for parents and press to understand schools' performance (Sammons, 2008). Children's Centres and extended schools sought to support children prior to the age of compulsory education and outside of the school day. The Children Act (2004) brought LEAs and social services together within Local Authorities (LAs) and the *Every Child Matters* initiative sought to protect children, though there were also concerns that in so doing the State was becoming more interventive and regulatory (Parton, 2006). An indication of the extent to which New Labour had moved from its more socialist roots can be seen in the passage of the 2006 Education and Inspections Bill, which required the support of Conservative MPs in the face of Labour rebels.

By 2007 the DfES underwent another rebranding, this time to emerge as the Department for Children, Schools and Families (DCSF) in order to reflect a commitment to social justice embodied in a coherent multiagency support network around each child. Higher Education was moved to a new department. The professed emphasis was on an integrated system based on cooperation rather than competition (Abbott et al., 2013). For older children the Education Maintenance Allowance (EMA) was introduced to support the education of 16–19-year-olds from low-income families. In an apparently contradictory move, top-up fees were introduced in Higher Education to allow universities to charge up to £6,000 a year. Vocational diplomas were introduced in an effort to revitalise applied learning for 14–19-year-olds, but the attempt was doomed, not least because the complicated portfolio qualifications were neither understood nor accepted by education professionals or employers. Towards the end of the first decade of the new millennium, New Labour's star was beginning to wane: under Gordon Brown the 'hyperactivity' of initiatives and reforms that characterised the Blair years gave way to tired introspection in the struggle for survival at the top (Heath et al., 2013).

COALITION, CONSERVATISM, CONTINUUM

The 13 years of Labour government came to an end in 2010, though the victory for David Cameron was hardly convincing as he needed a coalition with the Liberal Democrats to secure his hold on power. For some this suggested that the brakes might be applied to the march of neoliberalism, but this was later – and emphatically – demonstrated to be a misconception, as the Liberal Democrats performed a spectacular U-turn in supporting a vote to raise university tuition fees to £9,000 – 'the only sensible way to fund universities' (Butler, 2021). They demonstrated more consistency with their core supporters in meeting a manifesto promise to introduce a 'pupil premium' in 2011. This targeted funding for disadvantaged children (an umbrella term that is explored more fully in Chapter 10) was intended to raise the attainment of disadvantaged children and close the so-called disadvantage gap (Foster and Long, 2020). This was welcome money for schools; less welcome was the incoming Secretary of State, who would prove to be as memorable and divisive as Chris Woodhead had been in the 1990s.

Michael Gove's first act when taking up office was to push through the Academies Act (2010), which allowed for all schools to become academies and took away any say the LAs might have in the matter. The DCSF was renamed again, becoming the Department for Education (DfE), and the *Every Child Matters* agenda was quietly dropped, though the DfE was careful to say that the sentiment behind the initiative remained. Any hint of a soft edge to his department was decisively removed by Gove, who ushered in a harsh 'I know best' approach that brought neoconservative voices into the prevailing neoliberal arena. A 2010 White Paper, *The Importance of Teaching* (DfE, 2010) asserted that the quality of teachers is the most important factor in achieving a 'world class education system', but it balanced the devolution of power to school leaders with clear emphasis on accountability measures. Committed to saving money, Gove abolished the Education Maintenance allowance and cancelled the *Building Schools for the Future* programme, a move that was later judged by the courts to have been an abuse of power.

The Importance of Teaching set the pattern for the years to come, prompting reviews of, and changes to, the taught curriculum and examinations, vocational qualifications, initial teacher training and special educational needs provision which was extended to cover birth to 25. There was a new focus on children's behaviour as well as the performance of teachers, whose morale generally declined as a result of Gove's style as much as his speed: a rapid programme of reforms and changes was expected to be implemented with little or no notice.

Most significant and long lasting were the changes to the curriculum and qualifications. Module exams during the course of the academic year were removed, coursework abolished and re-sits ruled out. A swathe of vocational qualifications were consigned to history, and the A*-G grading system was revamped, replaced with a new 9 to 1 system at GCSE. The emphasis was on traditional values and a 'knowledge-based curriculum' in which knowledge is transferred from experts to children, who then demonstrate their under-standing in high-stakes, one-off, end of course examinations. To justify his decisions Gove rejected the views of some education academics, but cited one of their own as he referred to the work of Michael Barber, Tony Blair's former adviser (in a speech to Policy Exchange in July 2014). Once again we can see the continuous thread of the standards agenda between governments of different political colours.

Michael Gove was in office for four years, but the outworking of his reforms continued to be felt right up to 2020 as successive cohorts of learners progressed along their educa-tional journey. The COVID-19 crisis in the summer of 2020 exposed the drawbacks of a single final exam to assess attainment: when GCSEs and A levels were cancelled there were no consistent, robust data to fall back on, save the professional judgement of teachers which had been so clearly rejected by Gove six years earlier. Gove's successors retained much of his philosophy, if not his abrasiveness, and any potential moderating influence from the Liberal Democrats was lost in 2015 when a general election returned a Conser-vative government. Lessons had been learned about the pace of change, however, and the frequency of new initiatives diminished. Between Gove's departure and 2020 there were just four Education Acts, one introducing a regulator for Higher Education, the Office for Students (OfS), and another dealing with the processes to follow should an FE College find itself insolvent. These, combined with an act to speed up conversion to academy status, bore all the hallmarks of neoliberal ideals, leaving just one 2016 Act to actually deal with children's education.

Justine Greening was a short-lived Secretary of State (2016–17) who brought a glimmer of hope in these later years to those seeking justice in education, with her *Unlocking Talent, Fulfilling Potential* plan to improve social mobility through education. This recognised inequities within the system which she summarised as 'where you start … determines where you finish' (DfE, 2017, p. 5). Less than a month after its publication, Greening had lost her position, but not before injecting a note of caution into government policy and issuing a call to challenge the status quo that had been developed over the previous 40 years. Knowingly or otherwise, she perpetuated the thread spun by Disraeli in her conclusion: 'Britain will only succeed if we unlock talent and fulfil potential for all' (ibid.: 36).

CONCLUSION

This chapter has explained how 40 years of education policy development came to be dominated by the concept of the market. Political leaders have identified the principle of choice as a driver of improvement, and all claim to have seen standards of education improve during their tenure. The remainder of this book examines how these views have shaped some of the smallest details of practices and behaviours in England's nurseries, schools, colleges and universities.

FURTHER READING

Education Policy in Britain, by Clyde Chitty (2014), provides a clear overview of the development of educational policy from a historical perspective. It emphasises the idea that policymaking is always influenced by knowledge and experience of the past, and it analyses and dissects policy through this lens.

4

ACCOUNTABILITY: THE STRUGGLE OVER THE TEACHER'S SOUL

CONTENTS

This chapter includes:

- An exploration of the implications of a national standardised testing regime and the associated performance (league) tables.
- A discussion of the introduction of a robust inspection mechanism in the form of Ofsted, along with the way in which teachers' performance is measured.
- The implications of high-stakes accountability systems and how this generates a performative approach to education.

INTRODUCTION

The 1988 Education Reform Act (ERA) handed significant responsibility and autonomy to school leaders. This changed the nature of their roles as we will see in Chapters 5 and 6, but it was not a generous gift, nor was it universally received with grateful thanks – though not many of today's leaders would want to hand back the independence they now have. In return for certain freedoms, school leaders were to be held accountable for the way in which they carried out their duties. There is undoubtedly a strong argument for good stewardship of public resources, but few would have predicted the ways in which an accountability culture would come to permeate the entire system, from the highest levels of organisational leadership right down to specific activities in individual classrooms. It has been argued (Ball, 2003) that such reform goes beyond changing the behaviour of the sector's professionals, ultimately changing their professional identity. Ball calls the internal conflict between principles and performance 'the struggle over the teacher's soul' (2003, p. 217).

Such ethical dilemmas are a natural and unavoidable consequence of the educational quasi-market. Markets function as disciplinary frameworks, complete with implicit reward and punishment, creating winners and losers and a tendency towards self-interest (Gewirtz et al., 1993). Accountability measures, whether employing absolute scales or relative comparisons, give added strength to the controlling disciplinary framework and by design will be used by those with authority to make judgements and take action as they see appropriate. This response, which can appear cold and somewhat heartless to those on the receiving end, does not sit comfortably within a body of professionals who may feel that their idealistic and pragmatic reasons for choosing a career in education are being challenged (Priyadharshini and Robinson-Pant, 2003).

Since 1988, there has been little sign of any move away from a plethora of performance measures. On the contrary, there is a sense that the genie is out of the bottle, never to be pushed back. In 2003, 15 years after the ERA, accountability measures remained controversial but the Department for Education and Skills (DfES) stated quite clearly that 'testing, targets and tables are here to stay' (DfES, 2003, p. 20). A further decade and a half later arguments still raged (Gewirtz et al., 2019), and they will surely continue. But in a so-called information age that delights in putting unimaginable quantities of data into the public domain, the chance of education being shielded from a performative use of these data is vanishingly close to zero.

TESTING AND TABLES

John Patten was one of a string of short-lived and poorly remembered Education Secretaries of the Major years. By the end of his term of office he was described as 'hapless and accident prone' by the TES (Sutcliffe, 1994), but despite the contemporaneous lack of confidence, history credits him with an enduring legacy: that of publishing educational league tables. Publication of the first league tables for schools came early in Patten's term of office and was the result of some frustrating and difficult work by Kenneth Clarke, his predecessor. Clarke became a senior father figure for the Conservative party in later years and is remembered for greater things, but as Secretary of State for Education between 1990 and 1992 he oversaw the creation of performance measures for schools in the form of Ofsted inspections and a national testing regime. Results of the tests were to be published, in John Patten's words opening the 'secret garden of education' to the gaze of the public (cited by McCall in the Times, 2017). Despite initial government protestations to the contrary, it was always clear that once numerical data were available for schools, there would inevitably be a compulsion to show them in a rank order, by the press if no-one else. So the school league tables were born. The government continues to label them performance tables, but even on its own website users can sort schools into a league or rank order, based on a variety of metrics, at the click of a button.

Data for secondary schools had always existed in the form of examination results from the GCSEs (and their predecessor exams) and A levels, but from 1992 these were collated centrally by the DfE and published in the autumn after pupils received their grades. The GCSEs in particular, based on the new National Curriculum, provided a comparison measure for children's attainment that had nationwide consistency. For primary schools, prior to the 1988 ERA, there were no consistent national – or indeed local – measures which would allow for comparisons between schools. The introduction of standard assessment tasks (SATs) for children at the ages of 7, 11 and 14 aimed to provide metrics by which children's (and therefore schools') performance could be directly compared at the end of each of the newly established key stages: twice in the primary phase and twice in secondary.

The stated need for this testing regime was rooted deeply in neoliberal ideology: the principle that if parents could 'break into ... Fort Knox' (Major, 1991) and be furnished with data about the effectiveness of schools they would be able to choose which schools they would like to send their children to, with school funding following the children. In turn this would provide a stimulus to those schools which were performing less well to improve the quality of education in order to better compete in what would then be an open market. Commentators frequently refer to the 'quasi-market' in education (e.g., Exley, 2014; Institute for Government, 2012; Whitty, 1997) because of course this ideal-istic theory does not translate neatly into practice: even if the data are reliable, the better schools would become full and oversubscribed, while those perceived to be weaker might simply run out of money and close, resulting in a demand for places that cannot be met by the popular schools. This would be exacerbated if there were geographical variations in schools' performance. In addition, data are of course historical, yet what discriminating parents really need are indicators about the future of a school once their child has joined, not its past performance (Leckie and Goldstein, 2009). It has also been argued that the market model favours the middle classes who are better able to negotiate the rules around applications and therefore give themselves a choice that is not available to less affluent families (Reay, 2004). In effect, it is the popular schools that have choice in the system; they are able to select, through their published admission policies, a subset of children from their many applicants (so-called 'cream-skimming', Allen, 2008, p. 109). In the rhetoric of parental choice in the marketplace, this ability for some schools to choose their pupils is often overlooked.

Whatever the political philosophy behind the introduction of testing, the practicalities presented their own headache. Aside from fierce opposition from parents and professionals, the task-based nature of the Key Stage 1 SATs made them both time-consuming and unreliable – and in the view of some professionals, damaging to children's education (Abbott et al., 1994, p. 166). A Key Stage 1 science task that involved floating and sinking became a particular focus of derision, with children's conclusions that 'some things sink and others float' appearing to merit the highest available assessment level. Secretary of State Kenneth Clarke consistently referred to the SATs as 'tests', both to appease some of his more conservative colleagues who were wedded to the idea of written pencil-and-paper exams, but also as part of a determined drive to simplify the tasks. He described the proposed Key Stage 3 SATs as 'elaborate nonsense' (cited in Whetton, 2009, p. 143) and swiftly set about transforming them into terminal (end of Key Stage) written exams. In hindsight this can be seen as an early nod to neoconservative values which would raise their head much more dramatically under Michael Gove 20 years later. Over subsequent years, and under various governments, the SATs have continued to evolve. Now referred to as 'National Curriculum assessments', they have survived teacher boycotts, seen the balance shift between teacher assessment and externally marked exams, and had their content reduced in line with a slimmer National Curriculum. Key Stage 3 SATs disappeared altogether, but the spirit remained, and national phonics tests were introduced for children in Year 1, along with an Early Years Foundation Stage Profile (EYFSP) for children in Reception classes. National Curriculum assessments at Key Stage 2 continue to be reported at school level in league tables, to 'allow for comparison between schools' (Roberts, 2017).

CHANGING PRACTICES

The exact nature and shape of National Curriculum assessments may have changed over the last three decades, but their introduction brought about a lasting step-change to the practice of primary school teachers. Prior to the 1988 ERA, infants' teachers had been seen to have had 'little or no experience of formal assessment activities' (Wyse et al., 2008, p. 12). Within two or three years all teachers (primary and secondary) quickly became familiar with summative assessment, and in fact became highly skilled in the practice, even if they hadn't been before. While the progressive practices described in the Plowden Report were far from ubiquitous, the idea that 'at the heart of the educational process lies the child' (Plowden, 1967, p. 7) was subjected to challenge, as the most important aspect of education now seemed to be the measurement of a child's learning rather than the experience of learning. This renewed emphasis, as much as a National Curriculum, drove a change in the content and style of teaching as we will see in Chapters 7 and 8. While some will say it drove a new professionalism, others will say that the emphasis on processes and procedures around testing and assessment gives rise to an internal conflict within teachers who may feel the need to set their own values and beliefs to one side, in order to be seen as a consummate professional (Woods and Jeffrey, 2002).

For secondary schools, which had been entering 16-year-olds into external examinations for many years (GCSEs, and before that the CSEs and O levels), the league tables were less about a change of practice and more about a change of emphasis and importance. Suddenly the grades of each teacher's pupils became important, as these would affect the school's ranking in the league tables. No matter what moral high ground might be claimed by resistant headteachers, nobody wants their school to be at the bottom of any league table, or listed among 'England's worst schools', as the popular press likes to label them (Miller and Evans, 2019). Consequently, secondary schools became focused on the accountability measures which would determine their league table rankings, primarily core GCSE results but in addition, for many schools, performance at A level as well.

For a decade the main measure of secondary schools' performance was the proportion of children gaining five or more 'good' grades at GCSE, later refined to include mathematics and English. While attainment measures, as indicated by GCSE results, have been tinkered with by successive ministers, the basic principles of recording a core group of subjects including the key skills tested by mathematics and English remained the national benchmark measure. Between 2010 and 2014 Michael Gove changed both the content and the examination of GCSEs, as well as their grading system, but retained attainment measures through an 'attainment-8' score. This maintains the same basic philosophy of counting the number of children who have achieved a certain standard in GCSE exams across a range of subjects, in this case 8.

PROGRESS MEASURES

From the beginning, however, school leaders argued that simply measuring the attainment of children does not necessarily indicate how well the school has educated them. Grammar schools, whose intake represented only the most able 20% of children and whose results therefore should show all pupils achieving five good GCSEs, were being compared directly with secondary modern schools in the same area, where achieving grade C or better in GCSE was a significant challenge for many pupils. The same effect is seen across all schools: those with an intake of higher average ability (as measured by prior attainment) are much more likely to see higher GCSE grades for that cohort, even if their educational efficacy is exactly the same as that of schools with lower prior attainment cohorts. This basic measure also incentivises schools to focus their efforts on a small group of pupils: those for whom a small difference in grades will make a large difference to the overall school measure. For many years this meant that schools invested in children working at the C/D grade boundary, potentially ignoring other pupils whose D/E or A/B performance would make little difference to the school's league table score.

Progress measures were introduced in 2002 in an attempt to quantify the educational advancement that a school's pupils have made in comparison with similar children in other schools. The methodology for calculating progress is both complex and contentious, and the preferred method has changed a number of times: from simple 'value added' in 2002 to contextual value added in 2006, expected progress in 2011 and progress-8 in 2016 (for methodological details, see, for example, Leckie and Goldstein, 2017). There are shortcomings with each of these methodologies, some of which relate to them being 'difficult for the public to understand' (DfE, 2010, p. 68) and others which concern specific statistical borderline effects or anomalies (see, for example, Perry, 2019). None of these accounts for a persistent political distrust of measures which might appear to give excuses for the low attainment of children from particular socioeconomic groups, and easy to understand attainment baselines remain the primary currency in popular and political discussions.

The introduction of school league tables spawned a small industry that revolved around monitoring children's progress towards specific performance measures. Individual children were set targets in each subject which would ensure good outcome measures for the school, and these translated into targets for those teaching them. Schools focused their activities around 'war boards': initially whiteboards prominently displayed in staffrooms, with cards showing Venn diagrams of children on track (or otherwise) to achieve their targets, grouped according to their performance in maths, English or other key measures. These evolved into sophisticated software versions which enable teachers and school leaders to track individual children across multiple subjects – and intervene where a trajectory does not appear to be satisfactory (McGill, 2016). Schools looked for silver bullets which would guarantee a meteoric rise-up the league tables and sought to understand which interventions would best accelerate children's progress (Hattie, 2012). Through the Education Endowment Foundation (EEF) the government funded research to quantify the effects of different aspects of schools' work in terms of months of progress (EEF, 2021a). Local Authorities began to monitor the performance of schools much more closely, and at a national level schools falling below certain benchmark values (variously called threshold levels or floor standards) have been identified in a 'name and shame' attempt to drive up standards (Judd, 2011). The treasury found funding to support so-called failing schools in the form of a variety of initiatives, including the *National Challenge* which identified secondary schools in which fewer than 30% of children achieved five or more C-grade GCSEs including English and mathematics. The number of schools in this category fell from 909 to 247 over four years (Bolton, 2010), partly as a result of the £400 million that was invested into the *National Challenge* in 2008, but also because schools became better at targeting support for individual children and getting them over the C/D borderline.

The practice within schools of strategically targeting individual children and using techniques to maximise league table standing – such as repeatedly entering children into an exam until they passed – was sneeringly referred to as 'gaming' the system and potentially led parents to make inappropriate decisions for their children (Waters, 2015). Politicians – Labour and Conservative – condemned such practices and acted to block them (Harrison, 2013), perhaps ignoring the inevitability that, in a quasi-market where choice might be driven by schools' league table standing, the schools would use every means possible to look good on those tables. It could be argued that the political drive towards marketisation was the very cause of an emphasis on results rather than children. The focus on results also sparked another debate, around 'grade inflation'. As schools got better at encouraging particular children to jump through certain performance hoops, grades improved nationally. Far from celebrating the achievements of schools and young people, exam boards were castigated for allegedly making their tests easier. This prompted a perpetual cycle of examination reform, followed by a few years' improvements as schools and pupils got used to the new tests, before returning to examination reform once again (Cuff et al., 2019).

Although the performance of schools is measured primarily on attainment and progress, the range of measures that have been shared with the public is now very large. From a position in 1988 where schools appeared to operate in the secret garden behind closed doors, and little was known about any of their vital statistics, we can now interrogate a bewildering array of metrics in a variety of ways, using complex statistical tools or, more commonly, unsophisticated high-level comparators. In 2019, interested users of the DfE school performance tables were able to download more than 1,000 columns of aggregated data for each secondary school. Despite the ostensible transparency that this generates, revealing such data for public sector organisations like schools has been described as being on a par with opening Pandora's box, allowing data to be deployed crudely as part of the 'rough and tumble of political debate' in an attempt to govern by numbers (Jackson, 2011).

Among the somewhat obscure and technical data in the multitude of indicators are some that might be of more interest to parents, such as the average attainment on entry (which might give a clue as to how selective an oversubscribed school is) or the number of children on the special needs register, which might be thought to indicate how well children's individual needs are accommodated. Of course, many assumptions underlie any such reasoning, but that does not stop people from drawing conclusions, however invalid they might be. Included in the data are the number of children excluded in the previous year and the average attendance. These data are certainly scrutinised by one audience in particular: those who inspect the schools.

INSPECTION

Everyone working in education is now familiar with the idea of inspection through the regulator, Ofsted, which came in to being through the Education (schools) Act of 1992. Prior to this, each Local Education Authority (LEA) had its own inspectors who would visit schools making comments and recommendations, but the prevailing view at the highest levels of government was that these were inconsistent and insufficiently challenging, as each Authority was inspecting its own schools to its own standards. Nationally, Her Majesty's Inspectors (HMIs) were a group of highly respected individuals who, having been appointed by order of the Queen through the Privy Council, were entirely independent of the government and LEAs, and consequently exercised 'discursive power' that encouraged some schools and gently rebuked others (Ozga et al., 2014). However, HMI were seen by the Thatcher government as the 'priesthood' of progressive orthodoxy (Baker, 1993, p. 168), too willing to offer advice (which did not have to be accepted) to schools and reluctant to challenge or make judgements. Consequently a new architecture for inspection was constructed in the form of the Office for Standards in Education, with a promise of regular, rigorous, nationally consistent inspections, and an inspectorate that would behave more like referees than coaches (Sutherland, cited in Ozga et al., 2014, p. 64). After a muted start, which initially maintained the feel of HMI inspections, Ofsted came of age and showed its teeth under the leadership of its second Her Majesty's Chief Inspector (HMCI), Chris Woodhead, in 1994.

Chris Woodhead was determined that Ofsted was a force for improvement in English schools, though some independent research suggested that its first five years made no difference to the GCSE grades of the comprehensive schools it inspected (Shaw et al., 2003). Given that Woodhead stated the two key aspects of Ofsted's work were regulation and advising the Secretary of State (Ofsted, 1995b) – but not advising the *schools* – a causal link between inspection and school improvement was not necessarily inevitable. Two decades later there was still no clearly established causal link between Ofsted inspection and school improvement (Jones and Tymms, 2014). Importantly, Woodhead did reassert the neoliberal rationale for inspection: 'to provide a service to parents of pupils' (ibid.: 11), although he did not feel the need for a National Curriculum. He was deliberately combative, hitting national headlines in 1995 after his first Annual Report (Ofsted, 1995a) when he stated that there were 15,000 incompetent teachers in schools who should all be sacked. He argued for a 'traditional understanding of education', castigated teaching unions, and asserted that grade boundaries for examinations were deliberately lowered, leading to an 'educational cloud cuckoo land' of grade inflation in which sentimentalists applauded hard-working teachers and pupils (Woodhead, 2002). The effect of Woodhead's approach to inspection and judgement was debilitating to teacher morale (Webb et al., 1998), and Ofsted came to be seen as a ruthless, faceless, disciplinary machine, to be feared rather than respected, by the profession.

Fear of the inspectorate was not necessarily misplaced. While the evidence for teachers leaving the profession as a direct result of Ofsted inspection is weak and anecdotal, the pressures of preparation for Ofsted and the related stresses within a school certainly contribute to feelings of anxiety and uncertainty among the workforce (Jeffrey and Woods, 1996). The impact of Ofsted inspection on headteachers and school leaders is more direct. Although headteachers are generally more positive about the principles of inspection than other staff (Scanlon, 1999), a poor inspection report could lead directly to restructuring of leadership teams, in which one or more individuals might lose their jobs. This unforgiving system remains: even Ofsted HMCIs recognise the fear that they engender (Wilby, 2018), and while the inspectors don't sack headteachers directly, their reports can be 'catalysts for personal disaster' for leadership teams (Barton, 2018). Other leaders take pre-emptive action, choosing to leave as they read the metaphorical writing on the wall in their own school self-evaluations, when they see that they will not meet Ofsted's exacting standards (Flintham, 2003).

The nature of Ofsted inspections has changed over two and a half decades, under frameworks designed to 'establish the optimum in consistency and objectivity' (Davis, 1996, p. 5). The frameworks lay out the form and process for inspection for different sectors, from Early Years providers through to universities. Initially providers were given several months' notice of an impending inspection, giving them ample time to prepare and put their house in order. Visits lasted for up to a week, during which time individual teachers were observed, graded and given feedback by inspectors. Inspection teams were large and included lay inspectors, who did not have a background in education and were therefore viewed with scepticism by some (despite the power they had 'to say "that person is a dud"' – Hustler, 1999, p. 172). The brown envelope from Ofsted would trigger a flurry of activity, in which policies would be rewritten, classrooms redecorated, boxes of evidence collected, and staff and pupils groomed: for some this period was 'a living hell' (Perryman, 2007, p. 179). Over time the teams have got smaller, visits shorter and notice periods reduced. This may have reduced the time available for intense preparation activity, but has probably done little to reduce the pressure on individual teachers, as the emphasis on classroom teaching has been increased (though teachers are no longer graded individually on their lessons) and schools are expected to have extensive and accurate (by Ofsted's measures) self-evaluation processes. HMI have been brought into the Ofsted fold, and in 2015 the inspectorate underwent a significant cull in which hundreds of inspectors were dismissed, with the remainder undergoing retraining, part of an ongoing process of slimming down and toughening up (Elliott, 2012). Ofsted has always used performance data to inform its judgements of schools, and while the degree of influence has waxed and waned, this raises the league table stakes even further.

The 1992 promise was of regular inspections, and for the first five years of its existence Ofsted's challenge was to ensure that each school in the country was inspected at least once. Thereafter the original four-year inspection cycle broke down, partly by design and partly because Ofsted simply could not resource such a high number of inspections. This led to a situation in which some schools which had been graded 'outstanding' by Ofsted could then go through a decade or more without a visit – during this time a whole generation of children would pass through their hands, and the quality of their experiences could potentially be very different from that seen by the inspectors. In the meantime, inspection teams focused their work where there seemed to be most needed: on schools which were underperforming (by the standards of the day) or 'coasting' (DfE, 2016). It took a surprisingly long time for Ofsted to recognise this disparity and begin to re-inspect the neglected schools.

If one of the original intentions for Ofsted was to put more information, factual and judgemental, into the public domain (Ouston et al., 1997), then that aim has been consummately achieved. Alongside educational providers' inspection reports which are published and available online, Ofsted also publishes annual reports summarising key findings and statistics, reports on particular themes, reports on Multi-Academy Trusts and Local Authorities, and an increasing number of research-based documents. We have seen that the evidence that this raises standards in schools is contested at best; indeed from its earliest days, school leaders perceived inspection as an accountability process rather than a mechanism for school improvement (Dean, 1995). Politicians are keen to point out that there are ever more pupils in outstanding schools, thus supporting their claims to efficacious policy. In this instance they conveniently neglect the grade inflation argument that they are quick to apply to GCSE grades, and they appear blind to the fact that while outstanding schools remained exempt from re-inspection, their numbers could only go up, not down. In 2018 a DfE insider pointed out that half a million children were being taught in 'good or outstanding' schools which had not been inspected since the 2010 election eight years before (Andrews, 2018). Despite occasional disagreements between HMCI and the Secretary of State for Education, Ofsted's claim to be impartial and independent is challenged by the perceived behaviour of the inspectorate, which simultaneously adjusts to fit the political backdrop while maintaining a discourse of inspection which puts it at a 'respectable distance from its political masters' (Baxter, 2014, p. 35). While this paradox remains, it is unlikely that Ofsted will ever be seen as anything other than a political intervention.

PERFORMANCE MANAGEMENT

A national system for teacher appraisal was introduced as a statutory requirement in 1991. Prior to this appraisal practices (where they existed at all) varied from one LEA to another and, in line with LEA inspections of the time, were viewed by the Conservative government as symptomatic of permissive 'sloppy-mindedness' (Bartlett, 2000). The Education (School Teacher Appraisal) Regulations 1991 introduced appraisal with two stated purposes: to assist teachers in professional development and to inform decisions about the management of teachers. Appraisal processes included target setting and review, combined with at least one observation of teaching, all conducted confidentially – which made it difficult to use in management decisions. As the decade progressed so the requirements around appraisal were amended, both to remove some of the limitations of confidentiality and to establish some national consistency and consensus around the expectations of teachers.

As appraisal was being introduced, the requirements for newly qualified teachers (NQTs) to complete a probationary year was being removed, in what might appear to be a contradictory action. However, the freedom of NQTs was short-lived as Standards for the award of Qualified Teacher Status (QTS) were introduced in 1997. Probation had been viewed as ineffective (Tickle, 2000), and the new QTS Standards, all of which had to be achieved by those completing initial teacher training (ITT) from 1998 onwards, were intended to provide a non-negotiable competency baseline for ITT graduates. These were complemented by Induction Standards which NQTs would have to meet by the end of their first year of teaching. Although there was a delay between probation disappearing and QTS Standards being introduced, some felt that their introduction was unnecessarily hasty (Martin and Cloke, 2000). While the sector had been cursorily consulted, there were concerns that democracy was being undermined and discomfort that the New Right had been consulted to help with the political positioning of the Standards (Hextall and Mahoney, 2000, p. 325). In the educational world, the Standards for QTS were viewed as a technocratic approach to the assessment of ITT students which would only be appropriate if teaching were to become 'a unidimensional and context-free knowledge based profession' (Martin and Cloke, 2000, p. 189). While a competency-based approach to the assessment of new teachers might support public confidence in the profession, teacher educators felt that the QTS Standards presented a limited vision of teaching at best and attempted to objectify good teaching to make it quantifiable instead of using a developmental language of critique and possibility (Stevens, 2010).

Performance related pay (PRP) was introduced across the public sector by the Conservative governments of the 1990s, and New Labour applied similar principles to teachers from 2000 onwards. After the introduction in 1996 of a national pay scale for teachers overseen by a pay review body, teachers progressed annually up a series of nine increments on the scale. The new PRP policy allowed for a maximum of six increments up to a performance threshold: to progress beyond this, teachers had to demonstrate, through an application process, their professional skills and abilities as demonstrated in the performance of their pupils. The threshold divided those on the main pay spine (mainscale teachers) and post-threshold or upper pay scale teachers. Its introduction was unpopular with teachers but that did not prevent them from applying to go through the threshold – which would result in a £2,000 salary increase (Farrell and Morris, 2004). The Threshold Standards provided a further dimension to the range of standards that was being developed, and by 2007 there was a professional Standards Framework with a distinct hierarchy, each layer of which had clear competence descriptors detailing attributes, skills, knowledge and understanding (TDA, 2007):

Q: qualified teacher status
C: core standards for main scale teachers who have successfully completed their induction
P: post-threshold teachers on the upper pay scale
E: excellent teachers
A: advanced skills teachers (ASTs).

By 2012, the Coalition government had condensed the Frameworks matrix into a simple list of Teacher Standards as a benchmark for all in the profession, whatever their career stage. NQTs had to meet these standards by the end of their training and still had to complete an induction period to be fully qualified (which was lengthened to two years in 2020).

While the Teacher Standards seek to support teacher professionalism and uphold public trust in the profession, it has been argued that they promote a 'tick-box' approach to professionalism, in which the emphasis on what is measurable enables technical compliance that might be undermined by a lack of professional wisdom (Goepel, 2012). Over a period of 20 years appraisal for teachers lost its focus on the development of teachers and became a tool for managing performance, reduced to crude metrics which focus on behaviours instead of intellect, attitudes or understanding (Evans, 2011). The consequence of this, the obsession with pupils' test scores and the need to demonstrate compliance rather than competency to a hostile inspectorate, all conspire towards a reduction of humanness in teaching (McQueen, 2014). The move away from the caring aspects of education (Hebson et al., 2007) and the drive to behave in a particular way in order to be seen to perform give rise to a tension which is now endemic throughout the system: performativity.

PERFORMATIVITY

England is not alone in having developed an emphasis on a compliant workforce, a judgemental inspectorate and league tables to provide performance indicators for a market that is ostensibly the parents. These features are now common in many Western nations, and suggest a global trend towards treating education as a quasi-market. Standardised, high-stakes tests and a 'punitive' inspection system are characteristics of what Holt calls a story that has been peddled for over 25 years: only a system of rigid, standards-based accountability will cause standards to rise (Holt, 2017: 111). Such measures also allow for comparisons to be made between nation states, and political leaders use international comparators such as the OECD's PISA (Programme for International Student Assessment) statistics to support or justify policy developments. Though it is popular, the idea that putting outcome measures into the public domain necessarily engenders a self-regulating system through market forces does not seem to be borne out in practice. Academic studies generally suggest that the evidence for such performance measures driving improvement is weak: Propper and Wilson (2003) conclude that in the United Kingdom and United States at least, there is virtually no evidence of such schemes improving the efficiency of public services. Academics argue that the attempt to create context-free objective measures simply results in rankings that identify policy failures without revealing anything of substance regarding the policies or the consequent practice (De Vries, 2010).

This is not to say that the neoliberal drive to raise standards by creating a competitive market has not changed practices – of schools but also of individual teachers in classrooms. We have already seen that when schools have sought to develop practices to give them a better showing on the performance tables, they have been accused of playing the system. This exemplifies, at a school level, the principle of performativity.

The idea of performativity was developed by Lyotard (1979), a philosopher who suggested that knowledge was becoming increasingly saleable, and that in our post-modern era knowledge is becoming a dominant economic factor in the wealth of a nation. As in a mechanical process, the efficiency of the production of knowledge – which only exists in the minds of people – can be measured in terms of the ratio of input/output, and it therefore follows that in order to maximise this efficiency any input energy that does not contribute to the measured output is wasted. Hence, the value of knowledge is no longer intrinsic, of worth in and of itself, but is a function of the output measures. In fact, the generation of any new truth, whether through research or education, that challenges the accepted measures can be seen as irrelevant at best, with no operational value, and disruptive at worst. In what Peters (2004) describes as his prophetic and seminal work, Lyotard characterises post-modern education as the transmission of a canon of knowledge, which is no longer the preserve of scholars and students. Hence, education is relegated to a transactional process, only of value insofar as it can be measured.

Performativity is not simply an esoteric philosophy that might be debated along with the number of angels that can dance on the head of a pin. In the educational marketplace, the commercialisation of knowledge (Lyotard talks of mercantilisation) makes particular types of knowledge more valuable than others: what can be measured in league tables reigns supreme. It is therefore incumbent on those working within the system to produce this particular knowledge, or in other words to make sure that pupils pass the relevant exams to the right levels that give the school the potential to generate more income. To bring this right down to earth in a simple phrase, performativity is about teaching to the test.

Teaching to the test is a phrase commonly used in the United States and Canada to summarise the practice of preparing children for high-stakes examinations, at the expense of other learning which might, in another context, have seemed important.

Activities might include drilling for the test, neglecting curriculum content not covered by the examination, and long practice sessions on past paper questions (Volante, 2004). The emphasis is on declarative knowledge and basic skills, rather than the application of knowledge and higher-level skills (Jones, 2004), and this behaviour is often seen to undermine the professionalism and independence of teachers. More than this, the need to meet certain standards and achieve specific benchmarks is said to undermine teachers' creativity in the learning process (Burnard and White, 2008).

It is not just before key examinations that performative behaviour is seen. Throughout a pupil's educational journey they may set targets and actions to help them achieve the milestones that have been deemed critical by society and politicians in particular. This can result in a school culture that is dominated by tracking of attainment and progress, using spreadsheets and databases which may be focused on precise aspects of the curriculum which will have the most impact on the school's performance measures. The abundance of data is translated into appraisal targets for teachers and senior staff, with the consequent potential of rewards and sanctions. Each day's work is carried out in this context, so that every minute represents an opportunity to make further progress towards the targets, and therefore should not be squandered. For some teachers, this provides a security within which to operate and there is evidence in the United States of pleasure in performativity (Holloway and Brass, 2018), but for many it challenges some of their original reasons for training to teach.

As we have seen, the data are not the whole story, and schools will be aware that at some stage they will be inspected by Ofsted. With only a short notice period before inspectors walk through the door, there is a need to be ready for inspection at any time. Some providers estimate when an inspection is due and carry out 'mocksteds': internal inspections based on the Ofsted framework in order to identify potential shortcomings and put them right before the inspection. Others engage in such activities on a more regular basis, and many will have frequent departmental (or subject) reviews, lesson observations, learning walks and work scrutinies, all to check that standards are constantly being upheld. For some teachers such ongoing scrutiny conspires to result in 'demotivation, annoyance and resentment' (Clapham, 2005).

The constant surveillance that educators experience has been described using Jeremy Bentham's idea of the panopticon (Bentham, 1791), often using the interpretation of Foucault (1977). In the panopticon a hypothetical prison is constructed with a central chamber from which guards can see into all of the prisoners' cells which are arranged in a circle around it. This can be viewed as a metaphor in education, where a central but invisible disciplinary force is able to maintain compliance through individuals modifying their own behaviour because they never know if or when they are being observed. Some writers have extended the metaphor further, moving from a position where central power is exercised by government or state to one in which the market itself intervenes and structures the behaviour of the State (Courtney, 2016; Gane, 2012), with suggestions that this 'post-panoptic' model is even more pernicious and less tolerant than panopticism, speaking to values of neoconservatism as much as neoliberalism.

However their experiences might be described by philosophers, many teachers and school leaders experience the challenge of ensuring they meet externally set standards while maintaining their own value systems, which may be very different. Some are able to adopt the neoliberal viewpoint and work comfortably within the educational panopticon, knowing that their approaches conform to expectations. For others they are trapped in a dilemma in which they need to 'perform' in two different ways (Locke, 2015): they have to demonstrate performance in the sense of achieving the requisite results; and they have to engage in a performance in which their actions are contrary to how they really feel. Such performances are equally apparent at school level (Perryman et al., 2018), though the one-off fabricated show is increasingly being replaced with perpetually renewed veneers of success in order to maintain a state of constant readiness.

The emotional impact of allowing oneself to become 'colonised' by the inspection process can be hugely damaging, even if inspectors attempt to present a more humane face (Woods and Jeffrey, 1998). Some people express an ongoing fatigue that undermines their ability to do their jobs well; others describe a pressure that goes beyond manageable stress, and such feelings undoubtedly contribute to some leaving the profession (Case et al., 2000). The issue is not one of quantity of work, but instead relates to the nature of work in which the need to perform in a hyper-critical managerial environment leads to feelings of inadequacy and undermines wellbeing (Perryman and Calvert, 2020). Ultimately, the root of the unease is a clash of values, where for some the performative framework urges inauthentic behaviour. The daily choice is between what Hennessey and MacNamara call 'the silence of assent' (2013, p. 17) or challenging the system: in other words, compliance or resistance.

This black-and-white choice has led to a debate which has become increasingly polarised. On the one hand, there are those who promulgate a view of education which appears to be a transactional technical process, whose aim is to ensure that standards are achieved, while on the other are those who feel that education is much broader and deeper than this functionalist approach. To use an aphorism, we are in danger of valuing what we can measure when we ought to be trying to measure what we really value. To some degree this is an age-old debate because it asks what the purpose of education is. The answer to that question informs the mechanisms we might use to understand how well society has been educated. As we will see in subsequent chapters, the neoliberal and neoconservative responses to this fundamental question will also be heard in relation to curriculum and pedagogy: to what is learnt and how it is taught.

CASE STUDY: NOTTINGHAMSHIRE COUNTY COUNCIL

Nottinghamshire County Council is a Local Authority which includes schools in post-industrial coalfield towns as well as rural areas, though not the city of Nottingham itself. The following case study is drawn from the Authority's strategy for improving educational opportunities for all children; it clearly embodies the accountability agenda.

The vision of the County Council is for the county to be a region where children can grow up free from deprivation and disadvantage, where they are not held back by circumstances of birth.

Accountability

Education providers are closely monitored and held to account for the attainment and progress of all learners, including their most vulnerable groups. This is done using Department for Education performance tables and the Ofsted inspection framework. Schools are required to publish on their website details of how they are spending the Pupil Premium funding and the effect this is having on the attainment of eligible pupils in their school. Local systems of accountability operate to hold individual schools to account where additional 'high needs' funding is sought in regard to children and young people with SEND. Key partners and Local Authority (LA) teams are held to account through the Improving Educational Opportunities for All Performance Board which monitors the impact of their contribution to the strategy. In turn this Board reports to the LA's Leadership Team, the Children's Trust Board and the Children and Young People's Committee.

Success criteria

The Local Authority determines that success will be measured if the following objectives are achieved:

- An increase in the take-up of funded places for eligible two-year-olds.
- An increase in the percentage of children receiving a 2–2.5-year-old health and development review.
- An increase in the proportion of disadvantaged children (those eligible for free school meals in the last six years and Looked After Children) who achieve the expected level of development in literacy in the Early Years Profile.
- An increase in the take-up of supplementary funding targeted at the most vulnerable children and families.
- An increase in the number of children with SEND and those known to the Early Years schools and families support teams who are accessing full time school at statutory school age.
- Progress of disadvantaged children in reading between Key Stage 1 and Key Stage 2 is at least in line with national outcomes for comparable groups.

- An increase in the number of schools who use appropriate tools to measure progress of children and young people with Special Educational Needs and Disabilities (SEND) over time, where schools and families support teams are involved.
- An increase in the number of Emotional Literacy Support Assistants trained and working in Nottinghamshire schools, so children and young people receive timely emotional literacy support within their school setting.
- An increase in the number of schools involved with the Attachment Aware Schools Project including supervision networks, so school staff use an evidence-based relationship-based approach.
- An increase in the proportion of children receiving specialist support remaining in mainstream school, enabling pupils with SEND to access education in their local community alongside their peers.
- The progress of disadvantaged children at Key Stage 4 is above national outcomes for comparable groups.
- A reduction in the percentage of young people in Years 12 and 13 whose Education, Employment and Training status is not known.
- A reduction in the percentage of young people in Years 12 and 13 who are not in NEET.
- The percentage of young people aged 19 qualified to level 3 is at least in line with national outcomes.
- The percentage of young people not achieving a level 2 qualification in English and mathematics who go on to achieve this by age 19 is at least in line with national outcomes.
- An increase in the number of young people with SEND who secure sustained employment following a supported internship.

Study questions

1. Which (if any) of the measures of success appear to be driven by centralised performance measures, and which by the moral imperative to do the very best for the children in the Authority? Are these categories mutually exclusive?
2. Given that the majority of Early Years providers may be in the private sector, and most secondary schools are academies independent of the Local Authority, what challenges would you foresee in the Authority achieving its vision? How might these be overcome?
3. What do you think is meant by the phrase 'held to account' in the accountability paragraph? How does this go beyond monitoring progress, and how might it be effected in practice?

SUMMARY

This chapter has outlined the mechanisms and instruments of an educational system in which high levels of accountability encourage individuals and organisations to perform in ways which may be contrary to their own values.

FURTHER READING

The Education Debate (3rd ed.) by Stephen Ball (2017) provides a sociological analysis of early 21st century education policy in England. After setting policy developments in a global concept, and looking at the historical development of policies, Chapter 3 examines how technocratic solutions to perceived problems eliminate debate about value and purpose and lead to a particular vision for education which he outlines in Chapter 5.

5

LEADERSHIP AND GOVERNANCE: QUEST AND PARADOX

CONTENTS

This chapter includes:

- A discussion of Local Management of Schools through which the 1988 ERA transformed the nature of school leadership.
- The role of the headteacher which has increased precedence and is the nexus of the neoliberal system.
- Distributed leadership through which power is exercised in schools.
- System leadership, which examines the leadership strata above and beyond schools.
- Governance of schools in the 21st century.

INTRODUCTION

In 1988, the Education Reform Act (ERA) took power from Local Authorities and simultaneously moved it in two directions: upwards, as central government took a much more direct role in defining how schools were to be run, and downwards as autonomy and accountability were handed to schools. This generated a need to reinvent school leadership at every level, from subject leaders in tiny primary schools right through to headteachers of the biggest secondary schools. This 'new localism' (Corry and Stoker, 2002) generated cracks in the national–regional–local government structures for schools which soon fragmented the system that had evolved over the preceding 100 years. The situation is further confused by the fact that there was no system-wide step-change from one structure to another. Instead, schools dropped out of the Local Authority system in ones and twos, sometimes at their own instigation, and sometimes under compulsion, resulting in complexity and potential inconsistency across the nation.

Within this complicated educational landscape school leaders find themselves highly accountable as we have seen in Chapter 4, but in addition hugely responsible – for finances, personnel, building and assets, and of course children's education. A variety of circus metaphors have been used to describe school leadership, including a juggling act and plate-spinning, but perhaps the conjuror or magician might be a better representation for those who sometimes appear to suspend disbelief as they have to hold to ideals which are in tension at least, if not in direct opposition. Earley and Greany (2017) describe several paradoxes which school leaders face in attempting to lead successful schools. Their 'quest' or challenge, therefore, is to work out how to lead in a highly accountable context while recognising and resolving as far as possible the tensions that they face. And just to make things more difficult, some of those challenges change over time and at short notice depending on Westminster changes to education policy. For governors the quest might be to recruit individuals who are authoritative without being authoritarian, who can perform without being performative, who are challenging without being confrontational and who are sympathetic without being sentimental. Therein of course lies another apparent paradox: the need for superhuman qualities in those who simultaneously have all the flaws and foibles of ordinary humanity.

LOCAL MANAGEMENT OF SCHOOLS

Some of the effects of the 1988 ERA felt like a tectonic shift inside schools but passed almost unnoticed by those not working within education, and Local Management of Schools (LMS) was one of these. Also known internationally as School Based Management (SBM), LMS arose directly from neoliberal ideology and its disparaging view of the role of Local Authorities. At a stroke LMS removed the need for this middle layer of system leadership, paradoxically generating increased decentralisation while at the same time introducing mechanisms for much tighter central governmental control (Levačić, 1998). The principle of LMS was (and is) to put decision-making powers into local hands, through school leadership teams, parents and other stakeholders, undermining the influence of the Local Authority (LA) which, as we have already seen, was perceived to be overly progressive and insufficiently challenging. The hope was that this would, through the accountability measures that we have discussed, inevitably drive standards of education up:

> The purpose of local management of schools is to enhance the quality of education by enabling more informed and effective use to be made of the resources available for teaching and learning.
>
> (DfE, 1994, p. 7)

In the 21st century it is hard to imagine the pre-LMS landscape. Headteachers looked after the internal management of the school, organising the curriculum and maintaining pupils' discipline. Schools' budgets were not just monitored but controlled by the Local Education Authority (LEA), which also had responsibility for appointing and paying staff. Teacher trainees often applied to an Authority's 'pool' of teachers, from which they would be deployed to whichever school needed them the following September. Issues of staff discipline would be dealt with by the LEA, and the LEA was the owner of school sites, buildings and assets. Consequently, the LEA was responsible for the upkeep of schools, including new building projects, maintenance and repairs, and ongoing running costs and insurance. The LEA was also responsible for managing school admissions, transport, and support for children with special educational needs.

Not all of these responsibilities transferred to local school control overnight; some were dependent on a school opting out of LEA control, while others (such as school transport) remain the responsibility of the Local Authority to this day. What emerged over time was a spectrum, so that we now see some schools which are virtually totally detached from the LA, a minority of others which remain maintained 'community schools' under the LA's authority and a great many somewhere in between. This is further complicated by the fact that a number of schools make the choice to purchase some services from a Local Authority which may have reorganised to look more like a commercial service provider. This is not to underestimate the changes that have happened at LA level: this middle tier of governance has been stripped back over more than 30 years, both in terms of scale and influence. This leaves questions about whether a country-wide system can actually be managed without a strong middle tier (Woods and Simkins, 2014) – questions to which we will return in Chapter 12.

Wherever a school sits on the spectrum that runs from LA independence to embedded dependence, the nature of school leadership is not what it once was. To reverse the usual argument, if leaders are going to be held tightly accountable for the performance of their schools (however this is measured), then they need some freedom to direct and allocate resources as they see fit. In other words, there must be agency within school leadership where once it might have resided within the LA. The agency and activity of school leadership is somewhat diverse and distributed, including governance structures as well as the layers of leaders within a school's hierarchy, but it inevitably revolves around one individual: the headteacher.

HEADTEACHERS

The role of the headteacher (or principal) is multifarious. Over the same period that the role has become more clearly defined, so it has become increasingly complex and wide-ranging. While there has always been a collective understanding of a headteacher's responsibilities, these were largely unarticulated and ill-defined until the Education (No. 2) Act of 1986 and the Teachers' Pay and Conditions Act in 1987 (Le Métais, 1995). Over subsequent years, the position has been carefully clarified, honed and polished to produce the multifaceted role with which we are now familiar. Today's headteacher has to be a visionary, a leader and manager, a financially astute, politically aware advocate and salesperson (Moore et al., 2002). Add to this the need to know and understand children and adults, a good knowledge of curriculum, teaching, learning and assessment, and it can be seen that the role is unquestionably demanding and challenging. There is of course an expectation that headteachers act ethically and professionally at all times. We have seen how the freedoms of autonomous leadership have associated accountabilities for school leaders, and as the essence of leadership is embodied in the person of the headteacher the consequences of accountability have the same focus. This can mean that the role of the headteacher is as precarious as it is rewarding.

While there is of course a range of opinions and a balance to be achieved, there is a sense in which headteachers have not been entirely passive in the march to give them more independence and autonomy. On the contrary, there is evidence that they have pushed for increased freedoms with the argument that no-one else knows their school better than they do, so they should have the freedom to make their own decisions (see, for example, Thompson, 2010). Where they have been resistant to neoliberal reform, headteachers have learned to negotiate the system, using 'masquerade and reinvention' (Fuller, 2019, p. 31), amongst other techniques, to negotiate the system, minimising potential damage to their schools and reducing compromise of their own values.

The development of the headteacher's role has been described as a progression from administration before the 1988 ERA, through management in the first decade of LMS, to leadership after the 1997 change of government (Simkins, 2012). During the intermediate management phase, a new understanding developed of the skills required in headteachers, resulting in the publication of national standards for headteachers in 1997. While it has been argued (e.g., Male, 2018) that the standards were not based on robustly researched evidence, they became the foundation for a new headteacher's qualification, the National Professional Qualification for Headship (NPQH). It was suggested (Bush, 1998) that preparation for school leadership was one of the major educational issues of the late 1990s. Since then both the headteachers' standards and the NPQH have been revised and updated, but they remain a benchmark, in particular, for those newly embarking on headship. For a brief period (2004–12) NPQH was a mandatory requirement for all first-time headteachers, and although this is no longer the case, the NPQH still has substantial currency within the system.

During the early days of the NPQH the New Labour government made significant investment into the development of headteachers. A National College for School Leadership (NCSL – later renamed National College for Teaching and Leadership) was founded in 2000 and a purpose-designed centre built in Nottingham in 2002. More than a physical building, the College oversaw and commissioned delivery of the NPQH through regional centres, generated its own in-house research and encouraged a networked approach to professional learning supported by technology and the emergent internet. However, NCSL was never autonomous, but remained rooted in the Department for Education and Skills (DfES) as a quasi-governmental institution that upheld ministerial priorities. NPQH (and other 'programmes' which NCSL ran) was never an academic qualification (it was criticised for being undemanding academically: Bush, 2006), and NCSL never had the awarding powers of a university. It is notable that when the Conservative government finally wiped out the last remaining traces of NCSL in 2018 it was replaced with the Teaching *Regulation* Agency.

In its heyday, NCSL achieved its stated aim of providing 'a single national focus for school leadership development, research and innovation' (Southworth, 2004, p. 340). It wasn't a unique focus, and as a government mouthpiece it inevitably generated some criticism, but with annual funding that reached £111 million in 2004–05 (Thrupp, 2005), it would be surprising if NCSL had not had some influence on school leadership and societal understanding of the role of the headteacher. It certainly contributed to a supportive professional infrastructure for school leaders (Bolam, 2004). The headteacher standards became embedded in the collective psyche and as they developed over time (morphing through the national standards of excellence for headteachers) they came to embed the Teachers' Standards, effectively providing an implicit answer to the question of whether a headteacher needs to be a teacher, or whether they simply need to be able to run a business. The answer seems to be both: in law headteachers don't have to have QTS but the national standards expect them to be able to teach – as well as being able to manage the school, drive improvement, support governance and work in partnership with others (DfE, 2020a). One could be forgiven for thinking that the requirement is for someone superhuman: Michael Fullan (1998) suggested that 'miracle workers' would be needed to lead 21st-century schools.

The idea of superhuman miracle workers might be considered an extreme and perhaps flippant comment on post-ERA developments, but Fullan's words turned out to be prophetic, as the concept of the 'superhead' was celebrated by politicians and press in the early days of the 21st century. The New Labour government introduced the notion of transformation into the lexicon of school improvement – transformation of curriculum, standards and life chances – a concept that was absorbed by subsequent governments which extended it to transformation of the workforce and organisational structures of schools. The essence of school leadership was change management, and school leaders looked to business and commerce to learn how to move their establishments from good to great (Collins, 2001), turning to academics such as Michael Fullan and Andy Hargreaves, whose works theorised educational change in an attempt to influence practice in the general global trend to neoliberalism (Ahtiainen, 2017). It has been argued that the new orthodoxy of ongoing transformation demands 'spectacular' leaders (Bates, 2015), and with hindsight it is perhaps not surprising that a small number of seemingly superhuman individuals hit the headlines with stories of stunning transformation of schools. Although it quickly emerged that transforming a school's fortunes takes more than just the para-chuting in of a charismatic individual (see, for example, Perryman, 2002), the idea of a school's future resting in the hands of a single person continued. In 2011 Michael Wilshaw – then a headteacher but later to become HMCI – said:

> Take that scene in Pale Rider when the baddies are shooting up the town, the mists dissipate and Clint is there. Being a headteacher is all about being the lone warrior, fighting for righteousness, fighting the good fight, as powerful as any chief executive ... We need headteachers with ego.
>
> (in Barker, 2011)

The image is one of single-minded determination that will succeed against the odds: autocratic leadership where the head has a mysterious but exclusive understanding of what is best for the school. Where headteachers are successful (by the definitions of the government of the day) they are awarded public honours, with the usual media celebra-tions that highlight the actions of the individual, and in so doing perpetuate the myth of the hero head (Blackmore and Thomson, 2004). Add to this the identification of school-level accountability with the persona of the headteacher and it is easy to see why the construct of the superhead has been difficult to shake off, though the term itself is rarely used any more. Kaser and Halbert's 2009 assertion that 'the days of the heroic solitary leader "heading" the school are almost gone' (Kaser and Halbert, 2009, p. 7) looks to have been overly optimistic from the perspective of the 2020s, but the reality is that while the nexus of educational leadership has been and will continue to be the head-teacher, political idealism has driven an explosion of leadership roles, behaviours and structures above and below this focal point.

DISTRIBUTED LEADERSHIP

Middle leaders in schools – heads of department, heads of year, subject coordinators and so on – have been described as the engine room of school improvement (for example, in

Hall and Noyes, 2009). This metaphor seems to recognise that while the headteacher acts like a captain on the bridge of a ship, identifying the destination and issuing orders in order to ensure a swift journey, the middle leaders are working hard below decks, unseen and possibly unrecognised, but absolutely vital to the success of the venture. In the 1990s, as school management turned into school leadership, the school middle management tier had to undergo its own metamorphosis, changing from a collective of power barons who could obstruct and prevent change (Ball, 2012), to proactive leaders of sub-teams whose success would be key to a successful school (Brown and Rutherford, 1998). Terrell describes the middle leader's team in a large organisation as the 'seed bed for the development of culture' (in Leask and Terrell, 2013, p. 5), where the culture includes the thinking, beliefs and assumptions of the teaching team. There is a sense that in any large school some form of sub-unit, whether based on curriculum or pastoral divisions (so, subjects and year teams, respectively) is necessary, and there is a danger that this middle layer can be either subservient to and potentially squashed by the higher levels of hierarchy, or alternatively an inertial force that blocks proposed change. This was exemplified in a wide-ranging review which showed that 15 years after the ERA there was still evidence that middle leaders were reluctant to engage with whole-school priorities, and that in secondary schools in particular their preference to act as departmental advocates could still block large-scale change (Bennett et al., 2003).

By the turn of the century distributed leadership was emerging as an important dimension of the official discourse around school improvement in England (Frost and Harris, 2003). Some independent training providers were quick to recognise this and offer middle leaders' training: just as headteachers were finding themselves with roles and responsibilities which they had hitherto not considered or trained for, so too was there a tranche of middle leaders who needed training and development if they were to discharge their new responsibilities effectively (Brown and Rutherford, 1999). It took a while for the government to catch up, and just as the NCSL was contemplating its own demise a National Professional Qualification for Middle Leadership (NPQML) was introduced, along with a sister qualification for senior leaders, the NPQSL, in 2012. The NPQs therefore outlined a 'lattice' of competencies and training that provided for a national understanding of different types of leadership in schools, together with a complex set of interrelated supporting and developmental activities to supply and maintain current and future leaders (Supovitz, 2014).

The NPQ suite was subsequently expanded to include NPQEH for executive headteachers – those with responsibility for more than one school – and a further remodelling of the NPQs in 2021 disaggregated the generic NPQML into parts (specialist NPQs) to recognise different types of middle leadership. This demonstrates a recognition of an ongoing perceived need for investment into middle leaders. The NPQs, as their names suggest, are professional qualifications with no academic credits, and some might argue that there has been a missed opportunity to raise the academic standards of leaders within a degree-level profession. Successful completion of NPQs brings no automatic salary enhancements, though the NPQs do have currency in most schools as a recognition of someone actively engaging in their own professional development and improving their understanding of leadership at that level. The hierarchy of NPQs also indicates a career development journey for aspirant leaders, and it is not unknown for individuals to progress from NPQML to NPQSL and then NPQH as they gradually move up the promotion ladder. The DfE recognised this and embedded it into a 'golden thread' that links trainee teachers through the Early Career Framework all the way to senior leadership roles. Despite these developments over more than a decade, international research suggests that there is still little evidence to quantify the impact that middle leaders have in their schools (Harris et al., 2019), though there are tangible qualitative benefits of effective distributed leadership (Day and Sammons, 2016).

In the postmodern era of high stakes accountability, it is no surprise that responsibility and accountability for pupil progress and achievement are delegated to middle leaders in just the same way as strategic direction and oversight of an element of the organisation. Middle leaders are the faces that Ofsted inspection teams meet in their drilling down and deep dives under the skin of a school, and middle leaders will have to answer to hierarchy both inside and outside of the school for the results of the children in their care. Middle leaders will often be asked to provide regular evaluations of their areas of responsibility, and to write development plans identifying necessary improvements and how they will be brought about. They may be involved in the appointment of new staff and will be responsible for what their teams teach as well as how this is done.

As a consequence it can be in the middle leadership tier that the effects of performativity are most strongly felt: irrespective of their own personal values, middle leaders may feel pressure to conform to a headteacher's notion of transformational leadership which becomes an exercise in compliance (Thrupp and Willmott, 2003). This generates a paradox in which effective delegated leadership simply looks like an extension of the headteacher's power (Rolph, 2004); failure to conform can result in middle leaders who have been motivated by a sense of vocation being 'purged' in favour of teachers who are more willing to accept the discourse of audit and standards (Courtney and Gunter, 2015). This view may be insufficiently nuanced as there is evidence of an increasing number of professionals who are comfortable with performance measures (Keddie, 2017). Nonetheless high-performing schools may exhibit a 'mirage' of professional autonomy (Wilkins, 2015) in which middle leaders ensure compliance of the school community.

The tools available to the middle leader are the same technologies that Foucault identifies within all disciplining organisations: hierarchical observation and normalising judgement (1977, p. 170). The teacher appraisal system discussed in Chapter 4 provides the mechanisms for monitoring and evaluating the work of a school's teachers, and it is enacted through the middle leaders (who are in turn subject to the same procedures). In many schools the prevailing view of monitoring by middle leaders' is critically hostile, but there is a significant minority of schools where it is viewed as positive, both as a developmental opportunity in which shortcomings can be identified and addressed, and as a chance to showcase excellence (Rhodes et al., 2008). Either way, the fact remains that middle leaders can exert substantial power – something that they might not feel comfortable with. For many, demonstrable competence in the classroom, based on sound subject knowledge and an understanding of pedagogy, may propel them into a position of leadership and management for which they feel ill-equipped. We will return to the apparent disconnect that promotes good teachers out of the classroom in Chapter 6.

The world of the middle leader in schools is a complex one: squeezed from above and below, instruments of senior management yet still rooted in (and often popular with) the body of the staffroom. It follows that the development needs of middle leaders are equally complex as they strive to remain experts in subject knowledge and pedagogy while getting to grips with data analysis, leading a team and holding individuals to account (Thorpe and Bennett-Powell, 2014). NPQs may provide for some of these needs, but there will always be a sense in which new middle leaders will be learning on the job. Changes in school structures and greater flexibility for school leaders has generated a diversity of middle leader types within schools across the country: subject and pastoral leads go by a plethora of names and may have widely different responsibilities and freedoms, all of which make it more difficult for national generic training to prepare them adequately. Despite the many tensions and apparent contradictions, the role of the middle leader in schools remains pivotal, with its 'direct and potentially powerful impact on colleagues and students alike' (Fleming, 2019, p. 1). Whether as a passive cog in the machine, operating to the head's instructions, or with more autonomy and agency exercising genuine leadership, the middle leader's contribution to school improvement continues to be vital.

SYSTEM LEADERSHIP

Diversification amongst middle leadership overseen by the headteacher has been matched if not exceeded by dramatic change in the leadership of the system of which schools are a part, so headteachers find themselves at the pinch point of an hourglass with divergence and diversity above and below. The most farsighted of 1970s New Right adherents would surely have been surprised by the shape of 21st-century governance and system leadership that were sparked by the 1988 ERA. The intention to break the power and influence of Local Authorities became action in the 1990s, and 13 years of Labour government cemented and accelerated progress in the same direction, essentially confirming the neoliberal quasi-market approach as a permanent fixture of the English system. Deconstruction of the geographically based structure, and subsequent construction of new autonomous units working from individual schools upwards, has resulted in a picture that is inconsistent and, some would say, incoherent (West and Wolfe, 2019), with a rich diversity of structures and procedures that seems to embrace contradiction and conflict.

The resulting complexity with 'opaque networks of power' (Kulz, 2021) defies description by a simple diagram or organogram.

The key to understanding new models of system leadership and governance is the academy as a basic unit. As we saw in Chapter 3, academies are schools which are independent of the Local Authority, though use of the word 'independent' continues to fuel arguments when it is confused or conflated with independent (fee-paying) schools. Academies have much vaunted 'freedoms' or privileges which are not available to other schools, including:

- The ability to set their own staff pay and conditions;
- Greater control of their budget;
- Freedom from following the National Curriculum;
- Freedom to change the length of terms and school days.

All academies, along with community (or maintained) schools that are still run under the auspices of Local Authorities, derive their finances from the government through a formula that is based on pupil numbers. The difference is that academy funding goes direct to the academy, which uses it to purchase whatever services it may need. Community schools receive their funding via the LA, which withholds some to cover the cost of the services it provides.

This exemplifies the way in which power has been sapped from LAs using an economic technology. As the number of academies grew, particularly between 2010 and 2020, so the financial income that the LAs would have drawn from the government's Dedicated Schools Grant has declined. As well as acknowledging a philosophical stance in turning away from the LA, when a school becomes an academy it also reduces the funding in the Authority's coffers and reduces its capacity to carry out many of its functions. The law does not allow for LAs to hand over their responsibilities entirely: LAs have a wide range of statutory duties, including providing free school transport, identifying and prosecuting poor attendance, commissioning services to support children with special educational needs and disabilities (SEND), and school improvement. This last point illustrates contradiction built into policy: while an LA is technically responsible for standards and improvement across all the schools in the area, it has no right to intervene in the work of any of the academies and is reliant on their cooperation if it is to do any meaningful work with them. In such a scenario it has been recognised that 'relationships are king' as LAs try to persuade and motivate academy leaders over whom they have no inherent authority (Parish et al., 2012, p. 5).

Academies themselves are seen by the government as crucial to a national raising of standards, though the evidence to support this is contested (Gorard, 2009). A further complication is that in the early days of the academy programme there were two types of academy: *converter* academies, which chose to opt out of LA control and, on the basis of existing high performance, were given autonomy to do so; and *sponsored* academies, which were previously schools with a history of poor performance that were taken over by a 'sponsor' organisation in order to change the leadership and drive an improvement in standards. Initially such sponsored academies received additional funding from central government or the sponsor or both, though this burst of generosity was not long-lasting. The fact that some sponsor organisations were businesses or companies with no previous record in education added fuel to the fire of controversy, prompting suggestions that schools were being privatised for profit (for example, Silva, 2020; West and Bailey, 2013). Nevertheless, it was hardly surprising that the sponsored academies did show initial improvements in standards. Andrews and Perera (2017) identify this early improvement for sponsored academies, but conclude:

> It is evident that the structure of the school is less meaningful to the outcomes of pupils than what is happening within those schools

> (p. 42)

The explosion in the number of academies during the early days of the coalition government and the diminution of the middle LA tier gave rise to a new problem. DfE officials in Whitehall now had to manage direct relationships with several thousand schools (3,980 by July 2014 – DfE, 2015a) whereas in the past they only needed to maintain contact with 153 Local Authorities. The solution to this difficulty serves as an example of policy development that is driven from the bottom upwards. Some academies had linked together to form chains of academies, and some sponsors already had a group of academies under their wing. In addition, some highly performing academies had in turn sponsored new academies, resulting in a cluster of academies operating under the same leadership. These chains, or groups of academies, formed multi-academy trusts (MATs) where the trust has legal responsibility for a number of academies (see governance, below). Recognising the organisational advantages of this, the coalition government encouraged the growth of MATs, both by aggregation of smaller MATs joining together and by encouraging large successful MATs to accumulate additional new academies. There is an ongoing debate over the educational advantages of larger MATs and the optimal size of a MAT, with some leaders advocating 20 academies or more (Staufenberg, 2017). Independent research suggests that the size of a MAT has little significant impact on children's achievements, and that there is a possibility that, on average, pupils in large MATs may perform worse than their peers in standalone academies or schools (Bernardinelli et al., 2018). Research data have never stood in the way of government ideology or policy, and the drive towards an academy-only system based on relatively large MATs continues. It has been suggested that the growth of large MATs is unsustainable as it is dependent upon the altruism of Chief Executive Officers (CEOs) who need to be prepared for the risks involved in taking over an underperforming school (Simon et al., 2021).

In a pragmatic move that appears to deviate from the relentless progress towards central control and local accountability, new middle-tier players were created in 2014 in the form of Regional Schools Commissioners (RSCs). Working across eight large regions (confusingly, not the same regions as those used by Ofsted), the role of the RSCs is to take decisions on behalf of the Secretary of State (Durbin et al., 2015): in practice this means approving new academies and sponsors, brokering sponsorship of schools identified as failing, and challenging underperforming schools, academies and MATs. It is explicit that the RSCs are not responsible for school improvement activities (Foster and Long, 2016), but their remit to identify underperformance and arrange structural solutions – in other words new leadership for those schools – is clearly intended to support system-wide improvement. Working with a small advisory board of experienced headteachers, the activity of the RSCs has gone largely unnoticed by the general public, though its impact can be seen quite starkly when they intervene. Underperforming schools (or academies) are often closed and reopened with a new name, branding and uniform as they join the sponsoring MAT, and it is rare that the headteacher survives the transition. The timescale for these transitions can appear to be very short, though there will have been work going on behind the scenes before the new arrangements are made public.

While the rise of MATs may have been viewed with trepidation by some headteachers, for others it represented an opportunity. Successful school leaders now have the chance to take on leadership of more than one school – and in fact these opportunities preceded MATs as headteachers took on executive headteacher roles in LA attempts to provide school to school support to help raise standards (Harris et al., 2006). There has consequently been a blurring of the title of headteacher, which retains a specific legal definition, with other terms such as executive headteacher (generally accepted as relating to the leadership of more than one school), head of school (often the de facto head of a school but working under an executive headteacher) and associate headteacher (often similar to a head of school). In many academies and larger secondary schools, the label of principal might replace headteacher in some or all of these titles. The additional responsibilities and requisite skills of the executive headteacher have been recognised in the development of the NPQEH for executive headship. A further step that might be available to executive headteachers is that of CEO of a MAT, a role which takes the leadership of schools to a completely new level (Lord et al., 2016).

An additional development in the complicated mix of school types is the free school. Free schools were introduced by the 2010–15 coalition government as a means by which parents, teachers, charities and local communities (including religious groups) could establish a new school in their area. According to the then Prime Minister David Cameron this would give even the poorest parents a 'choice to escape poor schools' by establishing a new school, independent of the Local Authority (cited in Hatcher, 2011, p. 489). The appeal was directly to the neoliberal ideals of consumer choice and market competition. In the early days almost anyone could open a free school, though restrictions were later brought in to make sure that sponsors of free schools have some track record of school improvement, and in addition that there is some demand for more school places in the area. As a consequence, after an initial rush the number of free schools opening has slowed to a trickle.

Though the opening of a new free school might be controversial at the time, once it has been established it operates to all intents and purposes as an academy, with exactly the same funding mechanisms, freedoms and restrictions (and in common with other special types of academy: studio schools and university technical schools). Despite government ambitions, free schools and academies have not used the freedoms they might have because they are constrained by the same accountability requirements as any other maintained school (this will be discussed in more detail in Chapter 7). Where there is innovation it is more likely to be in management practices than in curriculum offer or pedagogy (Wiborg et al., 2018), so it is unlikely to have a direct impact on children's experiences of school.

GOVERNANCE

If the complexities of school, academy and MAT leadership are somewhat obscure to parents, the governance structures are all but invisible, and the advent of Grant Maintained (GM) schools and then academies introduced a similar complexity of governance models, relationships and structures. There is some irony in the fact that measures that were ostensibly introduced to give parents more control and ownership have simultaneously allowed them to have less say in what goes on in their children's schools.

Governance structures for community schools are relatively straightforward, with a governing body made up of 10–20 willing volunteers. In proportions that are dependent on the type of school, there will be elected staff and parent governors, community governors and LA governors. Some governors will be co-opted onto the governing body, and for church schools there will also be relevant church governors (DfE, 2020b). The role of the governing body is to act as a 'critical friend' to the headteacher, holding the school leadership team to account for budgetary spending, management of personnel, and performance and welfare of pupils. The governing body has legal responsibility for the school, and has strategic oversight; the role of the headteacher is to take day-to-day operational decisions. Some of these (such as pupil exclusions) are scrutinised and ratified by governors.

By contrast the governance structures of academies and MATs are many and varied. There is no legislation that prescribes in detail how a MAT must be composed, but as a charitable trust a MAT must have at least three members (similar to shareholders) and a board of trustees (or directors). The members have ultimate control of the trust and can appoint trustees, though they usually have little involvement in the running of the MAT on anything but the highest strategic level. The real power base of a MAT sits with the trustees who have the same legal responsibilities as community school governors: setting the vision and direction of the school, holding the CEO to account, and ensuring the trust is financially sound. Many MAT trusts delegate some of their responsibilities to local bodies which support each of the academies in the trust – they can do this to a greater or lesser degree for each academy according to the perceived need. Confusingly, in some trusts these local boards are called governing bodies even though they do not have the same legal status as community school governing bodies, so we will refer to them here as local advisory boards.

The composition of the board of trustees is open to interpretation, with few constraints. A MAT must have at least two parent representatives, either on the trust board or within the local advisory boards. This means that a large MAT, with perhaps 40 or more academies and many thousands of pupils, needs only have two elected parent representatives on the board of trustees. The other restriction is on the proportion of trustees that are 'local authority influenced', which cannot be more than one fifth – a very clear distancing from LA influence (NCTL, 2014). For the most part, trustees are co-opted onto the board and are not democratically elected, so it is unsurprising that MAT trustees are not seen to represent relevant stakeholders and that they potentially disenfranchise local communities (Baxter and Cornforth, 2021). Some of the larger MATs have no discrete geographical footprint, which makes it all the more difficult for trustees to represent each academy's local community effectively. While some trusts work hard to ensure local representation, overall the inadvertent impact of decentralising education has been to reduce local accountability. The deliberate implementation of the quasi-market, in which MATs are actively encouraged to compete rather than collaborate, could further undermine the imperative to meet local needs, as well as any possibility of learning from each other's practice (Baxter and Floyd, 2019).

Oversight of the activity of a number of schools is not uncommon globally and has been characterised as 'network governance' (Ehren and Perryman, 2017). In England, the growth of MATs has certainly achieved some of the intentions of 1988 ERA in that leaders are personally held accountable for their school's performance, and if they cannot bring about improvements, they are rapidly moved out of post: under Local Authorities such action would have been lengthy and convoluted (in part due to the balance of power between the Governing Body and the LA), and in fact this rarely happened. Accountability *within* MATs can therefore be very strong and actions swift, but the same is not true with regard to the accountability of the MATs themselves. Ofsted highlight a poor understanding of how to measure and monitor the performance of a MAT, which inevitably weakens the accountability of the MAT (2019, p. 23), and which potentially opens the possibility of illegal and immoral behaviour by trust boards (Male, 2019). There is an argument that in turn this threatens to undermine democratic structures, as MAT members are not elected and nor are there any criteria around their recruitment.

Faced with the ongoing government drive for more academies and MATs, some Local Authorities and religious foundations adopted an 'if you can't beat them, join them' approach, and actively encouraged groups of schools to work together to form a geographically based MAT. These have the advantage of being able to maintain many of the values of the original organisation, while taking advantage of any benefits of being in a MAT. There are now numerous examples of Church of England MATs, Catholic MATs and Diocesan MATs. It is more difficult to discern those MATs which developed with LA blessing, though these do exist; of course they necessarily retained some distance from the LA. The Johnson government latterly introduced provision for LAs to form their own MATs, perhaps in recognition that it would be the only way to achieve a 100% academised system by 2030. Across the country we therefore see a vast range of different types of school that have arisen through 150 years of policy development. A local area may have primary, infant, junior and secondary schools, selective grammar schools and comprehensive, schools with sixth forms and schools without. These could be faith schools with a church affiliation, they may or may not be academies or free schools; they might be standalone or in federations or MATs (a useful typology of schools can be found in Miller, 2011). There is no guarantee that the governance of two neighbouring schools may be in any way similar, and no assumptions can be made about the potential involvement of parents or other local stakeholders. Timid policymaking followed by inconsistently applied neoliberalism has certainly resulted in diversity within the system, though the actual choice available to parents is debatable. It could further be argued that the changes of the last 40 years have not reduced bureaucracy, but relocated it, and that growing MATs will serve to undermine the quasi-market by generating new monopolies and reducing choice (Wilkins, 2017).

CASE STUDY: OASIS COMMUNITY LEARNING

Oasis Community Learning (OCL) is a MAT with over 50 academies distributed across most of England. The trust operates a regional leadership structure and has developed a clear governance model which is described below using the trust's own words.

The Oasis model of governance

The Oasis model of governance is designed to ensure strong accountability and therefore great educational standards. Statutory governance responsibilities are held by the OCL Board, who ultimately govern each academy. These responsibilities are delegated to the OCL CEO, National Director of Academies and Regional Directors and then to Principals, taking responsibility for overall performance, financial viability, legal compliance and statutory duties.

The National Director of Academies is accountable to the CEO, assisting them and acting with their full authority to deliver education and governance across all Oasis academies. The role will deputise for the CEO and act as an ambassador for the organisation.

Regional Directors, on behalf of the CEO, line-manage academy Principals and Executive Principals. Regional Directors have responsibility for academy target setting and monitoring the progress that academies are making towards addressing improvement

(Continued)

priorities identified by the Monitoring & Standards Team. Regional Directors are accountable for ensuring an effective culture of safeguarding.

The National Director of Monitoring Standards leads a Monitoring & Standards Team informing school evaluation and providing academy leaders with key information on what their academy is doing well and what steps they should consider taking further to improve things.

The Oasis way of working is through Hubs, which seek to ensure individual people and whole communities have access to holistic and integrated support, economically, vocationally, academically, environmentally, socially, morally, spiritually, physically and emotionally.

In the local 'community Hubs', OCL aspires to ensure broad, integrated and quality activities. These include exceptional education through the academies and may also include youth and children's work, community empowerment, housing, advice and support, personal and spiritual development and health and well-being.

Each of the Hubs responds to the strengths and needs of their local neighbourhood, and community members are actively engaged in designing, delivering and leading services. Hub Councils play a key role in ensuring that OCL's priorities are driven by a local movement of people.

Hub Councils are a key mechanism for ensuring that OCL is accountable to the communities that it serves. They do not hold statutory governance responsibility for the academy; however, Oasis believes that the role of the Hub Council is a vital one because it is essential that people in a local community have the opportunity to discuss, reflect and become actively involved in supporting education in their community. They will do this by making links in their local community, building partnerships, considering the wider context of the pupils and families in the academy and practically responding to the support requested from Principals.

The Hub Council has the following functions:

- Shaping strategy – Ensuring community accountability, owning Hub priorities and playing a significant role in driving them forward.
- Supporting – Practically supporting key priorities of the strategy – by fundraising, volunteers, capacity growth.
- Gathering – Establishing one or two network events per year to grow the local movement of people who are engaged in the local Hub.
- Ethos – Supporting the Principal(s) and Hub Leader to ensure that the ethos is lived out in Oasis work.
- Connecting – Communicating with the national board(s), providing local intelligence.

Study questions

1. (How) does the Oasis structure challenge what Kulz called 'opaque networks of power', and where might there still be opacity in the system?

2. How does this MAT with a national footprint ensure local understanding and accountability? What is the value of Hub Councils that 'do not have statutory responsibility?'

3. This chapter began by noting the rise in significance of the headteacher or principal. How significant is the principal in Oasis academies, and where could you foresee relationship tensions within the organisation?

SUMMARY

This chapter has examined the key strata in the hierarchy of school leadership, looked at post-ERA school governance, and outlined how an individualised and decentralised approach to school leadership has resulted in a diversity of practices and structures and an increasingly fragmented system.

FURTHER READING

Earley and Greany's edited collection of essays in *School Leadership and Education System Reform* (2017) contains some pertinent and provocative discussions of what leadership and governance look like in today's schools (part 1). Part 2 discusses some of the specific responsibilities of school leaders, while part 3 is more forward-looking, considering some of the emergent issues for today's leaders.

6

RESOURCES: MANAGING THE UNMANAGEABLE

CONTENTS

This chapter includes:

- An exploration of the issues involved in employing qualified teachers in schools, including the training of teachers and the impact of the 2003 workforce reform programme.
- An overview of the roles of paraprofessionals: the range of adults employed by schools who are not teachers.
- A discussion of the material resources which must be managed by school leaders, including finances, buildings and estates.

INTRODUCTION

As we have seen, the 1988 Education Reform Act heralded a new era of leadership, with responsibility for resources taken from the Local Authority and devolved to headteachers. The concept of resources needs to be understood in its widest sense: Hedley Beare et al. (2018) would include money, people, knowledge, technology, materials, time and power under this heading. The law dictates headteachers must steward the first two of these responsibly; the remainder follow by implication. The content of the curriculum might be considered an additional resource over which heads have leadership and control; this will be discussed in detail in the next chapter.

The title of headteacher does little to convey the realities of the job. In times of extremity, heads may find themselves cleaning toilets, fixing doors or cutting hedges (Ferguson, 2019), but even when they are not doing these things themselves, they remain responsible for the school's material assets, so will need to ensure that someone else carries out these tasks. In turn this means that heads are responsible for a diverse range of staff, not just those who teach. While the governing body, academy trust, or, in a decreasing number of cases, the Local Authority, is the employer, the headteacher or Trust CEO is the senior line manager who, by definition, must deal with all aspects of employing a workforce. This runs from hire and fire to working practices and staff wellbeing. This cannot be done without money to pay for the staff and services a school needs to operate effectively, and finances, personnel and buildings are all targets of both local and national policy.

It therefore follows that a study of the policy–practice interface in schools would be incomplete without an understanding of how resources are managed. The Department for Education's (DfE) figures for 2021 show that teachers represent just under half of the school workforce (DfE, 2022c), so it is essential to understand what the other roles are and why they are there. Of all the activity that occurs in schools, teaching and learning is just a part. It will be seen that neoliberalism and Local Management of Schools (LMS) have conspired to generate a complexity that can appear baffling and hard to navigate, and which makes generalisations difficult. The constancy within the system is that wherever you look things will appear slightly different.

QUALIFIED TEACHERS

The core of a school – or indeed any educational establishment – is of course the team of teachers. These are the people who translate policy into practice every moment of the day, as they interpret the curriculum, develop pedagogy, and deal with every aspect of their pupils' experiences. This involves making decisions by the minute: decision-making has long been identified as 'probably the central feature of the role of the teacher' (Eggleston, 1977, p. 5). If they are to make wise decisions, it follows that teachers require a high level of skill as well as knowledge in order to know what legislation, policy, convention or guidance to draw upon, and then to apply that appropriately in the unique and specific situation which they face at that moment. Some of this is developed and honed by experience, but much of the basis for this competence comes from training, both pre-service and once they have qualified. British governments have repeatedly confirmed the view expressed in the 2010 DfE White Paper, *The Importance of Teaching*: 'no education system can be better than the quality of its teachers' (DfE, 2010, p. 3), and have focused some attention on ensuring consistent and effective training for the teaching workforce in schools. While the White Paper may express a certain common-sense truism, the actual relationship between pupils' academic outcomes and teacher 'credentials' is contested, with some American studies (e.g., Clotfelter et al., 2007) suggesting stronger correlations than we see in England (Slater et al., 2012) where issues such as parental involvement and class background often trump factors within the educational system (Wheeler, 2018). There is, however, an important distinction to note in terms of the White Paper terminology: it is the quality of the activity of *teaching* that is important, rather than simply the quality (however measured) of the *teachers* that a school employs (Jasman, 2007).

Around the world teaching is seen almost universally as a degree-level profession. There are some variations and subtleties: in Switzerland, for example, primary teachers need a bachelor's degree, while for secondary teachers a master's degree is required – and pay scales may also reflect these nuances. In the United Kingdom, teachers must hold a bachelor's degree as a minimum, supplemented in England with demonstrable ability in literacy and numeracy (and science for primary teachers). In order to achieve Qualified Teacher Status (QTS) additional study is required, often through an academic postgraduate qualification (such as PGCE) or alternatively as part of an integrated undergraduate bachelor's degree. In recent years it has become more common for new entrants to the profession to achieve QTS without a corresponding postgraduate award, though the bachelor's degree remains a fundamental requirement.

While the need for teachers to have a degree provides some reassurance in terms of the academic capabilities of teachers, there is a small minority of cases where this presents a hurdle which might prevent otherwise well-qualified candidates from entering the classroom. Examples would include those with excellent industry experience that could be relevant in school contexts, particularly as teachers of applied or vocational courses. For maintained schools there is a loophole which allows for such individuals to be employed as instructors, or unqualified teachers – though the corresponding unqualified teachers' pay scale may make this an unattractive career change.

The distinction between qualified and unqualified teachers has been blurred by neoliberal progress and its push to reduce central bureaucracy. Before the advent of CTCs and subsequently academies, all schools were bound by the School Teachers' Pay and Conditions Document (STPCD) for England and Wales, which dictated who could be employed to teach, on what terms and on which pay scales. The STPCD was supplemented by the so-called 'Burgundy Book', an agreement between unions and the Local Government

Association outlining the working conditions for teachers in schools. One of the freedoms that academies have is to be able to ignore the provisions of the STPCD and apply their own terms and conditions on teaching staff, including deciding on whether to employ unqualified teachers, and if so, on what pay scales. In reality, while maintained schools cannot ignore the STPCD they can and do bend the rules, which muddies the waters around teacher qualifications; conversely many multi-academy trusts (MATs) and academies stick closely to the spirit of the STPCD.

One of the ironies of the outcomes of *The Importance of Teaching* is that a document which described the teacher as 'our society's most valuable asset' (p. 7) and which underlined the importance of a qualified, professionalised workforce, simultaneously promoted more freedoms for academies which allowed them to employ almost anyone to teach. Unsurprisingly, this has led to deprofessionalising of the workforce: Martindale's 2017 analysis of DfE data shows that academies contributed to a significant increase in unqualified teachers in the school system, recruiting 1,500 more unqualified staff than maintained schools between 2010 and 2016 (p. 1028). Furthermore, a quarter of these were not educated to degree level (p. 1020).

As a consequence of national deregulation then, a range of employment practices for teachers is seen in schools. The variance is possibly not as large as it might be, due to what Mathou et al. describe as the 'diverse but convergent interests and norms' of the state, teacher unions and employers (2022, p. 301). There is no advantage to be gained by any party by employing teachers who cannot do their job well, though there will be dis-agreements over how this might be defined and measured. Similarly, there is nothing to be gained by exploiting people to the limits of their endurance, and budgets and market pressures would quickly push outlandishly high or low salaries back towards the system norm. The resulting equilibrium is that while they are not bound by the requirements of the STPCD, most academies do not stray far from it. This includes the basic principles around pay scales, hours worked, job roles and qualifications.

INITIAL TEACHER TRAINING

A second long-lasting effect of the 2010 White Paper was to change the nature of initial teacher training (ITT). Traditionally the preserve of teacher-training colleges and univer-sities, the 21st century saw a drive towards 'school-led' training for teachers that had its roots in *The Importance of Teaching* (though the school-based Graduate Teacher Programme had preceded this). The last years of Gordon Brown's Labour government had seen the development of plans for a Master's in Teaching and Learning (MTL). This would have been an ambitious national development that would have raised the expectations of teachers, developing their skills through professional development delivered in partner-ship with universities, and perhaps leading eventually to a master's-level profession. These ambitions were never realised, and the MTL was forgotten amongst Michael Gove's raft of controversial reforms when the coalition government took power. In creating school-led routes to QTS, Gove simultaneously sought to undermine confidence and power in the university sector (which he identified as part of the woolly liberal 'blob'), and at the same time develop a self-contained and self-sustaining school-based system. He stated that:

> Teaching is a craft and it is best learnt as an apprentice observing a master craftsman or woman. Watching others, and being rigorously observed yourself as you develop, is the best route to acquiring mastery in the classroom.
>
> (2010, cited in Furlong, 2013, p. 43)

Nick Gibb, who was Gove's Schools' Minister (and, tellingly, came back to the DfE in successive Cameron, May, Johnson and Sunak governments), was reported as saying that he'd rather see schools employ teachers with a good degree and no teaching qualification than those from 'rubbish universities' with a PGCE (Williams, 2010). This signalled a rising of the values of pre-war tradition and elitism, to which we will return in Chapters 7 and 8, and the attitude was adopted within Whitehall, resulting in the development of a plethora of school-based routes to QTS. These did not by necessity require the academic qualifications that universities offer or the study of educational practice which their courses contain. In the same way that the response of academies to permitted freedoms was relatively conservative, on the ground the changes to ITT did not diverge from traditional orthodoxy as much as the ministers might have hoped – partly because the universities had always included observing others and being observed at the centre of their ITT provision. Most school-based providers, such as Teaching Schools and SCITTs (School-Centred ITT providers), continued to work in partnership with universities to offer an academic PGCE award along with training for QTS – in much the same way as universities had always worked in partnership with schools who provided placements for ITT students. By 2019 the government identified 12 different routes into teaching, of which 10 could be described as school-based, accounting for about half of all new teachers trained (Foster, 2019). The introduction of a teacher-training apprenticeship further complicated the picture without adding much to the choice of potential trainees because entry requirements remained the same as for all other postgraduate routes. Nevertheless, policy developments certainly contributed to a rich mixture of ITT practices, and examples of a number of different approaches were often found within many schools which engaged in ITT. They did this for a variety of reasons, including commitment to refreshing the workforce, desire to train new teachers in their own image, benefit to the school from working with universities and other providers, and of course as a recruitment activity. By 2021 the abundance of routes into teaching was recognised as a problem, and a national 'Market Review' made recommendations to slim down the number, and rationalise and standardise provision (Bauckham, 2021).

As well as challenging the means by which teachers are trained, 20th-century governments have also paid attention to the content of their training. The Teachers' Standards were developed to provide a basic set of skills or competencies which all trainees had to attain, and which all serving teachers have to maintain. Originally introduced under New Labour, standards for teachers were subsequently slimmed down to summarise teaching on a single page of A4, in what some have described as a shift in seeing teaching less as a profession and more of a technical activity (Abbott et al., 2019), and one which empha-sises teachers' behaviour rather than their attitudes and intellect (Evans, 2011). National standards were also introduced for school-based mentors of ITT trainees and a core content for ITT – essentially the National Curriculum for teacher training – was imposed in 2019. A revised inspection framework from 2020 onwards ensured that Ofsted inspections of ITT providers focused on the curriculum and its impact. In a surprisingly joined-up move, the induction standards for newly qualified teachers were replaced with a two-year Early Career Framework (ECF) which follows seamlessly from the ITT core content and aims to ensure that entrants to the profession get the support they need to become 'effective and successful teachers' (DfE, 2021a). This centralised interference at a detailed level seems contrary to the 2010 White Paper ambitions to remove 'compliance with bureaucratic initiatives' in favour of more 'on the job' training (DfE, 2010, p. 19), but it serves to illustrate the growing tensions caused by rising neoconservatism in governmental thinking.

TEACHER DEVELOPMENT

In common with many professions, those teachers who are recognised as being good at what they do often end up being promoted to leadership and management roles which, by necessity, take them out of the classroom. For some this is a natural progression, and they turn their creativity and energy towards developing staff rather than children, but for others the reduced time in the classroom is a wrench which may take them away from what they see as their core purpose. The net effect of this is that there is a systemic tendency to push the best talent away from where it is evidently effective. To counteract this and to create incentives to stay in the classroom, the idea of the Advanced Skills Teacher (AST) was introduced in the early years of the New Labour government. The concept of ASTs was to create a role that could be achieved by passing a competency threshold, demonstrated through a robust assessment, that would be focused on demonstrating and sharing exceptional classroom practice, with financial rewards commensurate with those of school leaders. Unsurprisingly the notion met with some resistance from teacher and headteacher unions, though individual teachers, especially those new to the profession, were much more open to the idea (Blake et al., 2000). Initial take-up was slow, but against the odds the principle of ASTs was absorbed into the system. While the title no longer remains, similar roles continue to exist, whether they are called Specialist Leaders in Education, Lead Practitioners or by other names and acronyms coined by MATs and academies. The ambition of keeping such practitioners in the classroom, however, fell by the wayside relatively quickly (Sutton et al., 2000), superseded by an emphasis on leading pedagogical excellence both in their own schools and beyond. It is probably all to the good that the 'superteacher' label which was originally popular with the press and politicians has also faded into the mists of time, and that outstanding teachers are now seen as an in-house source of continuing professional development (CPD) that can be cheap, efficient and effective (Forde et al., 2006, p. 131). The role of lead practitioners in CPD to develop teaching and learning will be considered further in Chapter 12.

The day-to-day work carried out by teachers in schools goes well beyond teaching, including such diverse activities as chasing absences, collecting lunch money, putting up classroom displays, photocopying resources, processing reports, arranging examinations and absence cover... the list seems almost endless. A landmark agreement in 2003, between DfES and all but one of the major teaching and support unions, led to safeguards in the STPCD to ensure that routine and administrative tasks would be done by new school support staff, leaving teachers to focus on teaching (DfES, 2002). Part of a wider programme of 'workforce reform', the agreement banned 24 administrative tasks – including all of the examples above – and made provision for teachers to have leadership time and time for planning, preparation and assessment (PPA). While there was some initial scepticism that schools would be able to deliver the aims of the reform (for example, freeing up 10% of primary teacher's time for PPA immediately adds 10% to the staffing bill), there was an undoubted shift in what teachers were asked to do, and additional pay allowances became teaching and learning responsibilities (TLRs) which were very clearly focused on pupils' learning and progress, and not on administrative procedures. There was also a consequent explosion in the range and number of support staff roles in schools.

In terms of impact, Ofsted reported that by 2009 the workforce reforms had 'made a considerable difference to pupils' learning' as a result of schools deploying staff well and holding teachers to account for pupils' progress (Ofsted, 2010). The change process of workforce reform had brought about something of a culture shift in schools, though perhaps not a significant progression from 'years of compliance' and initiative overload (Collarbone, 2005). Some commentators remained unconvinced, arguing that allowing support staff to become more involved in teaching had deprofessionalised teachers (Thompson, 2006; Wilkinson, 2005), or even that the reforms were an act of organisational tyranny, designed to engender compliance rather than agency (Gunter, 2007). This view might be supported by Ofsted's findings, which certainly relate workforce reform directly to the increasing range of accountability measures.

While the detail and debate around the 2003 workforce reform fades into history, the legacy is very much evident in schools today. As we have seen, schools and academies can now have a relatively loose relationship with the STPCD, and consequently teachers can be found up and down the country who are engaging in one or many of the 24 banned tasks. Furthermore they may again have paid responsibilities that are outside of the original TLR definitions. What is more evident is that there are very many people now working in schools who are not teachers, and it is to this group that we now turn our attention.

PARAPROFESSIONALS

The wide range of roles which are found in schools encompasses those who help to keep a school site operating effectively and safely: the caretaking staff, cleaners, admin teams and lunchtime supervisors, and it also embraces the many people who support children's learning more directly. This group of support staff (i.e., those other than teachers) has grown considerably since the advent of LMS and in particular as a result of the workforce reform agreement: Simkins et al. (2009) cite DfES figures which showed that, between 1997 and 2007, the number of support staff in schools grew by 130% (p. 435). During the same period the number of teachers in English schools increased by just 9%. By 2009 a recruitment leaflet published by the Training and Development Agency for Schools (TDA) stated that there were 'more than 60 different support staff roles'. Schools use a range of umbrella terms to cover this group: support staff, non-teaching staff, AOTs (adults other than teachers) or the American-style paraprofessionals. This last term is used to describe someone who may be a professional in their own right, but works alongside a qualified teacher (para – from the Greek for 'beside'), and is seen to be less a hierarchical or judgemental term than support or non-teaching staff.

However they are labelled, there is no denying that this cadre of paraprofessionals provides a range of essential services in schools, which have become increasingly auton-omous and complex. The group of paraprofessionals most familiar to parents and pupils are those who support teachers in the classroom, usually known as teaching assistants (TAs), classrooms assistants or learning support assistants. The number of TAs in schools was growing even before the workforce reforms, fuelled by the need to support increasing numbers of children with special educational needs or disabilities (SEND) in mainstream schools after the Warnock report (see Chapter 9), and leading to a position where a quarter of a million school employees nationally are TAs (just under half of employees are teachers, DfE, 2020c). The nature of their work changed, as they progressed from being parent-helpers to professionals in their own right, with defined job descriptions and career structures.

Most schools value their TAs highly and would find it inconceivable to think of oper-ating without them. For over a decade questions have been asked about the value for money that TAs represent in schools, and whether they really support children to measurable educational gains. Ofsted (2010) identified that most TAs are asked to work with the lowest attaining pupils and those most likely to cause disruptions to lessons – which seems to be a logical deployment if it means the lesson can proceed uninterrupted for the majority of children. Conversely, it could be argued that these children are those in greatest need of the attention of the qualified teacher. A number of studies, both in the United Kingdom and around the world, suggest that the impact of TAs is inconsistent, and that in the least successful examples there is a negative correlation between the support given by TAs and children's progress (Blatchford et al., 2009; Farrell et al., 2010). Despite these warnings, a decade later the Education Endowment Foundation (EEF) found that in some schools the least able children still performed least well in classes that had TAs supporting them (EEF, 2021a). The rule of thumb seems to be that where TAs lead intervention work, often outside the classroom, there can be tangible learning benefits, but where they are deployed supporting pupils in a general 'everyday' classroom, learning gains are minimal at best (Webster et al., 2021). Possible reasons for these findings are immediately apparent: where TAs are working on a very specific intervention they can have the training and development needed for that particular task without needing to be fully qualified teachers; and an extra person in the classroom, working with the least able pupils, means that the teacher's attention is diverted elsewhere and away from those that need it most. While TAs may contribute to the smoother running of a classroom, which in turn may relieve some of the stress on teachers, this alone appears to be insufficient to secure significant learning benefits for the pupils.

TAs themselves have identified that simply expecting them to follow a pupil from one class to another, or to troubleshoot as issues arise in a classroom, undervalues their potential (Roffey-Barentsen and Watt, 2014). Supporting children without foreknowledge of the work to be covered is almost impossible, yet TAs are not entitled to PPA time, and may have to work outside of their paid and contracted hours if they are to go through planning with teachers and to prepare properly for the lessons they support. The best schools find ways of giving planning time to TAs, and include them in meaningful staff development and training, as well as employing them on proper contracts with possible career progression opportunities. For some this may be identifying a route to achieve QTS in their own right, while others progress to become Higher Level Teaching Assistants (HLTAs).

HLTAs, as their name suggests, are more highly qualified and work at a higher level than the majority of TAs in schools – though HLTA itself is a status rather than a qualification. The role was introduced along with the workforce reforms in 2003 providing what Ball et al. refer to as a policy career path (2012, p. 67). Over the next 15 years, more than 25,000 TAs met national standards and achieved HLTA status, and in return for a higher salary took on significantly more responsibility. HLTAs are used in a variety of ways in different schools, but the key difference between them and TAs is the ability to undertake what the regulations call 'specified work': planning, teaching, assessing and reporting on learning. In practice this means that HLTAs may teach small groups or even whole classes, and pupils (and their parents) may be unaware that they are not a qualified teacher. HLTAs inhabit a 'betwixt and between' position, neither TA nor teacher, providing opportunities for school leaders faced with tight budgets and enabling them to exploit the blurred boundaries that we have seen around the need to employ qualified teachers (Graves and Williams, 2017).

HLTAs are sometimes deployed to carry out another aspect of work which was outlawed for qualified teachers by the 2003 workforce reforms: covering the classes of absent staff. Where teachers' absences are known about beforehand (because they are on a training course or planned medical appointment, for example), the STPCD prohibits the routine use of qualified teachers to cover their classes. This leaves schools with a number of options: to buy in supply teachers, usually from an agency established for that purpose; to use other staff such as HLTAs; or to employ staff specifically to cover lessons – cover supervisors. The post of cover supervisor is another paraprofessional role that has been directly brought about by policy change and which is attractive to schools on the basis of more than just budgets. Cover supervisors have two advantages over supply teachers: they are much cheaper as they do not have to have QTS, and they are employed by the school so they know its routines and procedures. They don't have the subject or pedagogical knowledge of the teachers whose classes they cover, but in principle they are working to the teacher's instruction and plans, thereby supporting the special status of QTS while at the same time contributing to the blurring of the boundaries of teachers' jurisdiction (Wilkinson, 2005).

BEYOND THE CLASSROOM

Prior to the 1988 ERA pastoral care of pupils was considered a crucial part of the teacher's role – a key element of teaching lay in an understanding of pupils' personalities and their home and social environment (Hamblin, 1978). The relentless drive towards measurable achievements and then the 2003 workforce reforms put the teacher's time in the class-room at a premium and generated a pressure to move at least some of the pupils' welfare issues to other members of staff. This led to a 'segmentation' of roles in many schools (Edmond and Price, 2009) where pastoral leadership, in particular, was moved away from senior teachers (often Heads of Year, Heads of House) to a range of paraprofessional roles. These might be variously called learning mentors, welfare managers, or any number of creative labels, and may be more or less specialised depending on the size and needs of the school. Some may be trained counsellors or education welfare officers, while others may have fewer formal qualifications but an experience and understanding that they can bring to bear. Teachers have not lost this aspect of their responsibility altogether, and most will have a form or class which they will get to know well and whose needs they will be acquainted with, but the prevailing model now has a number of adults who surround and support the child in a variety of different ways. It might be expected that good wrap-around support for children would lead to improved educational outcomes, but the evidence for this is tentative at best, and is usually related to specific welfare interventions such as health education (Littlecott et al., 2018) or social and emotional learning (EEF,

2019). What is beyond doubt is that pastoral development is seen as separate but parallel to academic progress, even if the former may have an impact on the latter (Calvert, 2009).

Many of the remaining roles in schools relate to the maintenance and operation of what is essentially a business, with a turnover that will amount to several million pounds for a medium-sized secondary school. Large schools will have a business manager, who may in turn have finance or other assistants. Large campuses may have a site manager who looks after the caretaking and cleaning staff, and a team of administrators is likely to be overseen by the headteacher's personal assistant. The huge growth in the use of technology, to support both teaching and administration, will require a team of technicians to complement science or design and technology technicians, working under the direction of a network manager. Larger schools, and certainly MATs, employ individuals dedicated to issues around personnel and employment and may have their own HR manager. Such a description of the teams working in schools is a far cry from the bursar, secretary and caretaker that might have served a 1970s comprehensive school, and it illustrates how far we have come since the introduction of LMS. The language is that of the business and the markets, and it is not restricted solely to academies. Even small schools and those with a strong commitment to the Local Authority will have had to take on some of these roles themselves, as the LAs' ability and capacity to provide 'back office' support has been eroded by the incessant ripples and waves of neoliberalism. Terms and conditions for these roles vary considerably: as with teachers, the national local government terms and conditions ('Green Book') can be ignored by MATs and academies, but for paraprofessionals whose roles vary enormously there is little market pressure to push them back to the norm.

Schools can and do avoid some of the minefields associated with employing staff on a wide range of contracts by outsourcing or subcontracting. Outsourcing is a key behaviour in neoliberal economies (Cingolani, 2019): in principle, buying in services allows the school to choose the best value for money that the market has to offer and at the same time avoid the complications of employing staff directly. Schools have outsourced cleaning and catering contracts for many years, but the 21st century has seen the practice become more commonplace, with financial support, human resources, IT support, building maintenance and management, ground staff and specialist music and sports tuition all frequently outsourced. There are drawbacks to these arrangements: the school loses direct control over the staff so may find it difficult to change their practices, and there are criticisms that outsourcing is not a good use of public money, as the outsource companies need to make a profit from the arrangement. In England, some of these services have been monopolised by a very small number of companies (Crouch, 2015) thus reducing the moderating effect of the market, and there are concerns that outsourcing can have an adverse effect on workers' right, pay and representation (Hill, 2005). Some Local Authorities have used schools' ability and desire to outsource to their advantage by providing competitive services which the schools can purchase, even if they have distanced themselves from the LA by becoming academies.

FINANCIAL LEADERSHIP

If a school is run like a business, then the financial bottom line is important. Schools, including academies, are not permitted to make profits; any excess of income over expenditure must be ploughed back into the school (unlike some US and Swedish schools where profit-making is permitted; West and Bailey, 2013). Conversely, schools are not supposed to set deficit budgets where expenditure intentionally exceeds income. The need to tread this fine line to achieve a balanced budget year on year generates an imperative for school leaders (not just the business managers) to understand school funding – which at its most basic level depends on pupil numbers. This is where Ken Baker's 1988 reforms can be seen in their most stark form, unrefined by the passage of time. A per-pupil funding mechanism, combined with parental choice, becomes a tool in the invisible hand of the market which can cull weaker and unsuccessful schools whose numbers decline and, by the same token, reward the schools preferred by parents.

Although funding is based on pupil numbers it is actually calculated through a complicated formula, which is now common across the country and designed to be 'fair'. In reality the formula is highly complex, with factors including particular needs, small schools' allowances, premises effects and a geographic weighting. Various governments have changed and amended funding formulas at a detailed level, but none has moved away from the basic per-pupil principle which allocates huge sums of money to schools (£36 billion in 2017–18; Kelly et al., 2018) at a rate of £4,000–£6,000 per pupil (Williams and Grasyon, 2018). This means that recruitment of pupils each year is an important activity, especially for small schools and those in areas where the population of young people might be falling. In the early days schools embarked on marketing activities with little understanding and experience, almost as an act of crisis management (James and Phillips, 1995). Over time, practices have matured and the leadership and management of marketing has become a 'core function' in most institutions (Foskett, 2012), though it remains contested in many, and a necessary evil in the eyes of some staff (Maringe, 2012). The fears of unions and others that schools are becoming privatised have not yet materialised, but there is a strong argument that schools are being 'corporatised' (Courtney, 2015).

The way in which money is spent in schools is very much in the hands of leadership teams. Where once there may have been specific funds earmarked for particular expenditure, and close Local Authority oversight over income and expenditure, the amounts tied up in restricted funds has reduced, and there is more freedom to use money creatively. The vast majority of schools' budgets is spent on staffing, though an old rule of thumb (60% teaching staff, 20% support staff, 20% other expenditure) no longer applies – the wider range of staffing roles has contributed to a wider range of expenditure distributions. A summary of each school's spending is published annually by the government alongside the school's other performance measures. This holds insufficient detail to hold schools to account, but it provides a rich resource for those who wish to investigate how public money is being spent.

One of the neoliberal arguments for the introduction of LMS was that prior to 1988 school leaders had no vested interest in managing income and expenditure properly. In fact, in some instances a perverse incentive forced schools to spend money in order to avoid a reduction in income the following year. By 2010, analysts continued to argue that there was still not enough incentive to get spending right (Allen et al., 2010), though this related to the detailed spend rather than the balance sheet: important operational decisions of schools were found to be 'largely idiosyncratic'. This is not to suggest that school leaders are irresponsible, but that there is no uniformly accepted view of how money should be spent in order to achieve the best outcomes for children. The rising number of MATs continues to illustrate this same point, as they have a range of school support structures which result in further diversity in the way their funds are spent.

There is one particular targeted fund which deserves particular mention: the Pupil Premium. Introduced in 2011 by the coalition government in 2010, the Pupil Premium was additional funding given to schools to try to improve attainment outcomes for disadvantaged children. For these purposes disadvantaged families were defined as those that had claimed free school meals at any time in the previous six years, and subsequently 'ever-6' or Pupil Premium have become ubiquitous proxy indicators of disadvantage in educational circles. Money was allocated on a straightforward per-pupil basis, and at about £1,000 per pupil (depending on their age, Roberts et al., 2021) this could amount to significant sums of money in many schools. Schools have autonomy over how to spend this money, but are held directly accountable by Ofsted, and less directly by the requirement to publish a summary of Pupil Premium spending on their websites.

The extent to which Pupil Premium funding has contributed (or not) to social mobility and closing disadvantage gaps will be discussed in Chapter 10, but this restricted fund can be used to illustrate how school leaders approach spending decisions in schools. Research suggests that there are elements of both head and heart in leaders' decision-making, with some awareness of what has been demonstrated to have an impact, alongside well-meaning attempts to improve equity that may have no established causal link with attainment (Morris and Dobson, 2021). Of course, assessing the impact of a single initiative in a highly complex social environment with many cross-cutting factors is fraught with difficulty (Gorard et al., 2021), but it is clear that the money has been spent in as many different ways as there are schools: in some cases on staff, in others on materials, sometimes on off-the-shelf 'solutions', sometimes on in-school developments. Organisations such as EEF (2021a) attempt to provide a cost-benefit analysis of various interventions, but if there is a universal silver bullet, it has not yet been identified or adopted nationwide. Indeed, eight years after the introduction of the Pupil Premium it was still not clear that this additional injection of funds was making a significant difference to those whom it matters most (Copeland, 2019).

MATERIAL ASSETS

Of the physical assets owned by a school, the buildings and land are clearly of most significance – though depending on the governance of the school or academy the degree to which it has ownership may differ. In the case of community schools the assets are owned by the Local Authority; for church-supported Voluntary Aided or Voluntary Controlled schools there may be a complex scenario, with part owned by trustees and the remainder (often the playing fields) owned by the Local Authority. Academies usually occupy premises which they lease from the Local Authority (for a peppercorn rent – this is not a serious income source for local councils). To complicate the picture further, some buildings were constructed through *Building Schools for the Future* (BSF), a major New Labour policy intended to rebuild 3,500 secondary schools over 18 years at a cost of £55billion (Mahoney and Hextall, 2013). Though it was cut short by the incoming coalition government in 2010, BSF left a legacy in the form of Private Finance Initiatives (PFIs) which were used to fund the building. Under PFI a public–private partnership was established to transfer the building, maintenance and service costs to a private partner, who would be repaid from the public purse over the next 10–30 years. Controversial at the time, the PFI programmes meant that, decades later, schools and Local Authorities were still under a financial pressure as they struggled to maintain the repayments. From an operational point of view, PVI-funded buildings belong to the private partner until the lease has expired and ownership transfers, which can therefore put constraints on a school's use of the resource, potential development and ultimately educational activity (Granoulhac, 2021). This of course conflicts with the neoliberal ideal of putting power and autonomy into local hands.

This complicated picture means that any premises issues faced by a school will be highly dependent on its context and governance, and therefore utterly unique. Straightforward decisions about matters relating to the school site or building stock may be uncomplicated in one setting and intractable in another. Braun et al. point out that 'buildings, their layout, quality and spaciousness can have considerable impact on policy enactments on the ground' (2011, p. 592), which in turn means that these decisions may have an educational impact (though again, the direct causal link here is weak). The common factor across many schools is that constraints and restrictions arising from national policy decisions, whether from 100 years ago (in the case of church schools) or in the much more recent past, can lead to daily frustrations and feelings of impotence. Apparently simple changes to the physical environment can actually be impossible to effect in some cases – though where changes are made school leaders value the part in the decision-making process that they now have (Webb et al., 2012).

Whether managing people, places or property, school leaders are often in an unenviable position. They have been characterised as 'piggies in the middle', between political masters on the one hand, and increasingly demanding stakeholders on the other (Wallace, 2003).

The challenge to accept ambiguity and work with inconsistency may well leave them feeling that their job is, as Wallace puts it, to 'manage the unmanageable'.

CASE STUDY: BRIDGWATER AND TAUNTON COLLEGE TRUST

Bridgwater and Taunton College Trust (BTCT) is a small Multi-Academy Trust that includes primary schools, secondary schools and an all-through school. The Trust states that it has removed traditional performance management and replaced it with professional growth – a policy which it claims to be a different perspective and a new direction designed to challenge thinking, and promote deep reflection, collaboration and change for the better. This case study illustrates some of the principles and practices of BTCT's approach to 'Growing Great Teachers'.

Supporting great teachers

Bridgwater and Taunton College Trust aims to ensure that every child achieves, and states that in order to do this the staff team must be nurtured and supported. Teacher workload and staff wellbeing are recognised to be serious issues, and the Trust lists a number of initiatives which illustrate how they respond to these particular challenges:

- Teachers benefit from pay awards that are equal across the board and in line with or above nationally agreed increases.
- Teachers are given autonomy rather than being micro-managed, within the bounds of the Trust's shared values. Teachers choose a focus that is relevant to the children they teach, within the context of their school or subject priorities.
- Performance related pay has been eliminated, with progress up the pay spine guaranteed as long as teachers meet agreed standards for teaching and proactively engage with professional development activity.
- Lesson observations are low stakes, with no lesson grading. The emphasis is on developmental feedback, not judgements about effectiveness. Similarly work scrutiny exercises are based on professional curiosity and are not a checking-up mechanism.
- Strong and clear policies to support good behaviour, and highly visible senior leadership teams, counter the demands that poor pupil behaviour might have on teacher morale. In most BTCT schools, teachers do not have to run their own detentions, which are organised and supervised centrally.
- Collaboration is encouraged, so resources are shared, with centrally employed colleagues leading their development. However, there are no common lesson plan formats or central checking of planning.

- Assessment processes have been streamlined and unified across the primary schools, so teachers do not have to write these.
- Professional development avoids initiative roll-out and is instead a planned, bespoke and targeted approach to professional growth.
- A Leadership Qualities Framework supports the development of skills and behaviours that enable colleagues to progress to leadership roles. BTCT tries to appoint to leadership roles from internal colleagues first, before advertising externally.
- The culture of presenteeism has been replaced with flexible working, to support staff with caring responsibilities in particular.
- New parents are entitled to additional paid leave, and everyone can take paid time for funerals, medical appointments and unavoidable emergencies.
- A peer-review process between the academies supports teachers and leadership teams without making judgements.
- The academies have shared network access and technical support, as well as administrative support, that include data analysis.
- Over five years more than £16 million has been spent on buildings to create a clean, warm and pleasant working environment.
- Staff are supported through a staff forum and an online advice and counselling service. Principals have an open door policy, and a staff survey is conducted annually.

Study questions

1. Why do you think BTCT is so keen to state explicitly that performance management and performance related pay has been removed? What might be the drawbacks, as well as benefits, of this approach?
2. What other aspects of the accountability culture does this Trust appear to challenge? What are the dangers of doing so?
3. Does the BTCT model signal a laissez-faire approach to leadership and management? What (if any) are the indicators that might convince parents, visitors or inspectors that standards are robustly upheld?

SUMMARY

This chapter has reviewed the main resources which school leaders have to manage: people and property. The impact of neoliberal policy on employment practices, qualified teacher status, and paraprofessionals has been discussed. Finally, an overview of finances and material assets has exposed the complex roles of school leaders.

FURTHER READING

Bob Bates and Andy Bailey's practical handbook, *Educational Leadership Simplified* (2018), provides an insight into some of the complexities of managing resources (including people) in schools. Ostensibly for practitioners new to running schools, or those aspiring to become school leaders, this book is equally useful for educational scholars who wish to understand how policy affects practice as it actually happens in schools.

7

CURRICULUM: THE SUBSTANCE OF EDUCATION

CONTENTS

This chapter includes:

- An exploration of the National Curriculum and its constituent subjects.
- The impact of accountability on the curriculum in schools.
- Quasi-subjects' that schools teach beyond the National Curriculum subjects.
- The hidden curriculum in which children learn from the values and ethos of a school.

INTRODUCTION

The curriculum is at the heart of any education system. In simple terms the curriculum is what is taught, from the formal curriculum which determines the content of each lesson, to the 'hidden curriculum' which learners absorb through the ethos, values and behaviours of an organisation. Those who design curriculum content therefore wield significant power and carry huge responsibility: pedagogy will be designed around the curriculum (what is the best way to teach this particular content?), and assessments will be designed to measure how well the curriculum content has been learnt.

In 2017 Amanda Spielman, HMCI, said:

> One of the areas that I think we sometimes lose sight of is the real substance of education. Not the exam grades or the progress scores, important though they are, but instead the real meat of what is taught in our schools and colleges: the curriculum.
>
> To understand the substance of education we have to understand the objectives. Yes, education does have to prepare young people to succeed in life and make their contribution in the labour market. But to reduce education down to this kind of functionalist level is rather wretched.
>
> Because education should be about broadening minds, enriching communities and advancing civilisation. Ultimately, it is about leaving the world a better place than we found it
>
> (DfE, 2017b)

This holistic view of the objectives of the curriculum might have raised some eyebrows, coming from one of the enforcement agents of accountability within education. It did presage a remodelled Ofsted inspection framework which was tightly focused on the curriculum. Spielman's comments underline the fact that what motivates curriculum designers will be their own understanding of the purpose of education. As we saw in Chapter 1, there is no universal consensus on the purpose of education or the reasons for particular curriculum content. The issue has been surrounded by controversy from time immemorial and that continues to this day: in the same year that the Secretary of State for Education said that 'the purpose of education is to give people the skills that will lead to a fulfilling working life' (Williamson, 2021), his own Minister for School Standards stated that 'the purpose of education is to open up a pupil's mind to the finest examples of human endeavour' (Gibb, 2021).

For many in 21st-century England the idea of the curriculum will probably be synonymous with the National Curriculum, but in fact the National Curriculum only applies to maintained schools, and furthermore is only a part of what is required of those schools. Statute dictates that they must also offer aspects of Relationships and Sex Education (RSE), Religious Education (RE) and careers advice, depending on the school's age range. The requirements for academies are entirely different, as we shall see.

ENGLAND'S NATIONAL CURRICULUM

The National Curriculum for England and Wales (for 5–16-year-olds) was introduced after the 1988 Education Reform Act (ERA), with first implementation in 1989. The rationale for the National Curriculum included three principles which remain today with greater or lesser emphasis depending on the particular political agenda. These principles were:

- An entitlement for all children to a 'broad and balanced' curriculum;
- Curriculum coherence regardless of the characteristics of children or schools, or where they study across the country;
- Improving school accountability by providing national benchmarks for children's progress through the curriculum (DES, 1987).

This last principle was woven through the design of the National Curriculum, intractably tying it in to school accountability measures, and allowing for direct market comparisons for the neoliberal ideologues. It also provides the basis for a fourth principle which is to improve the public understanding of schools and offer a common basis for discussion of education issues (HC, 2009). It was through the introduction of the National Curriculum that Key Stages 1–4 were identified, and a complex structure of attainment targets and statements of attainment for each subject laid out the expectations for children in each year of compulsory education. The language around the National Curriculum implied more agency on the part of teachers and schools than was in fact conferred. For example, a percentage of time for each subject was identified but this was not prescribed by legislation. However, the statement that 'in schools where there is good practice' the government's model will be adopted meant that the non-statutory guidance effectively became compulsory (DES, 1987, p. 8).

The 1988 ERA went beyond the identification of a subject-based taught curriculum, including in its introduction the notion that a broad and balanced curriculum would be one which:

(a) promotes the spiritual, moral, cultural, mental and physical development of pupils at the school and of society; and
(b) prepares such pupils for the opportunities, responsibilities and experiences of adult life (GB, 1988, p. 1).

These two statements provided the basis for ongoing debate over the subsequent 30 years. The first, which morphed into Spiritual, Moral, Social and Cultural (SMSC) education, was for a period a focus of Ofsted inspections, and schools explored and developed a variety of ways to demonstrate their commitment to these values. There were discussions about if and how RE or assemblies could contribute to the spiritual aspect, and curriculum maps to demonstrate commitment to these values by each taught subject. The second statement is open to interpretation: for some it relates to the employability of school-leavers and their ability to contribute to the nation's economy, while others have a much broader understanding of what 'adult life' might mean.

It was probably inevitable that the huge, complex National Curriculum of 1988 would need to be refined and improved, and it underwent several revisions which both slimmed down the content and changed the emphasis and balance between subjects (Roberts, 2021). Over three decades the assessment mechanisms have been amended, partly due to the original plans (which had statutory assessments for all subjects) being too unwieldy and time-consuming to implement, but also because of successive governments' push towards more testing and less teacher assessment. As devolution took effect, Wales was able to diverge, and the most recent incarnation of the National Curriculum in England now contains citizenship education (secondary pupils) and computing (all ages) alongside the original foundation subjects:

Core subjects	
English	Key Stage 1-4
Mathematics	Key Stage 1-4
Science	Key Stage 1-4
Foundation subjects	
Art and Design	Key Stage 1-3
Citizenship	Key Stage 3-4
Computing	Key Stage 1-4
Design and Technology	Key Stage 1-3
Languages	Key Stage 2-3
Geography	Key Stage 1-3
History	Key Stage 1-3
Music	Key Stage 1-3
Physical Education	Key Stage 1-4

(from DfE, 2014a, p. 7)

The fact that some subjects are only compulsory for certain key stages reflects a reduced demand for primary pupils and the secondary schools' options process which allows for Key Stage 4 pupils to choose some of the subjects they study. While the curriculum content was reduced, its reach was extended as a curriculum for three to five-year-olds was introduced from 2000, and the Early Years Foundation Stage Framework (EYFS) for newborns to five-year-olds was introduced in 2008 (see Chapter 11).

The ambition for coherence across the country has certainly been achieved in large part, and the idea that schools could choose subjects and curriculum content according to favoured examination boards would now be almost unimaginable. A reduced number of exam boards, all working to the same curricular content, means that the differences between them are subtle and minimal, and a common primary school curriculum ensures similar experiences for all children. Things are not entirely uniform, however, because the National Curriculum now contains little detail for foundation subjects, where content is expressed over just two pages as a general programme of study. The content for core subjects is much more prescriptive; for example, the National Curriculum for Key Stage 1 and 2 mathematics covers more than 40 pages and lists specific mathematical skills, concepts and knowledge that must be taught to each year group.

CORE SUBJECTS

The earliest versions of the National Curriculum did not prioritise any particular subject areas beyond the implications of the non-statutory time recommendations. The bloated content across all subjects potentially led to a lack of focus on English and mathematics, and in 1996 two 'support projects' were introduced to help develop literacy and numeracy in the primary curriculum (HC, 2009). These developed into national strategies, expanded into the secondary phase and were the precursors to a much brighter spotlight on English and mathematics. The National Literacy and Numeracy Strategies had implications for pedagogy which will be discussed in Chapter 8, but they ensured that primary schools had dedicated time every day to teach specified content (Machin and McNally, 2008). Though the Strategies were not mandatory, few schools deviated from them, and long after their demise literacy and numeracy retain their dominance in the primary curriculum and in primary school performance measures.

In secondary schools the national emphasis on English and mathematics was driven through the accountability framework: the baseline measure of five A*–C grades was amended in 2006 with a stipulation that two of these grades must be from English and mathematics GCSEs. More recently the calculation for schools' Progress 8 value added measure has double weighting for English and mathematics qualifications. Despite this emphasis, there are frequent press reports of employers who claim that young people lack the basic literacy and numeracy skills required in the 21st-century workplace (e.g. Yeomans and Sylvester, 2021) and the CIPD reported that the United Kingdom sits just above the bottom of a Europe-wide league table of skills for 16–24 year-olds (CIPD, 2017, p. 13). The CIPD report makes it clear that measurement of skills is not the same as educational attainment, but there appears to be a mismatch between the taught curriculum and what might be called functional skills in English and mathematics.

The government introduced discrete Functional Skills Qualifications (FSQs) in 2007, and they are still offered alongside GCSEs to 'help students gain important real-world skills for the future' (DfE, 2019). This seems to imply a recognition that the content of GCSEs does not give school-leavers the employment skills that they need. FSQs are not offered by schools to the majority of students, because they do not count towards the accountability framework. Instead, FSQs are largely taken by students in Further Education (FE) who have not succeeded in their GCSEs, or adults who need to demonstrate a basic competence in English or mathematics and who have not achieved a good GCSE grade, for whatever reason. Some practitioners argue that 'it is not possible to teach young people all the skills of employability' (James, 2017, p. 37), and perhaps that is not the intention: the introduction to the National Curriculum simply states that 'it introduces pupils to the best that has been thought and said' (DfE, 2014a, p. 6), borrowing the phrase from Victorian poet and school inspector Matthew Arnold (1869, p. viii).

Of the three core subjects, science has been described as 'forgotten' by both primary practitioners (Tidd, 2016) and inspectors (Ofsted, 2021) who noted that science is being driven out of the primary curriculum due to 'disproportionate' amounts of time spent preparing for English and mathematics tests. Primary teachers are required to hold a GCSE in science (in addition to English and mathematics) in order to be able to teach the essential content of this core subject, but the fact that they are focusing on mathematics and English may suggest a lack of confidence in the subject (Sharp et al., 2011) and certainly underlines the way in which accountability drives school priorities. Science is much more secure in secondary schools, where it remains a compulsory subject through to the age of 16. After the removal of the artificial Key Stage 3 tests, many schools developed a five-year programme that enabled students to study 1, 2 or 3 sciences, culminating in the GCSE examinations. After the age of 16, the three science A levels are consistently amongst the most popular choices for students (Ofqual, 2019).

THE ACCOUNTABILITY CURRICULUM

While the National Curriculum is compulsory for maintained schools, academies are not bound by this prescription. However, all schools are judged by the same progress and attainment measures, which are intimately bound up with the curriculum which they teach. For primary schools, whether maintained by the Local Authority (LA) or not, this may mean an excessive emphasis on English and maths, especially in Year 6. For secondary schools, the accountability effect is much more obvious, and in their attempts to find the curriculum that best demonstrates pupil achievement according to the metrics of the day, they have been accused of 'gaming' the system (e.g., Ofsted, 2019b). While some have said that school leaders can't be blamed for trying to find the best way to show their school in a good light, in a system that was designed expressly to pit them against each other (Lightman, 2017), the view of the inspectorate is that they sometimes do this even when it is not in the best interests of their pupils. This raises the issue of a performative system that includes in its design a perverse incentive that puts the performance of an institution above the educational interests of children. Be that as it may, the simple fact is that for three decades the curriculum in all secondary schools, including academies, has been driven by accountability measures.

An early example – and perhaps justifiable casualty – was the GNVQ (General National Vocational Qualification). GNVQs were vocational qualifications available in a range of subjects at two levels, advanced (equivalent to two A levels) and intermediate, which was equivalent to four GCSEs. Given that the early benchmark measure for schools was the proportion of children who achieved five or more GCSE passes (at C or above) it was hardly surprising that some schools shot to the top of the league tables by ensuring that every pupil took one GNVQ (often in ICT; Wilson et al., 2006) plus one other GCSE. If further incentive were needed it could be found in the assessment mechanism for GNVQs, which were predominantly portfolio-based and marked in school, giving teachers the opportunity to coach pupils until their work reached the threshold level (de Waal, 2009). GNVQs were removed in 2007, and GCSE equivalences for other qualifications were reviewed after Michael Gove became Secretary of State in 2010, but their use illustrates the dilemmas that school leaders may face in constructing the school curriculum. The issue is not just one of content but also of timing and focus; once English and mathematics had to be included in the five good GCSEs measure, schools began to enter children for mathematics GCSE (in particular) in Year 10: those doing well could go on to take GCSE in additional mathematics (or indeed, focus on getting their English GCSE) while those who didn't make the grade could have another year to improve and have a second or even third attempt.

Consequently there has been an ongoing dance in which politicians amend performance tables to try to make them fairer and reduce schools' ability to artificially massage their figures, and in response school leaders seek to do the best for their pupils while maximising the school's league table position. Where these two ambitions are in conflict, it is difficult to criticise leaders who do not make the morally right choice; poor standing in the tables can result in them losing their job and the school being brokered to a high-performing MAT. The Attainment 8 and Progress 8 measures aimed to ensure that schools offered a good range of subjects within the secondary curriculum, and their introduction prompted another shift of emphasis for schools, this time towards the EBacc (English Baccalaureate, Gill, 2017). The EBacc is a suite of qualifications, including English and mathematics plus one each of a language, science and humanity subject, which has been encouraged by successive Conservative governments. Although mention was made of EBacc uptake by Ofsted, and it was included as one of many performance measures for secondary schools, it was its inclusion in the introduction of Progress 8 as a headline measure that pushed schools to take it seriously: the dance continues.

Similar tensions and movements exist regarding post-16 qualifications, but here the pace of change has been slower, and the performance measures are less clear. Schools may choose to highlight their standing in a variety of performance tables, often drawn up by newspapers. They may use varying metrics, such as the proportion of A*–B grades, the number of A/A* grades achieved or pupils' average point scores. FE colleges, which offer a much broader range of qualifications, are protected from league table drivers to some degree, though they face different pressures which will be discussed in Chapter 11.

SUBJECT CONTENT

Of course, examining a school's curriculum model only tells us so much about what is taught. The curriculum plan may show us the relative weight that is placed on different subjects and point towards any strategies that are being used to improve the school's performance measures. At a more detailed level it is for the school, and perhaps individual teacher, to decide on what the content is for each subject. For examination subjects, this may be driven by the examination board syllabus (technically called the specification) which, for National Curriculum core subjects in maintained schools, must include the Department for Education (DfE) prescribed programme of study. Even so, there are still decisions to be made around exactly what to teach, in what order and where to put the emphasis. Even at this level, it is clear that the system 'privileges that which is tested over any other expression of knowledge, which leads teachers to concentrate on teaching what is assessed' (Isaacs, 2014).

When it comes to within-school planning, the taught curriculum is not immune from the intervention of politicians, and this is most evident in the neoconservative commentary that was ongoing during the second decade of the 21st century. In 2011 Michael Gove launched a review and rewrite of the National Curriculum, ridiculing what had gone before with challenging statements, such as 'we have a compulsory history curriculum in secondary schools that doesn't mention any historical figures – except William Wilberforce and Olaudah Equiano' (2011). Similar comments were made about other subjects, and while the factual basis of his rhetoric might be open to challenge, nonetheless the narrative around curriculum content shifted considerably towards a traditional approach. It has been argued that this is 'trapped in an elitist past' (Young, 2011), with undue emphasis on 'facts' and an understanding of how 'our island' contributes to world history (cited in Beck, 2012). The obvious colonial overtones and reverberations of Empire attracted robust criticism (Heath, 2018), but the movement towards a clearly defined canon of knowledge progressed with some haste, supported by the Conservatives' changes to the National Curriculum. The idea of a knowledge-based or knowledge-rich curriculum gained traction (Sherrington, 2018), though the debate turned to issues of pedagogy – how the curriculum is taught – so will be examined in more detail in Chapter 8.

It is fair to say that the revised National Curriculum which emerged in 2013 was not entirely what had been planned or envisaged by politicians and the DfE. Strong opposition resulted in significant amendments, notably to the history curriculum (Smith, 2017). However, the impact on the way that subjects are planned and taught has been profound: in history children must be taught about certain key figures and will cover the linear progress of history, from the stone age in primary school through to the modern day by the end of Key Stage 3. The National Curriculum for English lays out expectations of reading, writing, spelling and grammar for primary children in levels of detail that are unfamiliar if not incomprehensible to their parents (Myhill, 2021), and while a specific list of writers was not included in the National Curriculum, examination boards felt sufficient pressure to remove renowned American novelists in favour of English authors (Kennedy, 2014). Arguments that the curriculum is too narrow are not limited to the academic community and teacher unions: pupils themselves also complain of dominant white British narratives that serve to make some feel excluded and fail to address issues of colonialism (Alexander and Weekes-Bernard, 2017; Savadia et al., 2021). In 1993, Stephen Ball warned that a curriculum composed of echoes of a political and cultural elite, which ignores the pasts of women, the working class and the colonised, would be a 'curriculum of the dead' (1993b, p. 210), which would reflect a romaticised Victorianism and undermine intellectualism.

An increasing emphasis on knowledge rather than skills became an existential issue for some subjects. The ICT curriculum, which Michael Gove claimed was 'universally acknowledged' to be unambitious, demotivating and dull (DfE, 2014b), was replaced with computing. The skills of using computer programmes (computer literacy) were replaced with an understanding of how computers work, including basic programming (coding) skills. As such, computer science became an acceptable science within the EBacc collection. Such changes have a significant impact on schools: not only do they have to change the content of the taught curriculum, but they may also find their teachers ill-equipped to teach the new content. In the case of computing, this was at least recognised by the DfE who provided some funding for teachers to improve their skills and knowledge.

The tension between skills and knowledge in computing is perhaps an example in microcosm of the wider debate around academic versus vocational qualifications that is conveniently ignored by some of the more strident voices of neoconservatism. The failure of the post-war tripartite system has left vocational courses in a strange limbo-land: vocational qualifications can provide good routes into employment, yet there is no place for most of them in the accountability framework for schools. FE colleges are able to manage this tension better than schools, mainly because schools cannot afford to sacrifice subjects which count towards performance measures for qualifications which don't have GCSE equivalence. Post-16 school sixth forms may offer BTECs, which are considered to be applied, if not vocational, qualifications, but they have been designed with A-level equivalence in mind and support students seeking university places just much as they might provide a route into employment (Kelly, 2017). There is a genuine dilemma if pupils are to keep their options open: applied courses can lead to a lack of theoretical knowledge and academic understanding which can hinder them in later life (Wheelahan, 2015) – a problem that is internationally recognised (Nylund et al., 2018) and which may exacerbate societal divisions. It has been suggested that even apprenticeships, which are clearly designed to provide direct access to employment through a skills-based training programme, can curtail the long-term life chances of participants because they assume or encourage an early rejection of conceptual knowledge (Brockmann and Laurie, 2016). This may be a concern for the more recently introduced T levels which are based on the same standards as apprenticeships, though they include a discrete qualification which includes core theory and concepts which may mitigate against the issue. Only time will tell if they successfully begin to bridge the academic/vocational divide in a way that the short-lived Diplomas of New Labour spectacularly failed to do (Isaacs, 2013).

Regarding optional subjects at GCSE level, there are, in principle, no limitations on what secondary schools may offer. In reality, after timetables have been partially filled with the necessary EBacc subjects there will only be time for the few 'open' slots that are left in the Progress 8 measure, so it is highly likely that schools will offer only those subjects which will count as GCSE equivalents in the final analysis. This may preclude more vocational alternatives, such as car mechanics, hairdressing or plumbing, though some schools may offer these for those students who are unlikely to succeed if they take a traditional academic programme, thus creating a particular curriculum for the (already) disadvantaged and adding to societal division (Wrigley, 2018).

RELIGIOUS EDUCATION

RE has a special place in the curriculum of all English schools and provides a good example of historical political decisions which continue to have an impact through to the present day, and which to modern eyes appear contrary to the logic which underpins the shaping of the current system. We saw in Chapter 2 how the 1902 and 1944 Acts each incorporated compromise with the church school systems, with the lasting effect that all schools must include RE in their taught curriculum, and all schools must hold a daily act of collective worship for all pupils – this is now interpreted very loosely by secondary schools in particular, as they often cannot bring the whole school together for such an activity.

While not part of the National Curriculum, RE is a compulsory subject for all children aged 5–18, though parents do have the right to withdraw them from these lessons without having to give a specific reason for doing so. This is the case for academies as well as LA-maintained schools, and most academies tend to follow the locally agreed syllabus which is compulsory for LA schools (Long et al., 2019). Faith schools and academies with a specific religious character are free to choose the content of their RE curriculum in accordance with their trust deeds or foundation religion or denomination.

In secondary schools, where all children are studying RE, there is a choice to be made over whether or not to enter them for examinations. Many choose not to (unless pupils take RE as an options subject), but some take the view that it is worth entering all pupils for the final GCSE examination. The extent to which they do this is affected by how the RE GCSE is viewed in school league tables: when it was made clear that RE does not count as a humanity in the EBacc component of Progress 8, the number of entries nationally dropped (Ofsted, 2013b), and schools reduced the number of specialist staff teaching the subject (Barker, 2012).

The case of RE illustrates the fate of those subjects not deemed to be worthy of inclusion in key performance measures. Despite being mandatory, a survey of teachers suggested almost half of all schools fail to meet the statutory requirements in Key Stage 4 (NATRE, 2019). This suggests that schools are reducing their RE teaching to what they consider to be the bare minimum, risking a negative comment on an inspection report but maximising their opportunities with regard to the performative system. This might be at odds with the needs of society which has moved on from the broadly Christian monoculture of 1902 and leads to consequences much more profound than the position of a school in the league tables. Dinham and Shaw (2017) argue that the 'policy muddle' has led to confusion over the purpose of RE in the compulsory curriculum, generating misunderstandings and religious anxieties which could exacerbate division, violence and oppression. One could argue in this case that an unintended consequence of a market-based ideology is a threat that undermines the fabric of stable society.

BEYOND THE NATIONAL CURRICULUM

Where schools have reduced the prominence of RE, they may well have subsumed it into other aspects of the compulsory curriculum, often under the overarching name of personal development or personal, social, health and economic education (PSHE). In turn, this may be taught in a regular timetabled slot, on a few drop-down days during the course of the year, or may be mapped across a range of other subjects (a cross-curricular approach). Other subjects and quasi-subjects included under this umbrella might include relationship education (RSE in secondary schools), health education and citizenship.

For maintained secondary schools, citizenship is a compulsory foundation subject but is rarely taught discretely and is more usually subsumed into PSHE-type provision. As with RE, the purpose of citizenship education is not well understood, and critics might suggest the National Curriculum content for the subject is rather parochial in a global age. Supporting this argument is the requirement for schools to promote 'fundamental British values' which was embedded in the Teacher Standards in 2012 and included in SMSC guidance in 2014. The danger is that global and cosmopolitan perspectives are challenged by more nationalistic points of view (Starkey, 2018), which can support the kind of narrow-minded viewpoints which these policies ostensibly seek to reduce, and highlight senses of 'strangers within': members of society but not belonging to it (Lander, 2016). Links between fundamental British values and the counter-terrorist Prevent strategy led to controversial accusations of state-sponsored politicisation of the teaching profession in an attempt to make them state surveillance operatives (Elton-Chalcraft et al., 2017). Such arguments tend to dominate perceptions of citizenship education, such that the content around managing money, contributing to society, and understanding human rights, the legal system and international law can be overlooked.

Sex and relationships education can be equally controversial, and this appears to be universal, not just limited to the English system (Robinson et al., 2107). Controversy arises from different cultural perspectives, religious beliefs, and perceptions of risk and appropriateness. In 2013 Ofsted reported that sex and relationships education needed to be improved in one-third of schools, with too much emphasis in primary schools on friendships and relationships, and a focus on the mechanics of reproduction in secondary schools (Ofsted, 2013a). Therein lies the dilemma for school leaders, who at the time appeared to have retreated to what is safe and least likely to provoke letters of complaint from parents (who do not have the right to withdraw their children entirely from relationships education). In response to Ofsted, the government acknowledged the importance of RSE and the lack of clarity within schools in its own report (HC, 2015), before publishing new guidance in 2019. This still leaves schools with an important duty, but it neglects some evidence that young people feel uncomfortable with RSE taught by authority figures such as teachers (Pound et al., 2017). What was once the role of parents – even though research suggests they did not do it well (Walker, 2001) – has become an essential but uncomfortable part of the school curriculum. In addition, the 2019 guidance covers health education, including physical and mental wellbeing, hygiene and healthy eating; again, all areas which would once have been dealt with in the home. It is unsurprising that after several decades of schools gradually including more life skills and societal understanding in the curriculum, there are claims that we have created a national expectation that schools fulfil the roles of parents (Nutt, 2018).

Also occupying this liminal space between home- and school-based learning and development is social and emotional learning. Internationally it appears to be well accepted that social and emotional learning is critical to students' long-term success (for example, see Mahoney et al., 2018), and during its final years, the New Labour government introduced a national policy for secondary schools: Social and Emotional Aspects of Learning (SEAL). Robust evaluation of the SEAL policy demonstrated disappointing returns: the programme 'failed to impact significantly on the social and emotional skills, mental health difficulties and pro-social behaviour of pupils' (Wigelsworth et al., 2012), though it was pointed out that the bottom-up pick-and-mix approach to implementation, poor trialling, and lack of regard to the evidence base all contributed to the failure of a policy that appeared to be successful elsewhere around the world. Since 2010 progress towards a national understanding of best practice in social and emotional learning has been slow, with independent commentators noting that England's competency-based approach is probably unhelpful and that disparate policies have led to a lack of clarity and coherence (Donnelly et al., 2020). The Education Endowment Foundation (EEF) has produced a guide for primary schools to encourage a more integrated approach to social and emotional learning (EEF, 2019), but there appears to be a reluctance on the part of central government to re-engage with this agenda, despite a Cabinet Office-commissioned report of 2015 calling for 'more purposive action' (Feinstein, 2015).

THE HIDDEN CURRICULUM

By definition the hidden curriculum is often difficult to pinpoint or quantify, but it is evident to all visitors to schools and other educational establishments. Explicit aspects of the hidden curriculum might include values statements, mission statements and expressions of ethos which appear over front doors, on walls, stationery and in children's books. Of more consequence is the way these are enacted in the life of a school: the real hidden curriculum consists of what pupils learn through the way they are treated, the interactions they have and the messages they take from school rules and procedures.

The phrase hidden curriculum was first used by Jackson in 1968, who described the need for pupils to 'master' the hidden curriculum in order to proceed satisfactorily through school (Jackson, 1968, p. 33). Jackson describes the hidden curriculum as a mechanism through which power is exercised, noting that rewards and punishments are often distributed according to compliance or otherwise with institutional expectations rather than in relation to learning and progress. This gives us a clue as to why the phrase is less commonly used than it once was: the reductionist approach to every aspect of school life, breaking it down into measurables – the metrification of schools – has extended to behaviour, reward and sanction. The neoliberal tendency has been to drag the hidden curriculum into the light in order to enumerate aspects and formulate development plans in order to drive improvements.

Generating quantifiable rewards and sanctions policies and practices in schools (and there are off-the-shelf solutions which provide these) assumes a behaviourist approach to teaching and learning in which positive behaviour is reinforced with rewards while inappropriate behaviour is discouraged by sanctions. Such an approach is part of our national psyche, for parents as well as teachers, but it can lead to conflict in the classroom, in particular if pupils perceive inequalities or inconsistencies. The behaviourist approach appeals to the traditionalist neoconservatives, whose 'spare the rod and spoil the child' attitude encourages enforced compliance. While this can clearly be beneficial to a degree, and lead to well-ordered schools, there are dangers that an atmosphere of fear and oppression can undermine the well-being of children and affect their learning. Contrasting ideas might suggest that good discipline is achieved through the taught curriculum which, if it is truly inspirational, leads to interest, engagement and ultimately compliance (Irby and Clough, 2015).

The right balance of care and support against discipline and control is difficult for schools to achieve, and it plays out in the minutiae of classroom life: the consequences of forgetting a pen or scoring highly in a test will provide indicators of the true ethos of a school, whatever the mission statement might profess. It therefore follows that the behaviour of teachers and school staff, and in particular the way that they teach and manage their classrooms – their pedagogy – will sit right at the heart of the school's hidden curriculum.

CASE STUDY: OUTWOOD GRANGE ACADEMIES TRUST

Outwood Grange Academies Trust (OGAT) is a large multi-academy trust (MAT) operating mainly in the north of England, with more than 40 primary and secondary academies. OGAT aims to ensure that all children enjoy a wide range of subjects and experiences through an inclusive and ambitious curriculum. This case study, drawn from the OGAT website, highlights the trust-wide approach to the curriculum.

Ambitious intent

Young people attending primary and secondary academies at OGAT are presented with an educational experience that is designed to be accessible and enjoyable, and to ensure academic success, develop life-long skills and offer rich experiences. Every child and young person is supported to grow as well-rounded and responsible citizens who can fulfil their potential and ability to play a positive role in society.

Across the curriculum each year is designed to build to the next. Curriculum planning focuses on core and subject content knowledge and skills to aid students' knowledge recall, build their subject fluency and deepen their understanding. Expert curriculum planning across all subjects as well as wider curriculum aspects such as Relationship, Sex and Health Education, Fundamental British Values etc. ensures that children's learning across each year and throughout their time at Outwood is clearly defined. A knowledge-rich curriculum supports students to access their next steps in education at every level: OGAT believes that the longer one continues in education and/or training, the greater the reward in health, happiness and social mobility.

The ambitious curriculum matches the demands of the National Curriculum at each stage so that students can meet and exceed age-related national expectations and progress well to their next phase of education. Across the curriculum expectations of the rich knowledge, skills and understanding that are required in each subject are carefully mapped. Teachers adapt schemes of learning to meet the needs of students in their classes. Across the wide range of subjects offered, progressive delivery is planned in order to secure students' learning and academic achievement. The primary programmes of study and secondary core and EBacc subjects are considered to be vitally important, so the Trust ensures that students' entitlement to these is strong. At secondary and sixth form, the curriculum architecture model is more locally bespoke, balancing breadth and depth with context. This approach ensures flexibility while taking into consideration any local or regional influences alongside parent and student choice and needs within the offer and design.

OGAT states that great schools are only sustainable within happy and healthy communities and that cooperation is vital to tackle the causes of under-achievement and disadvantage. The curriculum is rooted in local communities and goes hand in hand with the aims of being a family of inclusive academies in the heart of their communities where all children are cared for and where standards are raised and lives transformed.

Curriculum aims

OGAT aims to provide a high-quality education experience that is empowered by an ambitious, knowledge-rich curriculum that enables all children and young people to achieve well. The intent is, through the curriculum, to narrow gaps in achievement for all student groups, enable access and prepare children and young people well for their future steps. The curriculum aims to support students' learning by:

- Fostering an inclusive culture of responsibility, respect and safety with an ethos of praise, pride and purpose.
- Providing excellent teaching across a broad and balanced range of subjects to engage learners.
- Promoting mental well-being encouraging positive relationships and acceptance.
- Encouraging healthy lifestyle choices, self-regulation and personal accountability.
- Appreciating diversity and difference and valuing tolerance, democracy, liberty and law.
- Recognising issues that affect the world and acknowledging actions that can be taken.
- Supporting students' ambitions, and interests to open future study and career pathways.

The curriculum experience

Across each phase, the curriculum is designed to be broad and ambitious reflecting National Curriculum and qualification expectations. The provision enables students to hone their literacy and numeracy skills, deepen their subject study and support their personal growth across their schooling. Well-sequenced schemes of work clearly identify what students should know and be able to do by the end of each unit, term, year and stage in preparation for their next steps. Assessment is used to address gaps in students' knowledge and understanding to best secure key concepts, core knowledge and skills to move students' learning forward.

The curriculum design is localised to individual academies, ensuring it best meets the needs of the students and supports the social and economic priorities of the locality. Local interest is incorporated into subject topics. Each academy personalises its curriculum architecture in a way that structures key stages, subject delivery, time allocations, qualification pathways and staffing to ensure the curriculum implementation puts students first, raises standards and transforms lives.

Study questions

1. OGAT's expression of its curriculum makes little mention of specific subjects. Why do you think this is, and what does it tell you about the Trust's understanding or conceptualisation of the term 'curriculum'?

(Continued)

2. Where can you see statements that either support or challenge progressive, neoliberal or neoconservative ideals? How might these appeal to parents of different backgrounds?
3. How does the OGAT curriculum respond to Amanda Spielman's quote at the beginning of this chapter?

SUMMARY

This chapter has examined what the curriculum means and looked in some detail at the contents of the National Curriculum in schools. It has considered how accountability measures drive curriculum design and looked at those 'quasi-subjects' that schools include in their broader curriculum. Finally, mention is made of the hidden curriculum in which children learn from the embedded values and ethos of a school.

FURTHER READING

Ruth Ashbee's book, *Curriculum: Theory, Culture and the Subject Specialisms* (Routledge, 2021), takes a social realist approach to the curriculum which is constructed under the principles of 'powerful knowledge'. This sits comfortably with the neoconservative direction of political travel and leads to a particular interpretation of curriculum – and ultimately to a particular pedagogical approach. Of value here are the early chapters on the context and theory of curriculum, which should be examined in detail before turning to subject-specific knowledge.

8

PEDAGOGY: THE ACT AND DISCOURSE OF TEACHING

CONTENTS

This chapter includes:

- Notes on some of the long-lasting direct policy interventions that relate to pedagogy.
- A brief explanation of some of the common theories of learning.
- A discussion of the reality of bricolage pedagogy, rather than adoption of a single approach.
- Specific mention of digital pedagogies, which have become more prevalent without yet transforming education.
- A description of some common neuromyths and fads which are common in 21st-century education.

INTRODUCTION

The method and practice of teaching – pedagogy – is at the heart of the learning process. In this chapter we consider the craft of the classroom: the learning activities designed by teachers based on their training, their experience, and their knowledge of educational theory – but also rooted in their school culture and the wider policies of education. It is helpful to use the definition of Alexander (2008) to clarify the meaning of classroom pedagogy:

> Pedagogy is the act of teaching together with its attendant discourse of educational theories, values, evidence and justifications. It is what one needs to know, and the skills one needs to command, in order to make and justify the many different kinds of decision of which teaching is constituted.
>
> (Alexander, 2008, p. 47)

On a macro, national or global scale the idea of pedagogy can be understood as an ideological societal lever, to effect wide-ranging change, or the transformation of many by changing or challenging policy. This is seen specifically in the writing of Paolo Freire (2018, originally 1970) and the field of critical pedagogy that his work inspired (see Steinberg and Down, 2020). Conversely, at the micro level pedagogical practice with individuals and classes is inevitably shaped and defined by policy. The minutiae of the day-to-day world of the school classroom might seem light years from the Westminster circles in which ideology is debated and policy determined, yet teachers' everyday behaviours are fashioned by 40 years of neoliberalism and the growing influence of the neoconservatives. The realities of practice are subtle and nuanced, but debates around pedagogy are often polarised and extreme, characterised by themes lingering from 1960s progressive education which face challenges from an orthodoxy that is paradoxically both more traditional and more up to date. Arguments have ebbed and flowed for 2,000 years, since Plutarch suggested that the mind was not a bottle to be filled but tinder to ignite: every educator will have a different opinion (Plutarch, tr Babbitt, 1927).

In the 21st century, debates around pedagogy have become more open and public than ever before, thanks to the rise of social media. A 2020 survey of teachers showed that 65% of respondents used Twitter regularly for work-related purposes (Higgins, 2020), and the 'Edu Twitter' community has become the primary place to go for pedagogy-related opinion, encouragement and criticism. In principle, the open nature of social media allows for the most democratic of debates, but it has been argued (Watson, 2021) that the amplification of particular traditional perspectives by social media leads to a 'small-p populism' that distorts the arguments, which are based less on rational debate than on affective alignment (Papacharissi, 2015). This can sharpen the apparent dichotomy of views and may be confusing for students of education and practitioners alike.

The various social media platforms provide opportunities not just for debate and discussion but also for the formation of genuine professional learning communities for educators (van Bommel et al., 2020), and potentially for new forms of classroom pedagogy. The 2020/21 COVID crisis, when millions of children were out of school for weeks at a time, provided an impetus and acceleration of digital pedagogies, though some schools had already made significant progress in this regard. Time will tell whether the 'emergency learning networks' that were quickly established (Staudt Willet et al., 2021) will be long-lasting or transient, but it is clear that digital learning will remain as one of the many tools available to teachers in the classroom.

Understanding pedagogy requires a knowledge about how children learn, so it is inevitable that debate will be informed by theory as much as by policy. Education is a social science, with no immutable natural laws or binding formulae, which means that theories will always be controversial and contested. What may be viewed as important principles for some may be considered conceits, fads or myths by others (see, for example, Burkard, 2007). Theories of learning go back as far as the Ancient Greeks, and just as there were in ancient times there are modern-day disciples of particular thinkers and theorists, many of whom would claim to have the accurate, right or fairest way of understanding learning. As well as learning, pedagogy is also about authority; the role of the teacher is to manage the classroom and 30 or so children in such a way as to maximise learning and minimise disruption and distraction. This then introduces concepts of power and how it is exercised: at the classroom level neoliberalism has no view to offer, leaving a vacuum for the principles of neoconservatism to fill. For the individual teacher working late into the evening to prepare the next day's lessons, it is the outworking of ideology and theory in real-life personal interactions which has the potential to cause sleepless nights. Though shaped by policy, pedagogy is ultimately personal, and it is for this reason that the debates surrounding it are so passionate.

POLICY INTERVENTION

The period of time between the late 1980s and early 21st century has been described as a time of 'unprecedented central intervention' in English schools (Gibbons, 2017), directly challenging pedagogy as much as assessment and curriculum. This is not to say that from the mid-2000s onwards there have not been policy interventions that affect the classroom, but that in this more recent period the notion of policy intervention and centralised control has become the norm and therefore unremarkable. As Gibbons puts it, 'the fight has disappeared' (p. 2) and teachers have decided that it is not for them to make critical decisions about pedagogy. This is one particular analysis and others may disagree, but the reality of classroom experience is that its underlying shape is formed by historical policy interventions, just as it flexes and responds according to present-day policy.

We have seen how the National Curriculum was introduced to establish a coherent curriculum entitlement and provide for an accountability framework, set in the context of increasing right-wing discomfort with the perceived child-centred progressivism of the 1960s and 1970s. In principle the National Curriculum laid out the content of *what* should be taught, leaving the question of *how* it should be taught to the professionals. In reality, the new content, and in particular the assessment demands that came with it, necessitated a change to the way that teachers taught, bringing about lasting changes to practice which today we might take for granted: studies at the time noted much more formative feedback, leading to higher levels of explanation and questioning than had been the case before-hand (Alexander et al., 1996). As ever, change did not happen overnight, but was a gradual process, and there was no sharp discontinuity between old-style progressivism and modern traditionalism. The Conservative Government's own 'three wise men' report of 1992 noted that it would be inaccurate to think that 1970s primary schools were 'swept by a tide of progressivism', even as it recommended more whole-class teaching, supporting the idea of teacher as instructor rather than facilitator (Alexander et al., 1992). Be that as it may, the fact remains that for the next 30 years teachers were encouraged to take more charge of their classrooms and of learning and to leave behind the discredited child-centred approach.

The first really direct intervention by ministers into teachers' classrooms came with the introduction of the literacy and numeracy hours in 1998 – these were not mandatory, but schools choosing not to use them would have to demonstrate how their own systems were better. Primary schools were expected to set aside about an hour each for numeracy and literacy every day, with the contents of those hours tightly prescribed: predominantly whole-class teaching, including 20 minutes each for grammar and looking at texts in the literacy hour (Machin and McNally, 2008), and mental maths in the numeracy hour (Sharpe, 2005). These early attempts to shape classroom practice may have been clumsy and not entirely fruitful: while standards did rise, there were suggestions that the whole-class teaching was encouraging simple recall of information without leading to deep understanding, and that this was due in part to teachers not being well prepared or trained for new repertoires of responsive teaching (Mroz et al., 2000). Whatever the impact on learning, the National Strategies (as they then became) had a lasting effect on pedagogy: the three-part lesson (starter, main and plenary) stipulated in the 1999 numeracy strategy (DfE, 2011a) became the standard fare in all subjects across both primary and secondary schools, and literacy and numeracy hours were and are enduring *de rigeur* in the primary phase. The original framework document pointed out that the outline of a typical lesson 'should not be seen as a mechanistic recipe to be followed' (DfEE, 1999, p. 15), yet that was exactly what it turned into. The reasons for this are twofold, and both relate to accountability and performativity: it is easier to follow a prescription for what is deemed to be a good lesson structure than to carefully craft one's own approach and have to justify it; and for an observer it is straightforward to see that an accepted efficacious approach has been followed. Though the dangers of a formulaic approach are clear, leading in the worst cases to a sequence of fragmented and possibly unrelated activities (Adhami, 2003), evolution towards an approach that allows for a variety in type and number of what are often called episodes within lessons took considerable time (e.g., Butt, 2008).

SYSTEMATIC SYNTHETIC PHONICS

The introduction of systematic synthetic phonics teaching in primary schools is a good example of a direct government intervention that had a direct impact on pedagogy and which has survived changes of government to become a key activity in the primary and Early Years classroom. Despite the introduction of the National Curriculum and the literacy hour, by 2005 it was apparent that there was little evidence to suggest that children's reading skills were improving, and England appeared to be lagging behind international comparators in this regard (Stainthorp, 2020). An independent review concluded that teaching reading using phonics – already part of the national strategy – was not achieving its potential largely because teachers and support staff, despite being 'more than capable', were poorly equipped to teach phonics, having had weak, tokenistic training (Rose, 2006). In addition to this the review recommended a very specific type of phonics teaching: systematic synthetic phonics. Phonics in the English language is technical and complicated: synthetic phonics refers to the process of converting groups of letters (graphemes) into sounds (phonemes) and then blending them to make words, whereas analytical phonics begins with word patterns and breaks them down into smaller units. Internationally it was accepted that systematic approaches to phonics tuition could reap huge benefits: for example, the US's National Reading Panel identified five different typologies of phonics instruction, but noted the benefits of a systematic method in 2000. The panel defined a systematic approach as one which delineates a sequential set of elements, rather than introducing these incidentally and opportunistically (NRP, 2000, p. 8).

The idea that a systematic approach is more effective than an opportunistic one would appear uncontroversial, but the Rose report focused on one of the pedagogies in particular, seizing on a study which concluded that 'synthetic phonics was more effective than analytic phonics' (Johnston and Watson, 2004). This caused some debate in academic circles (Wyse and Styles, 2007) and arguments were still ongoing 10 years later with some studies concluding that the evidence for synthetic phonics over other methods was inconclusive (Glazzard, 2017; Torgerson et al., 2019). Policymakers were happier to accept Rose's recommendations and used a variety of mechanisms to ensure that their preferred methodology of systematic synthetic phonics was embedded in all schools. Initially phonics was used alongside other ways of teaching reading, but by 2010 the coalition government was funding approved phonics programmes, essentially making these the only options for schools. Systematic synthetic phonics was included in the statutory framework for Early Years and National Curriculum for English, required in the Teachers' Standards, and woven through the

Ofsted inspection handbook. A phonics check was introduced in 2012, DfE 'validation' of published programmes was introduced in 2014, and a 2015 government plan to develop reading skills commented that 'there is a substantial body of evidence which demonstrates that systematic synthetic phonics is the most effective method for teaching all children to read' (DfE, 2015b, p. 5). This latter report cited and overstated the US NRP findings from 15 years earlier and also used selective evidence from a DfE commissioned report (Torgerson et al., 2006), conveniently ignoring the finding that there was no difference in effectiveness between synthetic and analytic approaches. This level of policy intervention is probably unusual, but it illustrates a tendency towards micromanagement of teaching combined with compliance checking, ostensibly built upon a strong evidence base. The purported evidence-based nature of policy makes it difficult for practitioners to question mandated pedagogy or to investigate alternative approaches. Clark neatly summarises this quandary:

> While frequently declaring their policies 'evidence-based', evidence which does not support current policy is ignored by politicians who dictate not only what should be taught in schools, but how it must be taught. This is backed by an accountability regime which forces teachers to adhere to these policies, even if in their professional judgement they have concerns'.
>
> (2018, p. 33)

Systematic synthetic phonics is firmly established in schools as a result of more than a decade of policy intervention. While some teachers accept its efficacy and embrace the methods, others complain of having to 'teach to the test' and encouraging children to 'bark sounds' rather than to read for pleasure or understanding; half are not convinced that systematic synthetic phonics should be the only way of teaching children to read (Clark et al., 2018).

THEORIES OF LEARNING

In order to plan effective pedagogical approaches, it is important to understand how children learn. Even if they know no educational theories, every teacher will be making assumptions about the learning process as they plan teaching activities. The dangers of making unsupported assumptions are clear, but that does not mean that theorising learning is straightforward, and theories of learning are consequently contested to a high degree. When this academic debate is set into a political context the discussion can become heated and positions entrenched, leading to silos that are in theoretical and methodological opposition (Jacobson et al., 2016). Fundamentally, much of the division is caused by a continued insistence on trying to describe a highly complex and complicated social system with simple atomised reductionist models (Hager and Beckett, 2019).

As well as understanding how children learn, the development of pedagogy also embodies, either implicitly or explicitly, a consideration of *why* they are learning something, which of course relates back to curriculum. A teacher who is hoping that a new concept will be used and applied in novel situations might use a different approach than they would if the concept is simply learned in order to be examined in a written test paper. Likewise, content affects pedagogy and may lead to different theoretical models of learning: developing an understanding of Shakespeare's sonnets is unlikely to employ the same pedagogical approach as solving simultaneous equations, and may well be theorised in an entirely different way without either being 'better' than the other. The danger for educationalists is that they may become so enamoured with a particular theorist that they dismiss or ignore other approaches which might be equally valid and useful, albeit in different contexts.

The simplest learning theory is probably that of John Locke's 17th-century philosophy, in which he posits that the mind at birth is a *tabula rasa* or blank slate, upon which learning is written, this being derived from experience through sensation and reflection (Androne, 2014). The educator's role is to shape the child's personality not just by filling the mind with knowledge but also by providing moral instruction – and importantly doing so by way of modelling and example. Aside from arguments around how blank the original slate really is and whether Locke was the originator of the idea (Duschinsky, 2012), there are obvious difficulties with this model: once the child has begun to learn, the slate is no longer blank and new learning must be added to what is there, in either complementary or contradictory fashion. There is a logical step from this to the ideas of constructivism, a broad spectrum of theories which have as their common thread the notion that children construct meaning through experience and interaction with the world, building on and challenging what they already know (Fosnot, 2005). This can lead to a view that each child learns differently depending on their own starting point, and that there can be a large element of self-direction in their learning – the autodidacticism described by Rousseau in *Emile* (1762, translated Bloom, 1979). This may have contributed significantly to the child-centred progressive pedagogies of the 1960s and 1970s that were so derided by the Thatcher government, but is just one, perhaps extreme, aspect of the much wider topology of constructivism. The constructivist group of theories can usefully be categorised according to whether there is perceived to be a single reality or truth (as in pure mathematics) versus multiple interpretations or many realities (historical interpretation perhaps), and whether knowledge is developed individually or through a social process (Kanuka and Anderson, 1999). Much classroom teaching of the late 20th century, as well as more recent practice, would probably be described as social constructivism in which the child's construction of knowledge is the product of social interaction, interpretation and understanding (Vygotsky, 1934, translated Hanfmann et al., 2012; Dewey, 1938). The characteristics of social constructivist pedagogy are not an entirely laissez-faire approach in which the autodidact operates autonomously, but a respectful pupil–teacher relationship in which the child's engagement is facilitated by the teacher (Vygotsky's more knowledgeable other), where the focus is on learning rather than performance and in which assessment is a measure of the corporate shared understanding of truth (Adams, 2006). Pupil and teacher work together to construct knowledge, and by extension this can lead to children being involved in the design of lessons, choice of tasks and planning of part or all of the curriculum. For some this 'active learning' approach is a powerful educational tool, while others view the same activity as a dangerous intellectual experiment (Jenkins, 2000).

The Western world in the 20th century may have provided the ideal conditions for 'dreamers and visionaries' (Reese, 2001) to develop the pedagogy and practice of what we now call progressive education, but the mid-century emphasis on science and technology, rational thinking and computational processes also provided fertile ground for the development of an alternative approach to learning: cognitivism (Cooper, 1993). Cognitivism arose from a psychological understanding of how memory works in the human brain: in 1943 Kenneth Craik described a mental model of reality in which various scenarios can be tried and tested (cited in Mandler, 2002). In cognitivism it is the job of educators to enhance, polish and hone the mental model through instruction and practice: assessment can be used to understand the current state of the learner's knowledge, and feedback to guide and support accurate mental connections (Ertmer and Newby, 2013). Cognitivism has a strong emphasis on structuring and sequencing learning activities to promote optimal mental processing, storage and retrieval. This may include some learner autonomy, for example, around methods of revision, and knowledge of how to learn (metacognition), but essentially cognitivism is a transfer process in which knowledge is communicated to a pupil in an efficient manner. The final stage of cognitivism is to see external behaviours change as a result of learning: an internal prompt.

Behaviourism may seem to be diametrically opposed to cognitivism, in that it proposes that external prompts generate behavioural change, and furthermore that these external stimuli go on to influence learning. B. F. Skinner, one of the architects of behaviourism, noted that to trivialise the theory by reducing it to 'stimulus–response' was an oversimplification, but explained that while cognitivists see someone think and then act, behaviourism asserts that the environment and previous experience are all part of the decision-making process contributing to the probability of a given behavioural change (Skinner, 1985). In what is now known as operant conditioning, behaviourism uses reward and punishment to reinforce the learning process, which is seen as highly complex. Skinner asserts that behaviourism 'avoids the unnecessary problems of storage and retrieval' (1985, p. 297) – the details about how the brain actually works – and instead of being side-tracked by trying to describe the brain as a storage vessel, it focuses on reinforcing positive learning outcomes using external stimuli. Behaviourist techniques are immediately apparent in observations of parents or teachers who – seemingly instinctively – offer rewards or threaten punishment in return for particular actions on the part of their children or pupils. Such observations illustrate a key characteristic of behaviourism: a high degree of adult control, which can cast the learner into a relatively passive role as recipient of knowledge (Pollard et al., 2005). Behaviourism lends itself to whole-class teaching, though runs the risk of leaving individuals behind, either because they struggle to connect what they are learning with existing knowledge or because they are demotivated by too many negative reinforcements.

BRICOLAGE PEDAGOGY

Every teacher's class and classroom is different, and as a consequence teachers need to be flexible and agile in using a range of tools and techniques to respond to emerging needs and develop effective pedagogy (Reilly, 2009). Teachers move effortlessly between theoretical approaches, selecting techniques from one, combining with those from another, then discarding some and moving on to others, using whatever comes to hand in an attempt to achieve the best possible outcome. In this regard each teacher operates as a 'bricoleur' (Levi-Strauss, 1962) creating a uniquely personal bricolage pedagogy, selecting constituent parts from knowledge and experience. This has been described as an artisan quality of professional practice which is creative and responsive as long as the teacher has agency over decision-making (Campbell, 2019). The difficulty with such a characterisation occurs when teachers are forced to conform to a particular pedagogical approach, usually for ideological reasons which are mediated through policy reinforced by what Foucault would call disciplinary technology (1977, p. 227).

The rise of neoliberalism may be viewed as a resurgence of behaviourism at policy level (Garrison, 2016), in which rewards and sanctions are applied to schools, their leaders and teachers, and at a granular level to the children they serve. It would be surprising if the absorption of neoliberal principles into the collective consciousness of the educational establishment were not reflected in pedagogy, and this has certainly skewed bricolage pedagogy assemblages away from progressive approaches, though the principles of social constructivism have not been lost. More overtly, as we have seen in other areas, the initial wave of neoliberalism has been followed by a tough tide of neoconservatism, and this has challenged the bricolage approach much more directly. Calls for a return to traditional values and methods, alongside the accountability system which ostensibly measures the efficacy of those methods, have led to teachers feeling coerced into pedagogies which they neither believe in nor value (Cushing, 2021).

Ball (1993b) described the 'cultural restorationists' who sought a return to a traditional pedagogy, as embodied by an idealised Victorian model in which learning meant 'doing and knowing what you were told by your teacher' (p. 209). Over 30 years these ideas of common sense and anti-intellectualism gained sway, and from 2010 have been included in education policy with increasing explicitness. The Conservative government was unashamedly influenced by the thinking of E. D. Hirsch, whose mid-century analysis of American education concluded that pupils needed a 'traditional literate culture', based on a canon of agreed cultural information, such as battle dates and the names of American presidents (Hirsch, 1967, 1988). Hirsch's pedagogy is reduced to a sharing of facts, with the teacher being a curator of national heritage (McLaren, 1988). Such influences drove the development of pedagogy in English schools as well as the curriculum content (Neumann et al., 2020). The teachers' bricolage became increasingly dominated by 'knowledge-based' approaches, including frequent drilling and testing, use of resources such as knowledge organisers, and lower emphasis on practical activities (Cullinane et al., 2019). Ideas from publications in the popular press, such as Daisy Christodoulu's *Seven Myths About Education* (2014) were enthusiastically adopted by schools, which became increasingly articulate in their descriptions of expected pedagogy. The work of Doug Lemov in the United States (2010) gave teachers a new lexicon of terms to describe specific, actionable techniques that contribute to the 'alchemy that changes lives' (p. 2) by making the best use of classroom time and holding children accountable for their behaviour and their learning. In Lemov's words this is a pragmatic approach which amounts to working out what works and doing that, whether or not it is innovative or fits with any particular educational theory.

The techniques of Lemov rely on the teacher being in control of every moment of the lesson. They are essentially behaviourist, generating a stimulus–response classroom activity which is undoubtedly efficacious in terms of good use of classroom time, and are reliant upon a clarity of understanding of the exercise of power in daily classroom management. The top-down approach to classroom management led by the government in England is well summarised in a 2019 Ofsted summary which simply states that 'good behaviour is a necessary condition for learning' (Spielman, 2019). Over a decade this philosophy has resulted in stronger guidance for schools around the management of behaviour, the appointment of behaviour 'czars' to lead on behaviour, and what some might perceive to be an increase in punitive authoritarian behaviour policies in schools. The principles of no excuses (for bad behaviour) have been turned into zero-tolerance policies in schools; though beyond the advantages of a culture of consistency and clarity of expectation, there are concerns about simple one-size-fits-all policies which can cause teachers to focus on control at the expense of real learning (Graham, 2018). An EEF metastudy in 2019 recommended, perhaps unsurprisingly, a reflective approach by teachers and recognition of children's individual needs rather than a single strategy (Moore et al., 2019). Introductory comments included a reminder that ideas around the best way to manage children's behaviour in the classroom are contested and that while there is no consensus in the sector, much of the guidance and support for teachers oversimplifies a very complex issue (p. 4). There are suggestions that the tide is turning on the behaviour debate (Dix, 2017) though this might simply be a view from the anti-zero tolerance community. It is more likely that the debate will continue, so in the disagreements and confusion the skilled teacher will continue to use a bricolage approach based on a wealth of learning and experience.

DIGITAL PEDAGOGIES

Computers began to appear on classrooms in the 1980s, initially as a curiosity, then as something to be studied through the curriculum subject, ICT (Information and Communications Technology), later replaced by computer studies, but also as administrative and pedagogical tools. Early prophets predicted that education would be transformed by the new technologies, changing or reducing the role of teachers (Frick, 1991), but as time passed this began to seem increasingly unlikely. Even commentators who compared the digital revolution with the invention of the printing press found it difficult to conceive of machines taking on the role of the classroom educator, and some in fact argued that the teacher's role would become even more crucial (Collinson, 2001). New Labour policy supported the embracing of technology in the classroom with the establishment of the National Grid for Learning, a resources portal run and managed by the British Educational Communications and Technology Agency (BECTA) – abolished by the 2010 coalition government.

There was and is general agreement that some of the potential system-wide transformations of teacher practice and educational reform remain unrealised (Blundell et al., 2016): while the interactive whiteboard may have replaced a blackboard, and tablets or laptops may be used instead of slates or books, many of today's classrooms still exhibit recognisable characteristics of Victorian schoolrooms. One of the reasons for this may be that the first phase of what we might call the digital revolution was driven by hardware and new technology: a school may invest in tablets, for example, but at their most basic they are still just a reading and writing tool comparable with books. It is possible that a second phase might develop; one in which content, connectivity and decision-making are seen as the tools, rather than the hardware that makes this happen. This is certainly the vision of Michael Fullan, long time analyst and documenter of educational change, who foresees technology and pedagogy joining forces to achieve system-wide reform (Fullan, 2013). While the first phase of this revolution might have been limited by budgets and resources, the second has constraints that are more philosophical in nature. For practitioners, computer hardware is controllable and containable, while the internet, cloud storage, social media and artificial intelligence all seem to be fraught with danger, much of which has to do with lack of control. In a critical analysis of digital applications in education, Selwyn states that 'schools are first and foremost regulatory environments' (2011, p. 9) in which freedom of access and ready exchange of information and data does not sit comfortably. Proponents of digital pedagogies suggest that 21st-century children are 'digital natives' who grow up immersed in and surrounded by new technologies which may be unfamiliar or alien to their teachers, and that school pedagogy needs to change to reflect this. This simple view of modern children is open to challenge (Bennett et al., 2008) but there is no doubt that the teaching profession in general has a conservative attitude towards 24-hour digital connectivity. For traditionalists, embracing technology incorporates the dangers of focusing on engagement and enjoyment rather than learning gains, and the potential of learner autonomy and the ability to multitask actually leads to digression and distraction (Zierer, 2019).

The coronavirus pandemic of 2020–21, which closed schools and kept children in their homes, forced educators around the world to include digital approaches in their pedagogical bricolage whether they wanted to or not. Almost instantly digital resources were developed to enable children to learn from home, and teachers to carry out their roles from a distance. In England issues of access and support led to concerns that the most disadvantaged children were those most likely to lose out in this new way of learning (DfE, 2021b), but future thinkers were keen to push for lessons learnt during the pandemic to be applied to pedagogy when schools reopened (Zhao, 2020). In the event, when schools opened their doors again, children quickly returned to the old ways of learning for the most part, though teachers now had a new range of skills and resources which they could call into use for cover lessons, further COVID challenges or indeed the infamous 'snow days'.

Digital technology, whether interpreted as new machinery in the classroom or the programmes and applications which run on new devices, has certainly not been the saviour of a failing education system. Indeed, there are those that would question whether England's schools were ever as broken as the 'crisis accounts' suggest (Gorard, 2001). Classroom observers of the early 21st century will see spaces and activities that have emphatically not been transformed by technology, though there will undoubtedly be evidence of its use in pedagogy. Where teachers have agency and choice, digital approaches will be used within the bricolage assemblage, though there will always be schools whose internal policies press for either more or less technology according to their particular values and priorities. What Ball (2007) calls 're-imagineering' of schools is more akin to evolution than radical step change, and consequently the adoption of digital approaches by pedagogy proceeds at a somewhat slower pace than the absorption of information technology into wider society. Neil Selwyn (2011) identifies the rise of technology in schools as just one facet of societal change that has at its heart free-market capitalism: while neoliberalism does not promote digitalisation, its invisible hand may nonetheless encourage the involvement of global tech corporations and multinational social media companies in the education of our children.

NEUROMYTHS AND FADS

As our understanding of the brain developed in the latter half of the 20th century, educators inevitably looked for ways to make use of this to enhance learning. Popular interpretations of complicated neuroscience quickly led to a collection of misconceptions which together are now known as neuromyths and which often form the basis for well-meaning but ill-informed school initiatives. This is an international phenomenon, and while it is not new it continues to persist. It can be argued that neoliberal pressure to perform is one of the drivers: in 2002 the OECD reported that myths and misconceptions had arisen 'as a result of both pressure to improve overall school performance and excitement and interest about education that could be brain-based' (OECD, 2002, p. 69).

The OECD charts how reports of scientific developments, translated into the popular press, can result in completely false representations of the original findings. An example is the observed hemisphere specialisation of the brain, which led to ideas of right-brained and left-brained individuals who are respectively artistic or mathematically minded, when in fact both halves of the brain work together for most learning activity. Studies suggest that teachers are more susceptible to believing neuromyths when they are related to commercialised educational programmes, especially so if they themselves have some general knowledge of the brain (Dekker et al., 2012): it appears that enthusiasm for neuroscience can mean reduced ability to distinguish fact from fable. A development of hemispherical specialisation well supported by commercial products was brain gym – a series of simple exercises that claim to enhance academic learning, despite being based on little more than pseudo-science (Tardif et al., 2015). It is thought that the idea of VAK learning styles (visual, audio and kinaesthetic) derived from a similar base. VAK spawned a small industry developing resources to help teachers teach according to learners' preferred styles, despite the approach being widely discredited through lack of evidence of efficacy (e.g., Pashler et al., 2008). Schools appear to have accepted these findings and moved on, but use of various learning style typologies persists in Higher Education and also in management training programmes, prompting the question of why such myths persist without substantive evidence to support them.

Aside from the seductive advertising by educational resource providers who promise incredible outcomes if their methods are adopted, educators are also swayed by the prevailing zeitgeist. In the world of competition and targets, no school can afford to be left behind, so if others claim a particular approach is working wonders then it would be foolish not to join that particular bandwagon. It is easy with hindsight to criticise, but schools could hardly have been blamed for considering VAK in their pedagogy when Ofsted were highlighting 'outstanding' schools which used a learning styles approach, and the government actively promoted this. In 2004, the influential 'ped-pack' was published by the DfES (2004). This included a whole chapter on 'practical strategies that teachers use to accommodate pupils' preferred learning styles', and as recently as 2021 the DfE was criticised for continuing to promote the approach (Gibbons, 2021). The real questions are not why schools follow these trends, but why the evidence was not well examined in the first instance, and how such things became fashionable fads.

There has been a move towards examining the evidence that supports a range of pedagogical approaches, with some significant metastudies which seek to incorporate a wide range of evidence in order to understand the impact of different approaches. These include the Sutton Trust/EEF teaching and learning toolkit (EEF, 2021a) and John Hattie's *Visible Learning* publications (Hattie, 2012), which try to quantify the learning gains of a range of interventions. Though the ambitions are laudable, there remains the danger that pedagogical approaches that have demonstrated measurable impact might be seen as some kind of silver bullet, and that they will be highjacked and commercialised, morphing into something that has moved some way from what the original evidence suggested was effective. In its evidence review of cognitive science approaches, the EEF notes not only that some of the worked examples have little evidence to support them but also that it is possible to implement them poorly (EEF, 2021b). The policy line at Ofsted has always been that it would not support or encourage particular teaching approaches, but its evidence review for the 2019 inspection framework seemed to move the regulator towards advising, noting that retrieval practice, interleaving and adherence to cognitive load theory all support the development of pupils' long-term memory and the construction of new knowledge into larger concepts (Ofsted, 2019c). The language is qualified in terms of the strength of evidence, but it nonetheless provides a seal of approval for particular approaches, thus embedding cognitive approaches into school psyches and practices for the 2020s. The qualifying comment that cognitive load theory needs to be 'tempered by an understanding of the expertise reversal effect' (p. 22), making the cognitive approach less appropriate for expert learners, was conveniently lost in the search for a single universal truth.

A move towards a more evidence-informed profession, that looks for empirical support for pedagogical approaches, must surely be seen as a good thing. In reality, finding the evidence for or against particular interventions can be time-consuming and confusing, though some of the metastudies described here have helped by collecting evidence sources together and summarising their findings. Schools can of course carry out their own research to investigate the efficacy of an approach or intervention, but this carries with it a level of risk (Coldwell et al., 2017). School leaders may well feel that in a neoliberal performative culture it is not worth taking that risk, in which case they will follow the crowd and potentially contribute to the next educational fad. The OECD describes teaching as a professional triangle comprising the practice of teaching with theories of learning and of course the student experience, all embedded within a social field which results in a dynamic knowledge that flexes and adjusts as research and practice interact (OECD, 2017, p. 253). Tom Bennett, who, as one of the government's behaviour czars has arguably contributed to recent fads in schools, nonetheless said that 'a professional community of educators looks at the best available evidence bases and maps that onto the structured analyses of professional experience, and attempts to reconcile the two' (in Barton, 2019). This ongoing exercise is part and parcel of the craft of the classroom; it is what makes pedagogy more of an art than a science, and it is the reason for which the practice of teaching will go on being debated and discussed.

CASE STUDY: ARCHWAY LEARNING TRUST

Archway Learning Trust is a Multi-Academy Trust with nine schools in Nottingham and Derby. It operates a Trust-wide approach to pedagogy that is bound by guiding principles. These are outlined in the case study below.

Archway knowledge curriculum

The acquisition, retention and application of knowledge is the driving, underpinning philosophy of teaching and learning at Archway Learning Trust. The knowledge curriculum is detailed, sequenced and mapped deliberately and coherently. Retention and retrieval is embedded and integral to the curriculum. Teachers deliver the knowledge curriculum and adapt lessons to meet the specific needs of their classes.

Core expectations

The Trust's core expectations can be seen across the Trust every day and in every lesson. These aim to ensure that conditions for learning are optimised and allow teachers to focus on providing high-impact pedagogy.

- Routines to support learning
- Knowing your students
- Literacy in every lesson
- Inclusion of learning needs
- Clear feedback and guidance

High-impact pedagogy

The Trust uses evidence-informed, practical strategies to build and secure 'powerful knowledge' for its students. Teachers plan their lessons with a clear focus on these high-impact strategies.

- Retrieval to connect knowledge
- Instruction to build knowledge
- Questioning to check learning
- Scaffolding to support achievement
- Modelling to build expertise
- Review to consolidate knowledge

High-impact pedagogy is promoted through professional development and instructional coaching, and is not a focus for quality assurance. This is to engender innovation, variation and vibrancy in pedagogy.

Research-informed innovation

Trust staff are passionate about learning from and applying research-informed innovation into effective teaching and learning. Teachers read, watch, listen to and engage in vibrant

(Continued)

learning opportunities within and beyond the Trust, trialling, developing and sharing innovative practice.

Instructional coaching

Instructional coaching is an individualised, classroom-based, observation-feedback-practice cycle where a trained coach helps a teacher to improve highly specific aspects of their practice. It is developmental and not judgemental. A coach will observe a teacher frequently and provide them with very precise action steps which will improve their practice in incremental but meaningful ways.

Unlike other forms of coaching, such as relational or peer coaching, instructional coaching involves a recognised expert – typically a senior or middle leader or a 'lead teacher' – coaching a teacher who can benefit from their expertise.

Study questions

1. What theories of learning does the Archway policy include, either explicitly or implicitly? How much do you think teachers can use a bricolage pedagogy approach?
2. How and where does this approach appear to have been influenced by national policy and/or political zeitgeist?
3. Considering the full breadth of the curriculum, which of the core expectations and 'high-impact strategies' might be difficult to apply in some subject areas? Which, if any, should be non-negotiable in all lessons?

SUMMARY

This chapter has looked at what is meant by pedagogy in relation to classroom teaching. Some centrally imposed interventions that affect pedagogy have been discussed, and there is a brief introduction to common theories of learning. The way in which most teachers assemble techniques in a bricolage approach is outlined, and there is particular mention of digital technologies. Finally, some common neuromyths and fads are outlined.

FURTHER READING

Robin Alexander's *Essays on Pedagogy* (Routledge, 2008) takes a step back from the classroom to look at pedagogy in its widest sense. Six challenging essays consider pedagogy in an international context, the politicisation of pedagogy and the importance of talk, among other things. This book will provoke debate and stimulate thinking that moves pedagogy beyond the actions of the teacher.

9

INCLUSION: A FAILED IDEOLOGY?

CONTENTS

This chapter includes:

- The historical context of inclusion, explaining how practice has developed over the last 50 years.
- A discussion of the role of the Special Educational Needs Coordinator in schools.
- A description of Statements and Education and Health Care Plans.
- Consideration of the place of special schools within an inclusive system.
- Alternative Provision settings which meet the needs of children who are not included by mainstream schools.

INTRODUCTION

The concept of inclusion has become engrained in the collective psyche alongside neo-liberalism's quasi-market and accountability. Though they have emerged and developed over similar timescales, it must be appreciated that these are parallel and essentially unrelated developments, with different drivers. The move towards inclusion over the last 50 years has had an important and significant impact on the shape of our educational provision in England, evidenced both systemically and on a granular level within each individual educational setting. This has at times conflicted with some of the ideals of neoliberalism – and those of neoconservatism. Within education the term 'inclusion' is generally accepted as relating to children with special educational needs and disabilities (SEND), and for the purposes of this chapter we will restrict ourselves to this relatively narrow understanding. A wider discussion of inclusion as it relates to other characteristics such as race and socioeconomic background is included in Chapter 10.

Around the globe, the consensus seems to be that inclusion in education is something that is not just desirable, but essential for a fair and just world. UNESCO (2020) assert that ensuring schools are inclusive can be justified not just on educational and social grounds but also economically; they cite their globally influential 1994 *Salamanca Statement* which said that inclusive schools:

> are the most effective means of combating discriminatory attitudes, creating welcoming communities, building an inclusive society and achieving education for all; moreover, they provide an effective education to the majority of children and improve the efficiency and ultimately the cost-effectiveness of the entire education system.
>
> (UNESCO, 1994, p. ix)

The reference here to effective education for the majority of children (i.e. not all children) is a bone of contention for some: it potentially hints at a mediocrity of ambition, or even an attitude that it is acceptable to provide a less than effective education for some children. This gives rise to a question that is right at the heart of the inclusion agenda and which appeared at a relatively early stage in the global move towards inclusive schools: is this an admission that the philosophy is doomed to failure if it cannot meet the educational needs of all children? A 2006 report commissioned by the Conservative government described inclusion as 'a failed ideology' (Conservative Party, 2006, p. 12), rejecting what it calls a one-size-fits-all approach and favouring a continuum of provision that includes special schools alongside mainstream providers.

An educational system with both special and mainstream provision could still be considered a form of inclusion, and the Conservatives' statement serves to illustrate two different understandings of the term. Ruth Cigman (2007) defines universalists as those who would argue for all children to be provided for through mainstream schools – so inclusion is at the individual school level. By contrast she describes moderate inclusionists who would allow for the very particular needs of a small number of children to be met by special school provision, and notes that the Salamanca Statement allows for this. The moderates' view is that inclusion applies to the whole system, not necessarily to the individual components of that system. To some extent this is an argument about scale because even in so-called inclusive schools there is often special provision for particular pupils, and this is the root of an ongoing inclusion debate. At risk of over-simplifying, politically, the moderate view is adopted by more right of centre parties, while those on the left tend towards a more universalist approach.

Because the support for groups of children with particular needs is so dependent on resources and funding, issues of inclusion are inevitably bound up in national policy and therefore subject to the whims and vagaries of government to a very high degree. Political ideology and policy enactment can play out in ways which make a particular difference to individual children and their families, so inclusion policies may be unique in terms of the direct link between policy making and personal lived experience. In this area more than any other, the ability of articulate 'pushy' parents to understand and negotiate the system is key to children finding success in education (Norwich, 2017).

A BRIEF HISTORY OF INCLUSION

For a good understanding of current inclusion practice in England, it is essential to take a brief tour through the significant policy developments that have shaped not just practice but language around SEND. It is hard to imagine today that terms such as idiot, moron, imbecile, retarded and even ineducable were routinely used at a professional level to describe children who were different from the perceived norm (Williams et al., 2009). The 1944 Education Act used the term 'educationally subnormal' to describe children whose achievement was lower than expected, and they were commonly labelled 'backward' (Williams, 1965). At this time a deficit model identified children's needs through a medical lens – something that ideally could be fixed or cured by medical intervention. Over time we have moved more towards a social model in which it is the way our society is organised that defines an individual's special need or disability, and therefore something for society to address (see Caslin, 2017, p. 51). The transformation is neither complete nor universal: parents are often keen for a medical diagnosis or label to describe their child's condition, as the enduring controversy around attention deficit hyperactivity disorder (ADHD) illustrates (Pajo and Cohen, 2012). These views might be supported by research which suggests that children's self-esteem is adversely affected by a general SEND label but not by a specific label that relates to a particular need, such as dyslexia (Taylor et al., 2010).

The significant hinge point in England was the publication of the Warnock Report (1978), translated into legislation through the 1981 Education Act. Warnock used the broad term 'children with special educational needs' (SEN) to cover all of those who might need modifications not just to the physical environment and curriculum but also to the 'social structure and emotional climate' in order to thrive (p. 41). Her report encouraged the integration of children into mainstream schools on three fronts: locational, social and functional. This became the basis of inclusion from the 1981 Act onwards. Early in Margaret Thatcher's premiership the Act also signalled neoliberal tendencies, giving parents the right in principle to select the school they felt would be most appropriate for their child – though for many this was a compromise at best (Bajwa-Patel and Devecchi, 2014). For those with the most significant needs the Local Education Authority (LEA) would prepare a Statement of SEN, in which the support for the child would be specified and with which the named school must comply. For the vast majority of children the presumption was towards mainstream education, and the 1980s and 1990s saw the numbers of children in special schools fall dramatically, even as the numbers identified with various SEN increased (HC, 2006).

The Disability Discrimination Act of 1995 made it illegal to discriminate on the grounds of disability, and the direction of travel was further reinforced by the New Labour government which published the Special Educational Needs and Disability Act in 2001. This linked special educational needs with disabilities, requiring all educational providers to make reasonable adjustments in order to ensure that those with SEND had the same opportunities as all other learners. This underlined the presumption towards mainstream education for all, and the ambition for inclusion within schools, though many schools felt ill-equipped for the task. Some expressed concern that simply accepting children with SEND onto the roll of mainstream schools and then saddling them with the system's norm-referenced performance criteria served to disadvantage them further, by creating exclusive practices and inferior educational experiences (Lloyd, 2008). The *Every Child Matters* (ECM) programme, supported by the Children Act 2004, sought to inform inclusive practice, recognising that education was just one facet of children's lives and that coordinated multi-agency work was essential if all children were to come anywhere close to achieving their potential. ECM also broadened the concept of inclusion to include children who might have felt excluded from the system as a result of adverse childhood experiences or family circumstances, not just those with SEND.

The first decade of the 21st century marked the zenith for the universalist drive towards inclusive schools. The Conservatives and the coalition government had a more moderate policy of system-wide inclusion, with a commitment to 'remove the bias' towards inclusion and strengthen parental choice between mainstream and special schools (DfE, 2011b, p. 17). The impact of this policy change can be clearly seen in Department for Education (DfE) statistics. In 2010, 5.5% of children with special needs were educated in special schools; this had risen to just under 10% by 2018, despite the fact that the total number of children with SEND had fallen in that time (Black, 2019). Even those that hold to the universalist ideals of inclusive schools recognised that this might be a better compromise than forcing children into mainstream schools that cannot properly meet their needs, and in the most extreme cases struggle to keep them safe (Connor, 2016). In addition to government policy, the compromise solution is driven not just by resources, which mainstream school leaders claim are inadequate (Lauchlan and Greig, 2015) but also by accountability measures which may present schools in a poor light if a large number of children with SEND fail to achieve the required norms of performance. There are those that contend that school inclusion remains compatible with a national standards agenda, but rising neoconservatism would suggest that we are likely to see more differentiation and segregation, not less.

THE ROLE OF THE SENCo

In 1994, the DfE introduced a mandatory Code of Practice on the identification and assessment of special educational needs. Revised and updated under successive governments, the Code of Practice remains in place; it now includes disabilities, applies to children and young people from birth to 25, and includes both legal requirements and statutory guidance (DfE, 2015c). There have been concerns that the Code of Practice encourages bureaucracy; an alternative viewpoint might be that the Code uses documentation to support practice and thereby safeguard the rights of children and their parents (Bowers and Wilkinson, 1998).

A key requirement of the Code in all its iterations has been the need for each school to designate a qualified teacher with responsibility for SEN coordination across the school (SENCo) – in only the smallest schools is it permissible to share a SENCo. In addition to their teaching qualification SENCos must also achieve the National Award in Special Educational Needs Coordination, a masters-level postgraduate award that recognises the special place and responsibilities that a SENCo holds. The government describes the SENCo as an important role, identifying three specific areas of responsibility:

- Working with the headteacher and governors on the strategic direction of SEN policy;
- Day-to-day operation of the policy and coordination of individual provision for children with SEN;
- Providing guidance to staff, supporting parent and families, and working with other agencies to ensure that all children receive high-quality teaching and support (DfE, 2015c, p. 108).

By any measure this is a huge role, and while the recommendation is that the SENCo sits on a school's senior leadership team this is not always the case (Dobson, 2019). Other than headteachers, there are few front-line professionals in education who carry such a weight of responsibility, or potentially, such power and influence. In large schools, the SENCo usually has little or no teaching commitment, and may be responsible for a team of teaching assistants who will be deployed to meet the needs of children with special needs and disabilities. Because of the additional funding that flows to providers to support children with SEND there is an expectation that the SENCo is involved in determining how resources are used, though this is not always realised in practice.

A 2018 report suggested that while 'a fundamental expectation of a good SENCo is compassion for children's needs', the majority of SENCos did not have enough time to carry out their duties effectively (Curran et al., 2018), thus undermining their sense of ethical and moral responsibility. SENCos are predominantly women, often part time, and frequently underrated (Curran and Boddison, 2021; Dobson, 2019); they may have additional responsibilities as well as those for SEND, and their role may not be well understood within and beyond the school community.

These characterisations of a well-intentioned but poorly enacted policy would suggest that some of England's children with particular needs are not going to be well supported in schools. The Code leaves the classroom teacher with responsibility for children's progress, though of course the SENCo should be ensuring that they are well equipped to deliver this. In reality this can generate a twofold pressure to limit or minimise the number of children with special needs that a school can accommodate. Schools are reliant on a SENCo's 'psychological contract' (Smith, 2021, p. 33) which is fragile at best, and is put under extreme pressure by an in-school performativity discourse which threatens to marginalise children who might face barriers to learning or participation. This may place the SENCo at a unique nexus of tension, particularly if they are neither supported by nor part of the school's senior leadership team. Smith suggests that that this strain is further compounded in neoliberal regimes. It might be argued that, in insisting on a specific role focused on supporting children with SEND, the Code of Conduct has lifted some responsibility from the wider teaching team and created an impossible individual task that threatens to have the opposite effect to that intended.

STATEMENTS AND EHCPS

The introduction of Statements of Special Educational Needs (usually just called a Statement) from 1981 provided a legal basis for specialised support for a small number of children with more extreme needs. Within the Statement provision would be detailed, specific and quantified – in terms of the hours of specialist support needed. A Statement would specify any necessary curriculum modifications and specialist equipment, in addition to staffing requirements. Specific additional funding was linked to the support required, to enable schools to meet their legal duty to implement the requirements of the Statement.

The intention to give parents a guarantee of effective support to enable good progress in school for children with SEN may have been virtuous, but the outworking of the policy proved more problematic, ineffective and potentially damaging to children's education. Identifying and funding additional staffing (usually in the form of teaching assistants) led to children experiencing less time with qualified teachers, often in withdrawal groups away from the main classroom, with a consequent negative impact on their progress (Webster and Blatchford, 2015). A longitudinal study (Webster and Blatchford, 2017) found that although the support provided by teaching assistants was 'fuzzy', the deployment of teaching assistants was seen by schools as a key strategy in including and meeting the needs of children with Statements. Similarly, parental views were that their children would not be able to cope in mainstream settings without the personal support of a teaching assistant. A DfE report (Parish and Bryant, 2015) noted that the proportion of pupils with Statements varied widely between LAs, and that a negative correlation with levels of deprivation was counterintuitive, perhaps suggesting that the system was biased in favour of more affluent families.

From 2014, Statements were gradually phased out and replaced with Education, Health and Care Plans (EHCPs). As the name suggests, EHCPs should be more all-encompassing than Statements, recognising that education and health needs are often inextricably entwined. Like Statements, EHCPs are constructed by the LA, and must take account of the views of the parents and child or young person. They also specify particular needs in relation to education, health and social care, identify desired outcomes and establish how the various services will work together to achieve them. A notable difference from Statements is the concept of a personal budget: parents can request that some of the notional cost of support is not paid direct to the school, but is instead given to parents to choose how it is spent. There are clear neoliberal principles behind the idea that parents can make informed choices in the SEND marketplace, driving quality and value for money, but the reality is that very few are aware of this option, and even fewer choose to take it up (Cochrane and Soni, 2020). Proponents of personal budgets point out that they are not the ultimate form of personalisation of public services, but aim to provide a mechanism for service users to help shape provision (Martinez and Pritchard, 2019). Even then, the same authors state that 'the ability of personal budgets to deliver financial savings or improve outcomes in some circumstances remains unclear' (p. 47), which might suggest that the introduction of such schemes is driven more by ideology than by evidence.

Professionals working within education are generally in favour of the more holistic approach that EHCPs offer, though there are notable constraints including, unsurprisingly, budgets and time limitations (Palikara et al., 2019). More fundamental to the holistic principle are the challenges that surround multi-agency working in the assessment of needs and production of EHCPs. This task remains delegated to LAs, but it is complex as it involves developing a common language, a good understanding of roles and a commitment to shared outcomes, none of which is trivial for professionals that have become used to a more siloed approach. Once again, the focal point of this tension is often the SENCo, who may feel the responsibility to track down and secure appropriate support and provision with limited resources (Richards, 2021).

SPECIAL SCHOOLS

Whether or not they fit with the universalist's ideal view of an inclusive system, the fact remains that special schools have played an important role in educating children with SEND from 1918 onwards, though currently numbers in special schools are relatively small. In 2005 Baroness Warnock published a pamphlet that reconsidered 'the ideal of inclusion' (updated in Warnock and Norwich, 2010), re-igniting the debate about the place of special schools and prompting some to accuse her of a U-turn. Even a cursory reading of the original Warnock Report (1978) shows that she never subscribed to the universalist view of inclusion, and that although she advocated for more inclusion within mainstream schools, there was never any doubt that special schools would continue to be necessary. In a second 2005 paper Warnock describes the trauma faced by some children with Down's syndrome or Asperger's syndrome as they move to mainstream secondary education and face academic programmes with which they cannot keep pace, in addition to challenging environments and constant changes of teachers and rooms. Warnock concludes:

> 'I am convinced that for such children what is needed is a mixture of care and small-class teaching in the environment of a small school' and 'for such children "inclusion" is a nightmare'.
>
> (Warnock, 2005, p. 15)

Warnock is not of course the only voice on the subject, though she is one who carries authority and influence. Unless there is a dramatic change in policy it would seem that England will retain a small number of special schools in order to meet the needs of children with the most profound needs, and that the drive towards fully inclusive schools has lost momentum and energy. This is not to say that the universalist ideal is not achievable: there is evidence to suggest that other Western states, notably Italy and Canada, have made much more progress in this direction than the United Kingdom (Evans, 2004), but for England this may require more fundamental change to mainstream schools than the system is willing to bear. School-level inclusion may in that sense be considered a failed ideology, but that does not make it a failure. Those that agree with Warnock might suggest that system-level inclusion allows for targeted individual support that meets the needs of every child, albeit some in special provision, and that therefore inclusion is a successful practicality that holds special and mainstream provision in a delicate balance.

SEN in England are categorised into four broad areas (communication, cognition, social and emotional needs, physical and sensory needs) and special schools for children aged 11 and over usually specialise in one or more of these areas. Many identify further and more narrowly defined specialisms, such as autistic spectrum disorders or visual impairment, for example. Special schools are usually relatively small (typically less than 200 pupils, and sometimes as few as 50) and the curriculum they offer can vary widely – though they are still included in the government's performance tables using the same metrics as mainstream schools. Usually special schools have a strong emphasis on developing personal independence and life skills. Teachers in special schools often have a particular sense of vocation, and they report less stress than mainstream teachers, though the sources of stress are different (Williams and Gersch, 2004). Perhaps surprisingly, there are no national standards for teachers in special schools and no centrally defined training route for those aspiring to teach in special schools, other than the SENCo qualification which serves a different purpose.

While there are good examples of collaboration between mainstream schools and special schools that appear to demonstrate genuine system-level inclusion (for example, Gibb et al., 2007) there remain others which highlight the segregation that still exists. Doak (2020) highlights physical segregation not just between special and mainstream schools, but also within a special school setting that extends beyond segregation in learning to segregation of play, recreation and social activities. The importance of social segregation should not be overlooked: even if special schools meet the physical and learning needs of children with SEND, the fact that they are segregated by school can lead to stigma, bullying and a sense of social isolation (Norwich and Kelly, 2004) which undermines the moderate inclusionist argument. Because special schools are few in number, children may need to travel significant distances to access the provision they need, an issue highlighted by Ofsted (2015, p. 62) and described by one LA as 'unacceptable' (Duxbury and Bradwell, 2012). This may force more school-level inclusion at a local level, perhaps putting children into settings that are ill-equipped to meet their needs, or, if they choose to travel, cause them to be even more socially segregated.

It is clear that even though the existence of special schools within the English system seems to be irreversibly established, their place remains contentious, and arguments relate not just to policy and ideology but importantly to the lived experiences of children and their families (Shaw, 2017). Further tension is caused by accountability measures which take no account of the nature of special schools, and the lack of specialist training which means special schools must stretch their budgets if they want to source and purchase appropriate training for their staff. It is unlikely that a single policy solution exists to minimise the sense of difference children feel, while properly meeting their needs and supporting a fully inclusive society.

ALTERNATIVE PROVISION

So far in this chapter we have considered the inclusion and education of children with SEND. There is another group of children for whom inclusion is an important – perhaps life-defining – issue and that is those who, for one reason or another, become excluded from schools. The fact that there is strong intersectional crossover between these two groups is a sad indictment of the effectiveness of SEND policy to date, and although not all excluded children have SEND, the number that do is disproportionately high (Graham et al., 2019). The percentage of children permanently excluded from schools may seem vanishingly small, but the 2019 Timpson review (DfE, 2019b) points out that it is nonetheless 40 children a day on average, and the implications for each of those children are dramatic. On average a further 2,000 children are temporarily excluded; these numbers declined for a decade until 2021 but have been growing steadily since then.

Formal school exclusions (i.e. those following the legally defined process) usually result from either a single serious behaviour incident or a longer pattern of poor behaviour (called persistent disruptive behaviour), but there are children who are not in school due to other reasons. These may include pregnancy, physical or mental health issues, school refusal, and the relatively recent phenomenon of 'off-rolling'. Off-rolling is a direct response to the neoliberal accountability agenda which incentivises schools to exclude children who might have an adverse effect on performance measures (Done and Knowler, 2020). Although any form of unofficial exclusion is illegal, some schools have used a range of tactics to deliberately massage their school roll, resulting in a hidden underclass of children missing out on school – most of whom have characteristics of SEND or socio-economic disadvantage. It has been argued that in a fragmented system, the increase of academisation and decrease of LA oversight has contributed to this effect (McShane, 2020).

Alternative provision (AP) is an umbrella term that is used to include a range of educational providers established specifically to cater for those children who are not in schools. Pupil Referral Units (PRUs) are probably the most well-known form of AP. The concept of the PRU was introduced in 1994, though prior to this Local Education Authorities (LEAs) had a range of 'off-site units' with specialist support to educate children who could 'no longer be constructively educated in ordinary schools' (Hill, 1997, p. 28). Ostensibly PRUs aim to provide a temporary respite for children who have been struggling in their school setting, before being reintegrated into their mainstream school. In reality, the capacity of PRUs is very limited, they only deal with children whose problems have reached a critically acute stage, and they have to deal with extremely challenging behaviours. As a consequence, they may embark on a programme of educational compromise which further undermines young people's learning skills and behaviours and can make reintegration into mainstream settings more difficult still (Meo and Parker, 2004). A small number of children remain in a PRU permanently. Sadly, even the specialist provision in a PRU cannot accommodate some children, and they go on to be permanently excluded from the PRU. Even in the best cases, attendance at a PRU is likely to have been preceded by a period of months out of school, so learning habits are already broken (Pirrie et al., 2011), and although they may be on the roll of a PRU, children may actually be educated off-site by tutors, for as little as five hours a week.

PRUs are managed and run by LAs, but LAs are not obliged to offer PRU places for pupils in their areas. They may, instead or in addition, use other forms of AP. These will normally be an independently established provider, increasingly an academy or free school established specifically to provide an alternative route for children exhibiting challenging behaviour. The regulations around APs other than PRUs are somewhat vague: a 2019 government-backed review stated that APs 'may or may not be registered with the DfE and be subject to inspection by Ofsted' (Mills and Thompson, 2018, p. 7). Inevitably this gives rise to mixed practice in terms of provision and quality, though this is gradually being counteracted by an increasing responsibility of schools to account for the progress of pupils they have placed in AP settings.

Provision in APs may be full or part time, is usually in very small class groups and may be for a fixed period, usually around six months. For Key Stage 4 pupils, AP placements are often for the remainder of their time in compulsory education. The curriculum can be varied, though statutory guidance specifies that mathematics, English and science should be included. Most APs supplement this with some form of work-based learning or placement. Although APs do not have to offer the National Curriculum, deviation from this makes reintegration into mainstream more difficult, and therefore APs for Key Stage 1–3 children tend to align closely to it. Ofsted (2016) reported that pupils enjoy attending AP settings, but raised concerns about the quality of the curriculum offer. This is seen by some as an issue of equality and fair access to education (Malcolm, 2018), and there is a sense that pupils in AP settings might be contained and occupied, but they are no more part of an inclusive system than they would be if they were out of school entirely.

One particular group of children who are significantly at risk of being permanently excluded from schools are those who are legally in the care of the LA (technically called children looked-after, or CLA). Since 2014, LAs have been charged with appointing the headteacher of a 'virtual school' – not a school at all but the authority's looked-after children and those who have recently left a care setting. The role of the virtual head is to be an advocate for CLA, to be their champion through their educational journey and to help coordinate the multi-agency support they receive. Virtual schools also have a role in supporting parents and care providers, in a holistic approach that is unusual at the system level, but which seeks to ensure that some of the most vulnerable children are included (Drew and Banerjee, 2019).

It is straightforward to assert that society should be inclusive, and that as microcosms of society we might expect schools to reflect this. It is much more difficult to identify what our society means by inclusion, what is deemed acceptable, and where inclusion and integration overlap. The discussion is further complicated by an understanding of segregation within education as being a form of inclusion in a wider sense. What is not in doubt is that every child is entitled to an education – this is enshrined globally in the United Nations Convention on the Rights of the Child – but the role of policymakers is to translate this philosophy into policy and thence into practice. Inclusion therefore becomes an issue of human rights (Williams-Brown and Hodkinson, 2020), and is one aspect of social justice in education, which we take up in Chapter 10.

CASE STUDY: STONE SOUP ACADEMY

Stone Soup Academy is an alternative provision free school in the centre of Nottingham, serving students outside mainstream education in an environment that encourages their academic and personal development. This case study is taken from Stone Soup's 'about us' description on its website.

Stone Soup Academy

Stone Soup Academy is committed to the education and welfare of its students, with the goal of preparing them to be successful members of our communities as they enter the world of work, education or training after they leave. The focus and vision are about 'Creating Unimagined Futures' for everyone who passes through the Academy.

The Academy works with other local schools and LAs to ensure that students who fail to thrive in a mainstream school environment have a genuine educational alternative. Stone Soup subscribes to the view that every young person should have the opportunity to succeed by being motivated and inspired. With this as a fundamental belief, it aims to develop young people into unique, responsible, discerning members of society with a sense of their own value, and the school is structured to nurture the social development of all the young people it works with. All too frequently, students who are deemed to be difficult or disruptive are faced with a future of unemployment or social disadvantage.

The Academy holds at the heart of its work the ambition to create an environment that fully equips students for their personal and academic development. The goal is to empower each individual student to achieve in practical, functional and long-lasting ways, and to access future that, when they joined the school, seemed impossible to achieve. With this in mind, Stone Soup aims to:

- Provide a supportive environment that aids the learning and personal development of all students.
- Prepare younger students, where appropriate, for reintegration back into main-stream education.
- Support all young people to achieve their potential.
- Improve the behaviour and attitude of each student with both adults and their peers.
- Reinforce each student's self-esteem and integrity.
- Instil an understanding of fundamental British values for citizenship.

Curriculum

The curriculum offered by Stone Soup is matched to individuals' needs and is focused on achieving these goals through a wide range of courses to ensure continued student engagement and attendance.

The Academy believes that a diverse curriculum encourages students to develop integrated skills that will more truly prepare them for the responsibilities and experiences of adult life. As an alternative provision academy, creativity is encouraged to focus and guide learning. Functional Skills qualifications and core GCSEs in maths and English are combined with classes in creative subjects such as media, music technology and creative arts along with access to the local Further Education (FE) college and university. All of these are aimed at growing the skills and confidence of students as well as teaching them new crafts that could potentially turn into a career.

Students also have classes in personal, social, health and economic education (PSHE) and relationship and sex education (RSE) curricula which explore a wide range of topics aimed at equipping them for citizenship, and ensuring they understand fundamental British values including democracy, rule of law, individual liberty and mutual respect for and tolerance of those with different faiths and beliefs and for those without faith. While these are specifically addressed in form time and PSHE and RSE, these values are additionally embedded in the curriculum and environment of the Academy. This is apparent from the moment a student enters the academy, in the way in which they are greeted through to the way in which goodbyes are said. This work is supported through online resources, debate and resolution of conflict when it occurs.

Support

Alongside the academic subjects offered, there is also a system that ensures the welfare of students by providing services to them and their families. Most importantly, the policy is to tailor the learning career of each student to their particular needs and cross-reference initial assessment with future progress to maintain a positive learning experience.

Individual pastoral support is also available to students, as well as individual and group sessions with educational specialists. Regular contact is maintained with parents/caregivers and outside agencies involved in each student's welfare, in order to provide the best possible level of support and protection for all-round development, in keeping with the organisation's mission.

The Academy prides itself on personalising the education offered to each student, in the belief that by re-igniting their interest in academic studies and vocational practice they will make exceptional progress.

Study questions

1. From the information provided here, in what ways does Stone Soup contribute to the inclusion agenda? Are there aspects of its work and ambitions that might undermine inclusion?

2. How does Stone Soup create the 'social structure and emotional climate' that Warnock stated are essential for children to thrive? How and why is this different from mainstream settings?

3. Which government policies and ambitions – which were written with the mainstream majority in mind – might Stone Soup find challenging, and where can you see sug-gestions that these challenges are being addressed?

SUMMARY

This chapter has considered different meanings of the term 'inclusion' and looked at how schools gradually became more inclusive during the last third of the 20th century. The role of the SENCo has been discussed, and the support offered to children through Statements and EHCPs has been described. Consideration has been given to the place of special schools in the English educational system. The chapter concludes with a reflection on the need for alternative provision settings to ensure that some form of education is provided for every child, even if there are reasons why they may not be able to access mainstream schools.

FURTHER READING

Ruth Cigman's book, *Included or Excluded? The challenge of the mainstream for some SEN children* (2007), contains a collection of essays, many of which challenge the orthodox universalist viewpoint. A foreword by Baroness Warnock discusses the 'dangerous legacy' of her 1978 report and sets the context for a range of authors, including both academics and practitioners, to discuss what inclusion means for them.

10

SOCIAL JUSTICE: THE TRIUMPH OF EQUITY OVER EFFICIENCY

CONTENTS

This chapter includes:

- An introduction to examine what is meant by social justice and how it might apply to education.
- A discussion of social mobility as a common response to social injustice, to address issues of wealth and class.
- Short summaries of some of the dividing lines of social justice; race and ethnicity; gender and sexuality; religion and faith; geographical location.
- Finally, a recognition that all individuals will fit within numerous categories and that intersectionality must be considered.

INTRODUCTION

The deceptively simple term 'social justice' is one that has been heavily disputed and debated since the latter part of the 20th century. Alistair Ross describes a society in which 'structural inequalities are minimised, in which diverse identities are valued, and the outcomes (educational and other) for groups are broadly equal' (2021, p. 2), while critiquing a policy context in which efficiency trumps this idealised equity. Such an apparently clear understanding of equity and fairness in society is not shared by all, and the concept has been theorised and modelled in a variety of ways, some of them contradictory and many of them highly complex, if not complicated. A useful initial starting point is that of John Rawls, who points to the 'basic structure' of society in which people born into different positions, may have different expectations of life, dependent upon the prevailing political, social and economic environment (Rawls, 1971, p. 7). In this conceptualisation, the fairness of a society depends on how fundamental rights (and duties) are distributed – leading to what is known as the *distribution model* of social justice.

The distribution model is relatively straightforward to understand, relating as it does to a fair allocation of material and non-material resources. For some it has become synonymous with social justice, but others (for example Gewirtz, 1998) see distributional justice as only one dimension of a multifaceted construct. Alternative dimensions might include *relational justice*, which incorporates the ideas of how power is mediated through society and which might be dissected further to consider procedures and relationships, alongside notions of autonomy and identity. Wherever justice is discussed, there must be an implicit assumption that injustice is always a possibility. This may be built into Rawls's basic structure, pre-existent before current actors took to the stage, but it can also be accentuated and exaggerated by individual and corporate actions. This can lead to guilt-laden finger-pointing and accusation; more constructively, Young develops a theory in which 'all agents who contribute by their actions to the structural processes that produce injustice have responsibilities to work to remedy these injustices' (2006, p. 102). Young's social connection model is applied internationally on a global scale, but her sentiments will strike chords with those within education who feel a weight of responsibility to challenge injustice and to right wrongs insofar as that is their gift.

While academic arguments raged about the meaning of social justice, the neoliberal ideal continued its march through developed western nations, bringing with it a further understanding of social justice as it applies to education in particular. Instead of – or perhaps in addition to – distributional justice, which in this domain might be conceived as the right of all children to be able to access appropriate education, justice began to be redefined in terms of measurement and accountability such that outcome measures became the social justice indicators of choice. The inherent dangers of such an approach are immediately apparent: the actors in a system committed to *outcomes justice* (my term) might take the view that the ends justify the means, reducing or eliminating any considerations of relational justice. This may lead to school leaders who will do what is best for their school's outcomes, irrespective of the local collateral damage this may cause. The emphasis may be so much on the products of education that the experience of education is overlooked, though children will have to live that experience every day.

It is also argued that working towards outcomes justice can actually cause further injustice, on scales as small as classes within an individual school. Rezai-Rashti et al. (2017) describe how a particular Canadian policy, arising from a commitment to inclusion, led to the identification of 'at risk' groups and measurements of performance gaps, with pressure to reduce attainment gaps for those groups. The policy pushed responsibility for closing the gaps to local schools, but in choosing metrics relating to very specific sub-populations they rendered invisible the inequities related to other characteristics – in this case race and class. Governmental commitments to be seen to perform well in international performance tables (such as the OECD PISA tables) can compound this effect, as the driver for improvement is reduced to an average outcome statistic for particular groups, rather than the individual experiences of children or sub-groups of children.

Outcomes justice carries with it a more profound challenge for neoliberalism, based as it is on the invisible hand of the market: competitive markets only thrive when there is a limitation of supply, or where the market is rationed. Performative, accountability-based policies to reduce or eliminate gaps therefore serve to undermine the market: if there are no gaps there is no competitive edge. The ideas of underperformance, failing schools, pockets of underachievement and so on are essential to the narrative of neoliberalism even as its policies claim to promote social justice and raise standards for all. Connell (2013) suggests that the ideological requirement to create inequity and injustice through a series of winners and losers is fundamentally at odds with education. Be that as it may, successive UK governments have sought to close outcomes gaps with a variety of initiatives and policies that remain within the neoliberal ideal. Social justice itself is rarely mentioned in their discourses; instead they choose to use another term that is equally contested and carries multiple understandings: that of social mobility.

WEALTH AND CLASS: SOCIAL MOBILITY

Like social justice, the term social mobility can be expressed in a variety of ways, though again the fundamental face value concept is apparent: social mobility relates in some way to moving up the established social order. In England the Department for Education (DfE) defines social mobility as the link between a person's occupation or income and the occupation or income of their parents: where there is a strong link, there is a lower level of social mobility; where there is a weak link, there is a higher level of social mobility. More simply, Francis (2021) states that social mobility 'usually means a change in socio-economic position compared to the previous generation in the same family'. A variety of sobriquets may be used dependent on political leanings and the specific issues that are being addressed. The Conservative government of the 2020s liked to talk about the 'levelling up agenda'; when considering socio-economic outcomes justice the conversation usually involves 'closing the gaps'.

In order to quantify the notion of social mobility, it is necessary to define benchmarks against which different generations can be compared. Progression to Higher Education is a convenient proxy indicator of social mobility, as it works on both an individual scale (whether or not a student's parents went to university) and as a global measure: percentage of a cohort progressing to university. Though widely used, it is by no means the only indicator of social mobility. Others can be devised based on progression through the government's 8 socio-economic groupings (Office for National Statistics Socio-Economic Classifications), though it should be noted that some of these groupings relate to acquisition of a university degree. These probably replace historical ideas of class: instead of achieving John Major's 'classless society', we have merely reclassified society. Even when a working definition of social mobility has been accepted, there are further problems with identifying what is considered to be a 'good' rate of mobility, and yet more related to understanding and interpreting the data. Stephen Gorard (2008) illustrates the dangers inherent when one particular analysis of data is used to underpin national policy.

Whatever the current understanding of the rate of mobility, successive governments have maintained aspirations for higher rates. The Child Poverty Commission, established by the 2010 coalition, became the Social Mobility Commission (SMC) with a straightforward aim: to ensure that the circumstances of birth do not determine outcomes in life. The Commission aims to do this by challenging both education providers and employers – appealing to this latter group by stating that breaking down socio-economic barriers is 'smart business' as well as being a just cause (SMC, 2021). The SMC notes that the benefits of increasing gender and ethnic diversity in the workplace are well recognised, with only a footnote to state that in reality individuals may experience a multitude of factors which affect their standing in adult life. One of the dangers of a focus on a narrow definition of social mobility is that the wider aspects of social justice may be neglected. Furthermore, Francis and Wong (2013) note that there must be some movement down the social ladder in order to create room at the top for the upwardly mobile – and this may be unpalatable for those involved, which could generate a latent pressure against true mobility.

Education is frequently seen as a key driver of social mobility, and indeed in 2017 the DfE published its plan for improving social mobility through education (DfE, 2017). This identified four specific areas of work: the two perennials – closing outcomes gaps and increasing university participation – plus career development and improving literacy in early years. Calls from the political right to open more grammar schools in order to improve social mobility seem to be largely based on anecdotal tales of working-class children lifted from the dirt by grammar school attendance, and were not included in this Conservative policy. Robust research appears to support that editorial decision: for example, Andrews et al. (2016) conclude that grammar schools can widen attainment gaps, and that the focus of investment should be in early years and primary schools.

Pupil Premium funding was discussed in Chapter 6. This targeted funding was unashamedly focused on outcomes justice, using pupil achievement measures to identify gaps between the disadvantaged and their peers, and expecting schools to use the funding to close those gaps. Despite initial progress (at least with regard to GCSE performance), the government's own SMC has said that examples of success in this respect are 'staggeringly rare' (Riordan et al., 2021), and that since the introduction of Progress 8 as a performance metric, gaps have actually got wider. The Pupil Premium has had no more success in primary schools, where some commentators note that the dependence of cognitive development on socio-economic background is deep-rooted and unlikely to be affected by a small amount of per capita funding (Copeland, 2019). Of course, in total, the amount of money spent on Pupil Premium has been huge (£2.44 billion for 2 million pupils in 2020–21 for example, Roberts et al., 2021). Though well-intentioned, the targeted nature of Pupil Premium funding has perhaps been one of its biggest problems: the SMC has repeatedly asserted that the quality of a child's teacher is one of the most significant factors affecting their academic progress, yet schools cannot spend their Pupil Premium money on skilled teachers. Instead they must find interventions that only affect the disadvantaged children – the idea that a rising tide lifts all boats is not countenanced as it allows for attainment gaps to remain. Conversely, the implication of a closing the gaps approach, with an implicit ceiling on performance, is conveniently ignored.

Schools have become used to having Pupil Premium funding in their budgets and to looking for cost-effective interventions with the potential to close attainments gaps. It has become increasingly clear, however, that the sums invested into this fund have done little to encourage social mobility, and have made even less contribution to social justice. One of the problems with the Pupil Premium is the simplistic way in which eligible pupils are identified: their family must have claimed free school meals at some stage in the preceding 6 years. There is no differentiation between those who have needed to claim free meals throughout their school career and those who may only have needed to resort to this at odd moments of hardship. The fund applies in exactly the same way wherever children live, so geographical variations are not taken into account, and nor are the numbers of eligible children in a given school – it could be argued that schools with large proportions of Pupil Premium children may face a more difficult task than others. Stephen Gorard's work has highlighted various ways in which the Pupil Premium policy has been less than successful; in a 2016 paper he notes that there are problems not just with identifying the children who should receive the Pupil Premium but also with the way in which attainment gaps are measured (Gorard, 2016). This is not to argue for a removal of the Pupil Premium, but to note that its proponents are being 'unwittingly unfair' to many of the families that it was designed to help. The superficial nature of the policy's identifications of both need and success has contributed to a reconceptualising of social justice within education: practitioners may feel a performative urge to focus on efficiency and measurable outcomes which conflicts with deeper moral and pastoral obligations (Craske, 2018). Ultimately we may use the labels of class less than was common in the 20th century, but society remains stratified, and more than a decade of an expensive but simplistic approach has made little difference.

RACE AND ETHNICITY

Observers of the field of education might be forgiven for thinking that policy pays little heed to race or ethnicity, as reference to race has been largely absent from policy documents since the turn of the century. Warmington et al. (2018) chart a 20th-century rising of the awareness of race equality which briefly surfaced in mainstream policy around 2000, but then sank again, almost without trace. The trigger point which caused race to rise on the agenda was the racially motivated murder of teenager Stephen Lawrence in 1993 and the subsequent MacPherson enquiry which identified racial inequality in the public sector and institutional racism in the investigating police force. The Macpherson report informed the Race Relations (Amendment) Act 2000, but this was less a mountaintop moment than the brief surfacing of the tip of a huge latent iceberg. As with social mobility, discourses around race were reshaped by a gap-related standards agenda which tended to obscure the realities of race and ethnicity in England. The 9/11 attacks in the United States in 2001, followed by bombings in London in 2005, prompted a resurgence of patriotism and the identification of 'British values' by Brown's Labour government (Osler, 2009), which was enthusiastically adopted by the subsequent coalition and which arguably reduced any emphasis on race equality in policy debates. The Conservatives' narrowing of the curriculum with regard to history and culture further conspired to cover and hide issues of racial equity in schools. Critical race theory, imported from the United States – where the agenda and culture are different – and curriculum decolonisation in Higher Education, can be conveniently dismissed as intellectual academic conceits by those who are keen to see a 'colour-blind' society (Gove, 2013) and who advocate a closing-the-gaps approach to achieve this. However, ostensibly neutral 'colour-blind' policies will not necessarily create racial equity in education or wider society. While standards overall have risen since 1988 (relative to the contemporary benchmarks), over the same period the basic black/white attainment gap has remained, and at key moments following policy developments it has widened, even as political leaders claimed the opposite effect (Gillborn et al., 2017).

While there is a valid argument that there is no sound scientific basis for categorising people on grounds of race, the fact that it is essentially a social construct does not diminish the effects that are felt by people of different racial groups. In the same way, definitions of ethnicity, which may be somewhat arbitrary and relate to ancestral roots as well as to religion and culture, can nonetheless be useful in demonstrating the wide-ranging experiences and expectations of different groups of people. The DfE defines 18 ethnicities for the purposes of statistical analysis, under five general headings: Asian, Black, White, Mixed and Other. Definitions of ethnicity have been described as 'inherently contextual and likely to be transient' (Mateos et al., 2009) but the government's methodology and resulting list has remained largely consistent, with only minor changes over the last 20 years (it is reviewed and updated for each national census). Consequently descriptors such as White British and Black Caribbean have entered the lexicon as convenient labels of ethnicity and race.

The UK government has adopted what it calls a colour-blind approach to policymaking, rejecting specific interventions on the basis of race and ethnicity in favour of a focus on disadvantaged communities. This approach is not without its critics (for example, Khan, 2016) and the government's own school performance data would suggest that thus far the colour-blind approach is not yet having the desired effect. The appearance of headlines relating to racial and ethnic disparities is a depressingly regular occurrence, and robust qualitative studies illustrate the personal experiences that lie behind the broader statistics. To some extent, while highlighting some of the issues, such headlines may be contributing to a vicious circle, creating self-fulfilling prophecies. For example, there is evidence that teachers have low expectations of Black Caribbean children which generates an institutional racism: their needs are not properly assessed and this results in higher levels of exclusions (Demie, 2021). These reinforce the ongoing reports that the rate of exclusions for Black Caribbean pupils is three times that of other pupils, fuelling lower expectations in schools. The situation for Black Caribbean pupils is further compounded by the political and historical context, which includes a deficit-based 30-year discourse around 'underachievement', discriminatory ability groups which accentuate differences, and lack of teacher diversity and understanding (Wallace and Joseph-Salisbury, 2021).

The lack of racial or ethnic diversity among the school workforce has been well documented over a long period of time, even though it is now 'more diverse than ever' (DfE, 2018). The DfE noted that only 8% of teachers were from ethnic minority backgrounds, and that only 4% of school governors – who are legally responsible for hiring new staff – were from ethnic minority backgrounds. Figures are even more stark for school leaders, where over 96% of headteachers are classed as White. There is evidence not just that this may limit the aspirations of young people who might perceive through a lack of role models that education is not for them but also that leaders themselves might face isolation, microaggression and challenges to personal and professional development (Vieler-Porter, 2021). A 2020 report used DfE data to show that 46% of England's schools have no Black, Asian or minority ethnic teachers at all (Tereshchenko et al., 2020). The same report also suggested that teachers of colour faced a 'hidden workload' of coping with racism, and that this was a more significant factor than workload when it came to teacher retention.

It may be true that the lack of diversity among school leaders is no different from that seen in boardrooms across a wide range of industries, but that does not mean it should not be challenged. On the contrary, it surely provides further support for targeted intervention to ensure that leadership across all sectors better reflects the richness of wider society. This would require brave and controversial policymaking, difficult conversations and changes to practices and attitudes, all the way down to individual interactions with pupils. Attempts to celebrate diversity may actually sidestep issues of racism (Gorski, 2019) and seem to suggest we live in a 'post-racial' multicultural society when this is patently not the case (Warmington, 2010). Probably the most significant issue when attempting to address problems of racial inequity in schools, and more widely in society as a whole, is the need to challenge the dominant white hegemony: as Reno Eddo-Lodge notes in the preface to her searing critique: 'who really wants to be alerted to a structural system that benefits them at the expense of others?' (Eddo-Lodge, 2017).

GENDER AND SEXUALITY

The vast majority of state schools in England are coeducational and ostensibly offer equality of opportunity across the curriculum to both girls and boys. Most schools have a fairly even gender split, though there are local variations and fluctuations over time, especially in smaller schools. Where single-sex schools do exist they can skew the distribution in neighbouring schools which have a mixed intake. Broadly speaking though, we would expect our schools to offer a level-playing field irrespective of gender. It is perhaps surprising then to note differences in the academic achievements of girls and boys – where girls tend to outperform boys in each key stage – as well as gender differences in other measures such as exclusions (more boys are excluded than girls) and attendance (absence is higher for boys up to the age of 13, and higher for girls above 13).

In policy terms the push for comprehensive education in the 1960s and 1970s was accompanied by a move towards coeducational secondary schools. Single-sex grammar schools were closed and often combined. Mixed-sex comprehensives, 'schools for all', opened in their place (Sutherland, 1985), and coeducational secondary education quickly became the norm, just as it had been for primary children. This did not stop commentators and practitioners from calling for more segregation, within schools if it was not possible between schools. By the turn of the century single-sex girls' schools continued to top league tables, and analysis of attainment data that demonstrated endemic underachievement on the part of the boys prompted David Blunkett, the Secretary of State, to call for more research into single-sex classes within mixed schools (Woodward, 2000). A flurry of papers duly followed, but the general consensus was that while there might be marginal attainment gains for girls there was little to benefit the boys (Jackson, 2002), and certainly nothing to challenge what Blunkett called 'laddish culture' – there was the potential for this behaviour to worsen (Warrington and Younger, 2003). Longitudinal studies suggest that there are slight academic and economic benefits for girls who attend single sex schools, and moderate social benefits for boys who attend mixed schools (Sullivan et al., 2012), but neither of these is strong enough to support or drive policy change.

Within secondary schools gender differences are apparent in options choices, with a preponderance of boys choosing STEM (science, technology, engineering and mathematics) courses. This difference continues through Higher Education despite decades of interventions designed to increase girls' participation in the sciences (Smith, 2011). Becky Francis' analysis (2000) described traditionally defined 'masculine' subjects which were perceived to be objective, hard and scientific, in comparison with 'feminine' subjects which were subjective, soft and arty. She also identified a hierarchy of power and status which defined the 'feminine' subjects as less important and substandard, posing a double challenge to the pursuit of gender equity. Given the longstanding gender differential between science and arts subjects, it is tempting to subscribe to the populist view that 'men are from Mars and women are from Venus' (Gray, 1992) – in other words that female brains work in a different way from male brains, so there will be an inherent bias in the choices they make. Developments in neuroscience continue to challenge this narrative as they demonstrate no physiological differences between the brains of different sexes, but it is likely that misconceptions will persist. The reason for this is that choices are not made in a vacuum but are steeped in social context, and it must be this that drives the numbers differential: as Gina Rippon puts it, 'a gendered world will produce a gendered brain' (Rippon, 2019). Even in Francis's study only a minority of the teenage subjects thought that there was actually an intrinsic difference in scientific ability between girls and boys, but they were able to describe social pressures to achieve, or not, according to gender stereotypes.

There are other reasons to consider segregating girls and boys within a mixed-sex school. Physical differences lead to segregation and different sports in PE lessons, and pupils themselves state that they prefer at least some sex and relationships lessons in single sex groups, in both secondary and primary schools (Pound et al., 2017). This preference is not necessarily because girls and boys want to learn about different things, but because they feel more comfortable discussing the same subjects in single sex groups, including the meaning of gender itself. As societal understanding of gender has developed, so policy has evolved to become more gender-sensitive, recognising diverse realities (Mukoro, 2021), though developments in school practice are lagging behind. The traditional and historical structures of schools may be challenged by pupils whose thinking is generally less binary, raising very practical issues of justice – for example in relation to school uniform and boys'/girls' toilets (Ingrey, 2018). This results in reactionary practice in schools, which is often driven by parents and pupils themselves: where schools do not adapt, children identifying as trans or gender-diverse can be among their most marginalised and oppressed groups (Davy and Cordoba, 2020). In some senses schools can be seen as a battleground where progressive liberal policies (even those drafted by conservative politicians) conflict with the systemic leviathan that resists change. Debates about gender are being added to those about sexuality, which have continued for several decades: at issue is not just curriculum content – what we teach our children about gender and sexuality – but the very practice of schools which can demonstrate worth and value or prejudice and intolerance, implicitly or explicitly through words, actions and policies.

Most educational establishments would claim to be inclusive in the widest sense of the word, but the reality is that while they may teach the so-called British values of individual liberty, tolerance and respect, these are not always embedded in practice. It is claimed that half of LGBT teachers hide their sexual identity in the school workplace (Lee, 2020). While it may be true that pupils do not need to know about their teachers' sexuality, it is equally valid to say that teachers should not feel a need to hide this from pupils, peers or parents. Schools will inevitably educate children whose parents represent the full range of gender and sexual orientations, and may inadvertently discriminate against some of these if they do not allow open discussion of these matters. In terms of staffing, the Equality Act of 2010 defined protected characteristics such that employers cannot use them as a basis for discrimination: these include gender and sex, and sexual orientation. The parental body is beyond the control of the school, and within its wide range there will also be those with less-tolerant views who would want to see their children protected from liberal viewpoints. Debates about gender and sexuality therefore become framed in a context of parental rights relating to their children's education (Nash and Browne, 2021); often these arguments fall back on fundamental, but not necessarily mainstream, religious ideals.

RELIGION AND FAITH

Chapters 2 and 3 provide the historical journey that enables us to understand the complexity of the view from here in religious terms. In England the landscape of the state school sector is varied and confusing, with Anglican and Catholic church schools and a smattering supported by other Christian denominations, longstanding schools of other faiths, faith-based academies and free schools, multi-academy trusts with a religious character, and trusts which have a mixture of academies, some of which are faith-based. Among all of these are the many schools without a basis in any particular faith but which are required to hold a daily act of collective worship that is broadly Christian in nature – the United Kingdom is unique in being the only nation in the world that requires this of all maintained schools.

As a consequence of this huge variety there is the potential for particular religious viewpoints to conflict with schools' duties of inclusion, and this can be characterised in two opposing ways. Certain religious beliefs may be considered intolerant or bigoted; conversely individuals holding certain views may feel excluded by the educational community and therefore discriminated against themselves. This can be the case for both liberal families in conflict with conservative faith schools, as well as parents with a particular faith position that is challenged by a school's more liberal ethos. Despite the neoliberal mantra of parental choice, simply changing schools may not be an option for many families. Religious pluralism is a reality of society in the United Kingdom, but the multiplicity of school types seems neither to meet the expressed needs of its citizens, nor to educate and enable them to be more tolerant, respectful and inclusive. Debates about whether we should or should not have schools with a religious character or basis in faith are essentially academic, as a century of political compromise has demonstrated that there is no appetite to change the status quo. No school is ideologically neutral, so the challenge has to be how to recognise its own philosophy without marginalising those with different beliefs (Ameen and Hassan, 2013).

For faith schools, there are exemptions from the 2010 Equality Act, which some would interpret as fundamentally unfair. For example, where they are oversubscribed they may use faith-based criteria to select which children are admitted, so there is a bias in favour of parents of faith for popular faith schools. Similarly, schools with a religious character may give preference to teachers who demonstrate alignment with the particular faith, in terms of appointment, remuneration and promotion (Long and Danechi, 2019). Again, this is perceived by some to be discriminatory.

Objective analysis provides evidence that faith schools which do select children on the basis of their religion (and not all do) undermine ethnic integration and social inclusion: Anglican and Catholic families in particular are much more likely to lie in the top quartile of household incomes, so schools selecting those children will necessarily have a particular socio-economic bias (Allen and West, 2010). Similarly, where a faith is linked to particular ethnic backgrounds, the existence of faith schools can contribute to societal divisions and segregation. It would be overly simplistic simply to state that faith schools undermine social justice, though there is clearly the potential for them to do so. Under New Labour, the term 'community cohesion' was employed in attempts to somehow quantify the strength of community networks, but difficulties with its interpretation combined with the wide variety of faith school characteristics made it difficult to draw hard and fast, policy-influencing, conclusions. Faith schools are at the same time anomalous and central to the English educational system (Dwyer and Parutis, 2012), and policy developments are unlikely to overcome the inertia which will maintain their place. Arguments will continue to focus on the right of faith schools to receive public funding, and their potential to undermine social cohesion; but in the ethical, epistemological and political arena there will be no easy answers (Pring, 2018).

GEOGRAPHY

In principle, when everyone has a well-established right to an education with a National Curriculum, where schools must take uniform approaches to assessment, and where regulation is enforced through a quasi-governmental inspectorate, there is no reason why geography should affect children's educational experiences and outcomes. Not only is this not the case, but regional differences in outcomes in particular seem to have grown larger in neoliberal times: a 2016 report by the independent Commission on Inequality in

Education (Clegg et al., 2016) found that the geographic area which a child comes from is a more powerful predictive factor for performance for children born in 2000 than it was for those born in 1970. This is despite a large number of place-based policy initiatives, including Education Action Zones (1998), Excellence in Cities (1999), the London Challenge (2003) and Opportunity Areas (2017).

The early years of league tables and performance analysis initially identified problems in urban schools, and this is where funding was first directed (Barber, 2002). The London Challenge was the most significant geographical policy intervention in terms of both cost and effect, with up to £40 million annually invested over a period of 8 years, during which time Local Authorities in London rose from the bottom to the top of the national league tables (Kidson and Norris, 2014). Increasingly detailed geographical analysis, however, has revealed a much more nuanced picture, with a 2019 DfE review finding both strong and weak Key Stage 4 performance across 6 types of setting, ranging from hamlets to large conurbations (DfE, 2019c). Possibly as a result of two decades of government investments, outcomes are not necessarily poor in urban schools, but there is a general trend for coastal schools to show lower results than others. A number of factors are particular to coastal settings: population may be transient due to seasonal employment, transport and communication links may be more difficult than in more central locations, and staff recruitment may be problematic if only because the pool can be drawn from just 180° of hinterland. Coastal communities can feel shunned, vilified or left behind – and, in general, education may not offer the emancipation that residents might hope for (Parfitt, 2021).

Aside from these generalisations, it is clear that geographical differences are experienced on a more local scale and that in some cases these may be manifestations of other factors. Children's experiences of equity and social justice may depend on how close their home is to oversubscribed schools, whether they live in an area which still has grammar schools and selection at 11+, or what the Local Authority travel policy is. The national funding formula for schools still allows discretion in certain aspects, so per capita funding will differ depending on where children live. In many cases geographical differences are driven by more fundamental underlying causes, and these are often related to socioeconomic circumstances. For example, if a community of parents believes one particular school to be better than others, they may move house to be closer and improve the chances of their children being admitted, thus putting an upward pressure on house prices and creating socioeconomic variations in that area and changing the demographic of the school population (Gibbons, 2012). It therefore becomes impossible to disaggregate entirely factors based on location from those with other causes, forcing us to face the tricky concept of intersectionality.

INTERSECTIONALITY

Thus far we have taken a broad view of social justice and considered a number of factors that potentially affect equity in education, as though they are entirely independent variables. This is, of course, not the case: each child will have a particular and personal combination of gender, ethnic heritage, socio-economic background and so on, and could therefore be classified in a number of ways. Intersectionality considers the intersections or overlaps of different social groups to investigate how a combination of influences may affect experiences and outcomes for different individuals – for example, international studies show that the gender difference in STEM subjects grows as affluence increases (Charles, 2017). While this could lead to a more nuanced and sophisticated understanding of social justice, intersectional approaches may simply provide alternative labels that support a particular cause or agenda.

The case of 'white working class' underachievement is an example of an intersectional understanding that has been used in this way. Economic disadvantage – as defined by the proxy indicators of Pupil Premium or free school meal eligibility – is a ubiquitous factor that has an adverse effect on performance outcomes for all other groups. A 2021 report by the House of Commons Education Committee (Halfon, 2021) noted not only that educational attainment for disadvantaged pupils whose ethnicity is White British is lower than that for almost all other ethnic groups (apart from Gypsy/Roma and Traveller children), but that this is the largest ethnic grouping in English schools and therefore represents a significant challenge in terms of closing outcomes gaps. The report accused the educational establishment of muddled thinking in its approach, and suggested that the term 'White Privilege', which had been used to contrast racist experiences of the black community with those of dominant white society, was unhelpful in this particular context. While this dominated headlines and debates, the report's note that White British children were much less likely than any other ethnic group to be disadvantaged (and therefore more likely to be privileged) was conveniently overlooked, and for some it simply provided ammunition for a counterpoint to the Black Lives Matter movement.

As well as economically disadvantaged children, a second group that consistently underperforms is boys. It therefore follows that boys from disadvantaged households, and boys from lower performing ethnic groups, are doubly likely to struggle for success, all other things being equal. Obviously all other things are not equal, which is why it is important to understand context and intersectionality. Geographically, boys in London may outperform their peers elsewhere in the country, but they still lag behind the girls in their own schools. A 2018 report for LKMco (Millard et al., 2018) investigated two of London's least well-performing groups: boys from Black Caribbean families, and White boys eligible for free school meals, making seven recommendations to drive improvements. In common with some of the conclusions from the Halfon report, these did not revolve around targeted funding for particular groups, but instead focused on a much deeper understanding of the issues faced by different children. Both reports stressed the need for vulnerable groups to be supported from cradle to grave, rather than last-minute interventions just before key examinations at the age of 16. Millard et al. (2018) noted that a more diverse teaching workforce, with higher expectations and reduced bias, could contribute to what the government called levelling up; Halfon (2021) highlighted geographical disparities and called for better local understanding. Other recommendations such as working more with parents and families, and paying attention to social and emotional well-being and health, point towards a more holistic understanding of education, though the premise of both documents retained the overwhelming zeitgeist: that of outcomes justice, specifically outcomes at age 16.

These examples serve to highlight some of the complexity of social justice in education – and indeed in trying to use education as a lever to effect social justice in wider society. The problems are compounded by a lack of clarity in terms of what social justice means. Every observer and actor is coloured by their own experiences and philosophy, and educationalists work within a system that has had injustices built into it from the very beginning (Francis et al., 2017). This is not to say that England's system and problems are unique: every country has children that are marginalised and disadvantaged in some way. Not all have taken the neoliberal market-driven approach to try to resolve this, and as we have seen, there is evidence that such an approach can create further division and segregation. Some governments adopt a broader approach that seeks both equity and quality, inclusion and fairness, rather than assuming that market forces will generate these (Ainscow, 2016), but evidence of success is contested, and policy can be complicated. Valuing individuals and achieving inclusion as well as equity is a global challenge with no easy answers.

CASE STUDY: LANCASTERIAN PRIMARY SCHOOL

This case study is a summary of the vision and values of the Lancasterian Primary School, from the school's website. Lancasterian Primary School serves families in central London, in what it calls a 'diverse, welcoming and enthusiastic learning community'.

Vision and values

- Vision is the destination, where we want to get to and why.
- Values are the characteristics and behaviours which we all need to 'live' in order to achieve our Vision.

Below all of these sit our Three-Year Goals, School Improvement Plan, Subject Leader Plans etc.

Vision

We will make a fairer society:

- A society where everyone can reach the top of the mountain, because all of us understand that achieving ambitions includes learning from mistakes.

- A society where everyone has the skills and knowledge to open any door, because all of us break down barriers to opportunity.
- A society where everyone improves the world we share, because all of us seek creative solutions to the issues we face together.

To do this, we will make the best school:

- A school where every child embraces learning as a demanding lifelong journey, because all of us show them how to love challenge and growth.
- A school where every child feels proud of who they are and their own uniqueness, because all of us celebrate difference.
- A school where every child leaves the gate with fond memories, a creative outlook and a sense of excitement for the road ahead, because all of us have put them at the centre of everything we do.

Values

- Inclusion
- Lifelong Learning
- Integrity
- Growth Mindset
- High Aspirations
- Respect

Lancasterian Primary School's vision states that 'we will make a fairer society' and that, in order to do this, 'we will make the best school'. Above all else, children come to school to learn and we passionately believe that all aspects of learning are important – the study of academic subjects (reading, writing, maths and all the other areas) but also personal and social learning (getting on with each other, communicating well, managing difficulties effectively). We also know from employers that these 'soft' skills are highly valued and important in our ever changing world.

Whilst the national curriculum sets out clearly what we need to cover in our teaching of the academic subjects, there is less clarity on what we should teach children in terms of their personal development. In response to this, we have developed our school values in a rigorous and thoughtful way in order to teach the children the personal qualities that we feel are important to be happy and successful in life. These values – inclusion; lifelong learning; growth mindset; integrity; high aspirations; respect – drive and shape every aspect of school life. We use these values to identify and celebrate when children make good choices, and to support and encourage when they make mistakes, helping the children to reflect and think about how they might act differently in the future.

(Continued)

Study questions

1. In what ways does the Lancasterian vision challenge Rawls's 'basic structure' of society? Where is this made explicit, and where is it implicit within the vision and values?
2. Which kinds of social justice can be seen in the vision and values statements? Consider the models and dimensions of social justice, as well as groups which may experience disparities.
3. How would you expect these ideals to be expressed through the school's policies, as laid out in its 3-year goals, school improvement plan and subject plans?

SUMMARY

This chapter has briefly looked at social justice issues in England's schools, considering what is meant by the term and how it might be achieved. Several dividing lines within society have been used to consider commonly used comparison groups. These include a discussion of wealth and social mobility, differences between groups of varying race, gender, faith and geography, and a short discussion of intersectionality which recognises that each individual is unique and belongs to several of these groups.

FURTHER READING

Alistair Ross's edited volume *Educational research for social justice* (2021) dives deep into the issues of social justice in education in the United Kingdom, problematising the activity of research into social justice and casting both research endeavours and their findings in a critical light. Contributors discuss a range of social justice issues from early years through to higher education, and examine the ability of policy to bring about social justice in the name of the 'public good'.

11

NON-COMPULSORY EDUCATION: A JOINED-UP SYSTEM?

INTRODUCTION

Compulsory school age for children in England is from 5 to 16, but that is not to say that education policy confines itself to this period of someone's life. There has been increasing influence (some might say interference) in pre-school education, and significant changes to policy and provision for learners above the age of 16. As with the years of compulsory education, education policy for pre- and post-school learners is rooted in neoliberalism, and has become increasingly divergent across the four home nations. For the purposes of this chapter, we will define four discrete aspects of non-compulsory education, and consider the policy impact within each, recognising that in some cases there is overlap and that boundaries might be blurred – but the overall aim is for 'a joined-up system' (Augar, 2019).

Early childhood education covers the period from birth to the term after a child's 5th birthday, by which time they must be in full-time education in school. Many children begin school, either full- or part-time, before this, and they can do so at any time after their 4th birthday. Whitehall interest and influence over these early formative years is not a new phenomenon: in 1870 the Elementary Education Act allowed for children younger than three to attend school, and the 1908 Acland Report advocated nursery schools for some three-year-olds, whose home conditions were 'imperfect' (cited in West, 2020). Early policy revolved around what we would now call safeguarding, but from the mid-20th century attention was increasingly paid to children's learning. By 2008 the government had defined the Early Years Foundation Stage (EYFS) to cover the learning, development and care of all children from birth to five: this will be taken as the basis for discussion of early childhood education in the section below.

We saw in Chapter 3 that the school leaving age was raised to 16 in 1973. Somewhat confusingly, the *participation age* was raised to 18 from 2014, requiring 16-year-olds to continue in some form of education or training (including part-time training if they had begun work) until their 18th birthday. To add to the confusion, a DfE memorandum confirms that 'there is no penalty for young people who do not follow the duty' and that they are merely encouraged to comply (DfE, ND), so although participation is high, it is certainly not universal. Education beyond the age of 16 is usually referred to as Further Education (FE), though this might occur at any age. For 16–18-year-olds in many schools this would be called sixth form study, and some post-16 providers style themselves 'sixth form colleges'. For our purposes therefore we will use the term sixth form study to denote 16–18-year-olds and distinguish this post-school but pre-university or pre-work study from FE study later in life, which we will include under lifelong learning.

Higher Education (HE) has a much clearer definition, though it is defined by level of study rather than the age of the learners. The way in which education is funded can also be used to define what we mean by HE, but in this chapter we will stick to that used by Bolton and Hubble (2019) in a House of Commons report: 'HE covers education at undergraduate and postgraduate level in universities and colleges'. This allows for the fact that many FE colleges offer a small range of HE qualifications, and while the majority of undergraduates begin their courses aged 18 or 19, this definition of HE is broad enough to incorporate adult learners of any age.

Lifelong learning (or continuing education) relates to study beyond school age, and can include HE, though it predominantly refers to FE and skills development. Lifelong learning therefore includes learning through choice for personal reasons, as well as professional learning that may be a requirement of employment. An emphasis on skills developed through lifelong learning makes it an important focus for governments, as skills are intimately linked with the state of the nation's economy, but the prominence of lifelong learning has waxed and waned as the political direction has ebbed and flowed over 50 years or more. The semantics have changed (we rarely talk about 'adult education' now) as have funding mechanisms and incentives for both employers and workers, but there is universal agreement that learning in later life is a good thing. Evidence that the population in general appears to agree with this can be found in regular government surveys which suggest that 40% of adults are engaged in learning at any one time (Egglestone et al., 2018). Despite this widespread commitment to lifelong learning, policy thinking often seems muddled, and it has been argued that the ongoing drive for standards and school accountability generates school-leavers with no appetite to carry on learning (James, 2020). If true, this would be a sad indictment of 40 years of neoliberal policy.

EARLY CHILDHOOD EDUCATION

It is important to understand that although early childhood education (ECE) has become a universal provision, at least for over three-year-olds, providers operate in a genuine marketplace. This is populated by private companies, voluntary providers and independent schools (PVI providers), maintained nursery schools, and classes in primary schools (which may or may not be maintained). The introduction in 2017 of a national funding formula to support universal 15 hours a week early education for all 3–4-year-olds, and a further 15 hours for certain eligible children, aimed to create a 'level playing field' (West and Noden, 2019). The DfE itself, however, noted that common funding levels did not generate uniformity of provision: its social mobility plan recognised that school settings have more highly qualified staff and can potentially provide higher quality education than the unregulated PVI sector (DfE, 2017a). Further inequality is compounded by the market which allows parents to choose from a multitude of providers, so those with the means and motivation can travel to and pay for whatever provision is thought to be 'best'.

The quality and nature of education in early childhood has changed beyond all recognition over 100 years, with what was once forbidden now becoming a requirement. In 1908, the Acland report recommended that 'formal lessons in reading, writing and arithmetic should be rigidly excluded, and no inspection or examination of results in such subjects allowed' (Acland, 1908, p. 21). Contrast this with the 17 Early Learning Goals, originally introduced in 1996 as Desirable Learning Outcomes, which set expectations for children by the end of the EYFS and which include assessment of reading, writing and mathematics. Assessment of all 17 Early Learning Goals constitutes the Early Years Foundation Stage Profile (EYFSP), ostensibly to 'support a successful transition to KS1' and to inform parents about their child's progress (DfE, 2021c), though, of course, they are also used to provide a measure of a provider's effectiveness. An influential Ofsted report into the Reception year – for four-year-olds – said that the best providers put reading at the heart of the curriculum and that more attention needed to be applied to mathematics if the curriculum was to be 'fit for purpose'. That purpose was defined as being ready for school by the time children move to Year 1 (*Bold Beginnings*, Ofsted, 2017).

Ofsted inspects all early childhood provision, including nannies, childminders, nurseries and other forms of pre-school. While this may provide some reassurance from a safeguarding perspective, the associated accountability contributes to what some have called the 'datafication' of early childhood education (e.g., Roberts-Holmes and Bradbury, 2016), which can drive and define pedagogy and potentially undermine healthy personal development. The notion of school readiness is commonly used as a shorthand term to indicate that children have achieved the expected levels for their age in the Early Learning Goals, but although the term has global currency, its meaning is much less specific outside of the English system. UNICEF (2012) describes school readiness as a social construct that equates to how well children are able to settle into the school environment. Systems such as that in England are considered to be narrow pre-primary approaches focused on the school curriculum, whereas other 'social pedagogic' approaches support a broader development of children and at the same time support families. The OECD warns against 'schoolification' of early childhood (2017b, p. 254), which is sometimes evidenced in reduced playtimes and children sitting quietly at desks, suggesting instead that the rhetoric turns to looking at how schools ready themselves for incoming children. The criticism of Ofsted's review of 'what works' is that a circular argument is used to validate success as it is defined by the inspectors, rather than looking at the holistic development of children to determine what may or may not be effective Early Years practice (see Kay, 2021).

The issue of play in Early Years settings is a specific area of contention. Leaving aside the complex understandings of the term itself (see, for example, Bruce, 2018, pp. 39–46), the debate could be generalised by describing a polarisation of positions, with the acquisition of particular abilities and skills in structured learning settings set against play-based participation, exploration and self-initiated activities (Faas et al., 2017). For two centuries, at least since Froebel's *Education of Man* (1826), children's play has been seen by many to be the basis of learning itself. Some more contemporary researchers and commentators suggest that play-based activities support both cognitive development and emotional well-being (e.g., Whitebread, 2012), but the alternative view is that play punctuates learning, being an opportunity to both let off steam and gain refreshment.

The difficulty for those favouring learning through play is that sometimes the processes for and outcomes of learning are less than clear, which might invite detractors to see play as vague and unimportant in pedagogical terms. There is therefore a pressure on practitioners to be able to theorise and articulate a clear rationale for play activities, which need to embody challenge and progress for children – and, of course, enable key metrics to be evaluated.

There can be no debate around the need to uphold the highest possible well-being for children, and as we have seen this was at the heart of early ECE policy. The EYFS makes reference to children's well-being and includes measures at both summative assessment points, at age two and again at the end of the Reception year when the EYFSP is reported. However, the very way in which assessment is carried out has been identified as potentially harming children's well-being when this is understood in a more holistic sense (Street, 2021). Further concerns about policy regard for well-being are also prompted by the fact that Early Years educators can be the least well qualified of the education workforce: when our children are at their most needy and most formative, we entrust them to a diverse and possibly non-professional workforce. That is not to decry the abilities or commitments of ECE educators, but to note that policy does not have high requirements. In fact, the Early Years workforce is deeply passionate, but it is argued that the effective and affective aspects of their practice can bring them into conflict with the ubiquitous performance measures. Janet Moyles, in a seminal paper (Moyles, 2001), described the paradox that is inherent in the need for both professionalism and passion in ECE, and also points out that educational change can be slow: two decades on, ECE has still not achieved her vision in which passion inspires professionalism rather than being extinguished by it.

SIXTH FORM STUDY

We saw in Chapter 7 that there is a deep-rooted unresolved policy dilemma for post-16 study that revolves around curriculum: the academic/vocational debate. Despite efforts by various governments to the contrary, A levels remain the 'gold standard' for post-16 level-3 study (level 2 being the achievement of good GCSEs). There is some logic to this: A levels are understood and respected around the world (so there is an international market for the exam boards); A levels provide a similarly well understood currency for university admissions; and for the same reasons A levels provide a neat accountability measure of performance. Some schools in England adopt the European International Baccalaureate, a portfolio qualification which allows students to study a broad range of subjects to age 18, but most retain the age-old offer of 3 or 4 A levels. Occasional attempts to reform A levels have done little more than tinker with them: the 2015–19 reforms prompted by Michael Gove's (2012) concerns simply decoupled AS levels, making them standalone qualifications in their own right, and ensured that assessment was almost completely based on an end-of-course examination (Long, 2017). As with GCSEs, schools and colleges get better at preparing their students for A levels each time they are updated, resulting in accusations of grade inflation or lowering standards. This perpetuates the paradoxical societal position that expects fixed absolute standards, yet wishes to adjust grade distributions if too many candidates appear to achieve the thresholds. The uncomfortable reality is that this is exactly what happens: exam boards set nominal grade criteria (criterion referencing), but have enough leeway to adjust grade boundaries to make sure that grade distributions don't change much from one year to the next (norm referencing; Baird et al., 2000).

In contrast with the seemingly unshakeable stability of A levels, vocational, applied or technical qualifications seem to be in a permanent state of flux and the array of different qualifications can be bewildering for young people and their parents. Reforms from 2010 onwards attempted to clarify the issue with new criteria for vocational qualifications that specified content, assessment structure (which must include examinations) and size of the qualifications. However, this attempt to add 'rigour' also contributed to the confusion. At issue here is the pressure to develop high status, robust qualifications that prepare young people for the world of work – but by definition such qualifications become academically exclusive and also meet university entrance thresholds, so they lose their vocational difference. The unpalatable alternative would be to create lesser quality pathways to employment (Rodeiro and Vitello, 2021).

This difficulty is not unique to England. An EU report suggests that across the continent vocational provision is weak and held in low regard (Cedefop, 2018), and more widely Ruth and Grollmann note that in several developed countries vocational education and training 'has a low status and is perceived as a track for the "underachievers" and "losers"' (2009, p. 48). Given that such an attitude appears to be well embedded across many nations, it may seem surprising that government initiatives continue to seek quick and simple solutions. A 2016 report (Sainsbury, 2016) described 100 years of failure of technical education in the United Kingdom, criticising 'tinkering' and repeated failures to learn from other countries. The report called for fundamental reform, yet subsequent developments appeared indistinguishable from earlier iterations: employer-led apprenticeships and the introduction of a small number of technical T levels on a par with A levels (Foster and Powell, 2019). The fact that T levels are designed to enable university access merely underlines the persistence of the core problem.

Many school sixth forms largely sidestep the vocational/academic debate by focusing on a curriculum offer based on traditional A-level subjects. Post-16 study is funded at a lower rate than compulsory education, and a rule of thumb suggests that a school sixth form of about 200 students is sustainable with a reasonable curriculum choice. In reality, the income for the younger year groups may be propping up the overall budget or subsidising sixth form study. Colleges generally take a different approach that moves them beyond straightforward sixth forms: they make ends meet by offering a huge range of different types and levels of qualifications for learners of all ages. They may have thousands of students on roll, many part-time, studying a very diverse range of subjects in an equally diverse range of ways. Consequently FE colleges need a range of flexible options for timetabling and staffing, which can result in a casualised and, some would argue, depro-fessionalised workforce.

Colleges were taken out of local authority control in the early 1990s and have similar independence to academy schools, though with more true freedoms. They remain funded by central government and are subject to tight accountability measures (including Ofsted inspections), so autonomy is limited, as it is in schools. The 'tech colleges' of the 1950s now have a much broader portfolio, and though they are often seen to be skills-based educators, they supply one-third of the country's university entrants (Hodgson and Spours, 2019). On an individual level, it is recognised that the tension between lecturers in FE being both occupational professionals passing on expertise and teachers applying pedagogical theories and techniques (dual professionalism) presents a significant chal-lenge (Greatbatch and Tate, 2018).

The depth of the chasm between educators in schools and those who work in sixth form colleges is further illustrated by salary scales and working conditions. School sixth form teachers (who probably teach younger year groups as well) are paid on the teachers' pay scale, have induction entitlements and rights to PPA time (see Chapter 6). In contrast, those in FE colleges may be paid only for the hours they teach, and their hourly pay has steadily eroded over time so that it is almost 20% lower than in secondary schools (Dominguez-Reg and Robinson, 2019). The high emotional cost, which may include panic attacks, anxiety and poor work-life balance, has been directly linked to education policy that is focused on learner outcomes and neglects the needs of the workforce (Rasheed-Karim, 2020). The sense of being poor relations is further compounded by mixed messages from Whitehall, which continue to prioritise the A-level route to university: for example the 2022 Levelling Up White Paper addressed inequity for sixth formers by promising new 16–19 free schools run by providers with a track record of sending students to 'leading universities' (DfE, 2022a).

Successive governments have failed to establish policies which properly allow for both academic and vocational provision for 16–19-year-olds. The desire to match the academic standing of applied learning to that of the gold standard A levels creates conflict, and attempts to cater to the needs of employers, or students who would choose less academic routes, can be seen as of lesser quality. Schools are risk averse in terms of sticking to qualifications which support their accountability measures; sixth form and FE colleges pay a different price for offering a wider range of opportunities. In 2011, in his foreword to Alison Wolf's influential review of vocational education (Wolf, 2011), Michael Gove noted 160 years of failure in this regard, and despite his optimism at the time it is not clear that the dilemma has been properly resolved.

HIGHER EDUCATION

Higher Education in the United Kingdom was first established in mediaeval times in Oxford and Cambridge, and began 400 years later in Scotland. English HE saw expansion in the 19th century in London and the north and, like schools at the time, began to detach itself from its roots in the established church. Further expansion towards the end of the 19th century included the development of technical and vocational colleges alongside universities, and growth along both tracks of this 'binary system' (Carpentier, 2018) accelerated in the 1950s and 1960s, when polytechnics were introduced. Most of these became universities in their own right after the 1992 Further and Higher Education Act, resulting in a new binary system with most degrees being awarded by universities, but some HE being delivered in FE colleges. Various labels have been applied to different groups of universities (red-brick, plate-glass, post-92 and so on), but the formation of the Russell Group of 24 research-intensive universities in 1994 has been the most enduring.

After 1992, it was the New Labour government that shaped 21st century HE with two seemingly conflicting policies. Having been elected in 1997 with a pledge not to increase income tax, tuition fees (which had previously been abolished in 1976), along with maintenance loans, were reintroduced as a way to fund HE. In 1999, Tony Blair set an ambition to see 50% of school-leavers attending university – a goal that was achieved 20 years later despite Conservative ministers' attempts to distance themselves from it. Thus the 21st century began with another major expansion of HE, notwithstanding the need to pay tuition fees and take out loans which could accrue to over £50,000 for the poorest families (Belfield et al., 2017). Over 20 years, student fees have been raised such that, from contributing about a quarter of the cost of their tuition, they now cover the costs fully (Hubble and Bolton, 2018), and student numbers have grown at the same time. Unsurprisingly, university incomes have grown and are much less dependent on grant income than they once were.

Such commodification or commercialisation of HE is not unique; it is common across Europe and indeed more widely around the world. These, plus other characteristics of the 'trappings of neoliberalism' such as new public leadership, accountability and performativity, are generally viewed negatively by the academic community, but persist in the absence of viable competitive alternatives (Evans, 2018) and a mindset that assumes there is no other way (Maisuria and Cole, 2017). University students certainly see themselves as purchasers and consumers who expect a good level of service in return for their fees, and while this may add stress and adverse strain to the academic team, both parties demonstrate some recognition of the need to achieve value for money. This is more than a simple transactional arrangement, as it has given rise to greater recognition of student voice and an increased emphasis on the quality of teaching (Wilkinson and Wilkinson, 2020), though this can be interpreted as a market-oriented sector appropriating genuine student-centred concerns (Scullion et al., 2011).

The vast majority of university courses are not subject to Ofsted inspection and evaluation of their teaching. The Office for Students (OfS), a regulatory body for HE, was introduced in 2021 but even before this time attempts had been made to measure the quality of teaching in universities. The Teaching Excellence and Student Outcomes

Framework (TEF), which first reported in 2017, uses a gold/silver/bronze approach to grade HE teaching quality, through which it aims to inform choice for students and meet the needs of employers. The TEF was conceived as a 'transparency tool' which might allow university teaching to be funded on the basis of quality rather than quantity (Gunn, 2018), though there is little evidence that it has delivered this. The TEF provided a new metric to add to the plethora which have grown up around HE performance, probably starting with the REF (Research Excellence Framework) but including the NSS (National Student Survey), the GOS (Graduate Outcome Survey) and the KEF (Knowledge Exchange Framework). Each of these, as well as different combinations of them along with other measures, pits universities against one another in national and international league table competitions. Typical of neoliberal control mechanisms, it is not clear that such competition is more beneficial than collaboration between providers (Deem and Baird, 2020).

Higher Education is not immune to the debate and controversy around academic versus vocational qualifications. Somewhat inevitably, entrenched positions are formed resulting from differing opinions on the purpose of university education, some of which have their roots in the mass marketisation – or democratisation – of HE in the second half of the 20th century. Mass participation in what was once an elite activity posed existential challenges to HE as it was conceived 200 years ago, when von Humboldt described a community of scholars and students who could search for truth through a fusion of research and teaching. By the 1850s Newman was advocating the pursuit of knowledge for its own sake, establishing a viewpoint that the general training of the mind, albeit through specialised study, could support a wide range of career paths. A century later the Robbins Report (Robbins, 1963), which made the case that HE should be available for everyone who desired it and met the required admissions thresholds, stated that 'there is no single aim' for HE (p. 7), instead identifying four objectives which continue to be considered a concise summary of the purpose of HE. Those objectives are:

1. Instructions in skills, with a view to future careers;
2. Promoting the general powers of the mind;
3. The advancement of knowledge (or search for truth) through research;
4. Development of a common culture and standards of citizenship.

In essence the academic/vocational debate for HE revolves around the relative importance given to each of these four objectives. There are, however, important implications arising from a universal access to HE: functioning society needs people with specific skills, so it cannot sustain university provision which solely exists for the pursuit of knowledge. The huge expansion of HE over the last 60 years has necessarily driven the development of more applied learning. At the same time, neoliberalism, with its need for metrics on which to make judgements, prioritises those objectives which are easiest to measure: research activity (through the REF) and graduate employment (through the GOS), which can generate divergence both within and between institutions. Many universities take the approach of Archilochus's fox, attempting to be wise in every respect, while a smaller group have a narrower hedgehog focus – though the risks of this strategy are self-evident. There is a sense in which 21st-century governments' views are becoming increasingly utilitarian, promoting degree apprenticeships and higher technical qualifications while decrying 'low quality' courses which do not lead to well-paid graduate jobs (DfE, 2022b). Universities therefore have to decide whether to embrace more applied curricula, or stick to Newman's ideals.

While there are policy drivers that directly and indirectly influence curriculum design in HE, HE pedagogy has yet to come under the influence of policymakers. As a consequence, the type of teaching and learning activities that students experience when they leave school and begin university may seem at odds with the neoconservative-influenced pedagogy in schools (Chapter 8). Universities, for centuries known for their lecture-style delivery, are moving away from this transmission model of learning towards social constructivism, in which discussion and debate are prioritised over didactic lectures (O'Connor, 2022). Internationally as well as in the United Kingdom, flipped learning is 'trending' (Brewer and Movahedazarhouligh, 2018), 'radical' pedagogies such as SCALE-UP (Student-Centred Active Learning Environments with Upside-down Pedagogies) are shown to demonstrate highly positive outcomes (Foote et al., 2016), and team-based learning has migrated from medical education to other areas of the curriculum with claims of increased engagement as well as improved outcomes (Swanson et al., 2019). Such claims are not undisputed, and there are questions around whether different ways of teaching can be applied to all forms of knowledge , though these could be – and in practice probably are – addressed by adoption of the bricolage approach described in Chapter 8. The challenge in a commodified HE system is that students may begin to feel that if they themselves have to work hard for knowledge exchange, rather than simply receiving it in the one-directional transaction of a lecture, they may not be getting the value for money they are looking for. This in turn may put a more conservative and traditional pressure on HE pedagogy.

Half a century ago Jean-François Lyotard predicted the death knell for the age of the professor (Lyotard, 1979). He appears to have been right in identifying the way in which knowledge held by universities has changed in both content and teaching, which seems to marginalise the expert. However, suggestions that learning from and with machines would dominate appear to be over-exaggerations, even in our technological information-based age and after a COVID-19-enforced period of online learning. The performative principles defined and described by Lyotard thus far are achieved by what he calls interdisciplinary teams, perhaps reducing the role and influence of the academic, but not yet nailing the coffin closed. There is an area of growth within HE which might be considered an example of Lyotard's 'memory bank networks' (p. 53) and that is MOOCs (Massive Open Online Courses). The MOOCs offer an entirely different form of HE pedagogy, where students learn remotely and independently from material stored electronically. Costs to universities may be so low that courses can be offered with little or no charge, commercial viability being ensured by large numbers of enrolments. Some might hope that this offers a low-cost path through HE, but the reality is that MOOCs remain out of the ordinary; this, combined with extremely low completion rates, limits their ability to embody Lyotard's most extreme ideas with regard to both pedagogy and performativity (Roberts, 2019).

Despite the best efforts of the OfS, universities maintain an arms-length relationship with national policymakers, which limits – but doesn't eliminate – Westminster influence. They are large organisations and change is slow; in addition they are influential, often providing the experts and advisors which the government relies upon. It is probably not surprising that HE seems to show more resilience to some aspects of neoliberal and neoconservative thinking than other parts of the educational system, but it is not immune. The slower pace of change along with a general societal acceptance of market principles as embodied by schools for decades may contribute to lessened controversy, allowing for gradual evolution towards commodification of knowledge in HE.

LIFELONG LEARNING

For the purposes of this short discussion, it is important to understand the meaning of lifelong learning in the English context. It is not to be confused with Education for All, a global initiative which was instigated by UNESCO and other organisations to address children's education worldwide. In the United Kingdom what was once called adult education has gradually become lifelong learning – any formal study after compulsory school age. The change in name is more than semantics: internationally the emergence of lifelong learning in developed countries has been identified with neoliberal stances (Lee and Friedrich, 2011), and the phrase suggests an individual and personal responsibility rather than the collective state obligation that might be implied by the older term (Billet, 2018). Providers of lifelong learning include FE colleges and universities, but also third sector organisations and private companies. Some commentators would include in-work skills development, supported by employers, in lifelong learning. Lifelong learning might include leisure-time learning motivated purely by interest (life-wide learning) as well as vocational FE learning which is often related to specific employment skills. Policymakers tend to emphasise the latter, as evidenced by the 2021 White Paper which directly equates lifelong learning with 'skills for jobs' (DfE, 2021d). There is some evidence to suggest that as well as making a contribution to the economy, lifelong learning is also associated with wider unremunerated civic engagement (Rüber et al., 2018).

Some trace the development of lifelong learning policy in the UK to Churchill, who spoke in 1954 of the importance of adult education after the disruption caused by two world wars (Bynner, 2017). Twenty years later the Manpower Services Commission was established, with a mission to transform the workforce to support growing service- and knowledge-based industries. At the same time the Open University was becoming established, and universities, colleges and Local Authorities all began to offer a wide range of adult and continuing education provision through evening classes and night school, allowing for life-wide as well as lifelong learning. In the same way that compulsory education was dramatically transformed by the Education Acts of 1988 and 1992, the breadth and depth of lifelong learning was also constricted by centralisation of curricula, establishment of targets, and metric-based inspections and judgements, though it took longer for the tide to turn. One reason for this inertia was the clear divergence from the international mood, which was neatly summarised by Jacques Delors in a landmark UNESCO report:

> There is a need to rethink and broaden the notion of lifelong education. Not only must it adapt to changes in the nature of work, but it must also constitute a continuous process of forming whole human beings – their knowledge and aptitudes, as well as the critical faculty and the ability to act.
>
> (Delors, 1996, p. 19)

Coinciding with regime change in the United Kingdom, this attitude was supported by several domestic and international reports, allowing for a brief flowering of broader lifelong learning philosophy and policy before the inevitable onward march towards utilitarianism. The incoming New Labour administration set out ambitions which were refined and developed following the publication of Fryer's *Learning for the 21st Century*, a report which called for the development of a culture of lifelong learning for all (Fryer, 1997), but the combined forces of financial prudence, skills shortages and target-setting all conspired to ensure that any optimism was short-lived. It has been suggested that the vision for qualitative life-wide learning rested almost solely with the then Secretary of State for Education, David Blunkett, and that his departure signalled a return to the machine of quantitative measures of efficiency and progress (Tuckett, 2017). The closure of the Sector Skills Council, Lifelong Learning UK (established in 2002), by the coalition government in 2011 was less a change of direction than a recognition of the state of play by the end of the New Labour years.

The coalition and then the Conservatives maintained the focus on developing skills to support the national economy. In 2010 the Department for Business, Innovations and Skills – not the DfE – published a strategy document for the forthcoming parliament (BIS, 2010) which advocated the establishment of Lifelong Learning Accounts to allow adults access to student loans so that they could improve their skills. There was a passing reference to using the Lifelong Learning Accounts to record 'positive social contributions such as volunteering' (p. 41) but the real emphasis was on developing skills to build economic growth, asking individuals to pay for the privilege of playing their part. Lifelong Learning Accounts were never introduced, perhaps because lessons had been learnt from a disastrous attempt by New Labour to introduce Individual Learning Accounts in 2000 (NAO, 2002), but the idea is persistent and has gone by a number of names. By 2019, the Augar Review of post-compulsory education and funding was continuing to recommend an Individual Loan Allowance to be used at any stage of adult life (Augar, 2019, p. 41).

The 'independent' Augar review was wide-ranging, considering all aspects of learning beyond the age of 18 and thereby taking account of both HE and lifelong learning. Despite its admirably broad description of the purposes of post-18 education, however, its recommendations remained constrained by the neoliberal terms of reference including incentivising choice and competition, and developing skills for the economy.

The dominant narrative for lifelong learning in England over half a century, then, is that its focus has become increasingly narrow, with an emphasis on developing those skills that build the nation's economy at the expense of inspiring education that builds quality of life. Centralisation of resourcing along with performance measures for providers has forced many life-wide activities into the domain of 3rd sector organisations and those who can afford to pay for life-enriching activities. The notional democratisation of online learning through the internet has done little to address this socio-economic divide (Eynon and Malmberg, 2021). At the same time as removing personal choice for potential adult learners, successive governments have put responsibility onto individuals to improve skills and support the economy – which has been characterised as a subversion of the original social justice ideals of lifelong education, replacing it with a new form of neoliberal oppression (Barros, 2012). This is a far cry from the principle of emancipation which education appears to offer, but the simple fact is that 21st century lifelong learning policy has exacerbated social divisions, undermining social mobility and trapping the poor and the vulnerable (SMC, 2019). If this dismal cloud has any silver lining then perhaps it is the constant truth that education, from birth right through to adulthood, is what Augar called a joined-up system, inasmuch as it struggles to challenge social injustice at every age.

SUMMARY

This chapter has looked at neoliberal policy implications for non-compulsory education. The Early Years and lifelong learning sectors show more evidence of a genuine marketplace than schools, though this appears to stifle social mobility and exacerbate inequity. Post-16, sixth form study exhibits the ongoing academic/vocational curriculum divide which also plays out in pay and conditions for staff. Higher Education, post-18, comes relatively late to neoliberalism but appears to accept fees and marketisation, playing league table games while defiantly claiming independence and autonomy.

FURTHER READING

Ewan Ingleby's *Neoliberalism Across Education* (2021) considers specific aspects of neoliberalism as they apply to particular phases of the education sector. The application of technology to Early Years pedagogy, judgemental mentoring in FE and scholarship versus value for money in HE are all discussed with reference to relevant theory and empirical research findings.

12

CONCLUSION: 'THERE NEEDS TO BE GLUE'

CONTENTS

This chapter includes:

- Reference to international policy developments in education, both neoliberal and alternative.
- A discussion of the concept of the self-improving system to which England's policymakers aspire.
- An outline of the ways in which the education system is, and has always been, fragmented.
- Use of kintsugi as a metaphor to illustrate how the fragments can be held together in a more coherent whole.
- A brief overview of value and worth in England's educational system.

INTRODUCTION

The 1988 Education Reform Act marked a turning point for education policy and the foundation for the new neoliberal age, but it did not arise *ex nihilo*. In common with all policies, the ERA was of its time: a product of history, context and ideology. In their review of English education in postmodern times, Brighouse and Waters (2022) suggest that the hinge point for political thinking was Callaghan's Ruskin speech in 1976. As we saw in Chapter 3, the speech demonstrated some sympathy with Black Paper dogma, and Clyde Chitty's thesis suggests that some on the political right felt that the Prime Minister had appropriated their own agenda (1991, p. 174). It would be fair to say that in simple terms the speech set the direction for decades to come (including for the ERA), noting as it did a need to consider standards as well as to satisfy the demands of parents and industry. These are not the only points which continue to resonate with current discourses: Callaghan raised questions around curriculum content, lifelong learning, gender balance in different subjects, pedagogical approaches, applied versus academic learning, inspection, the nature of examinations, literacy and numeracy skills, and the list goes on. Therefore, we should not be surprised that the themes of the 'Great Debate', instigated by a Labour Prime Minister who borrowed ideas from the New Right, had a longevity that took them through Conservative, New Labour and Coalition administrations right up to the present day.

Policy enactment in England's schools has explored and pushed the boundaries of every aspect of the simple definition of neoliberalism that we adopted in Chapter 1. This challenges our understanding of terms such as liberty and freedom, and continually forces us to ask, what is the fundamental purpose of education? We have seen that the answer to this question may define the approach to education policy. Conversely, in our conclusion we might turn this around to see what the policy we have studied tells us about the implicit purposes of education. In the same way, since policy defines what is measured, it also tells us about what is deemed to be of value to policymakers, and this gives rise to a source of anguish for some practitioners if the things they feel are important are not recognised by the monitoring and controlling systems.

We have seen how metrics, benchmarks, thresholds and targets have become features of education, and it is through these that informed choice operates in the pseudo-marketplace. It has frequently been argued that marketisation, throwing educational providers into a competitive arena, has led to a fragmented system, a fundamental theme to which we will return and which is exacerbated by the deliberate erosion of Local Authorities, the so-called middle tier. The critical friend and organisational element which is represented by the Local Authority has been replaced by Adam Smith's ruthless invisible hand, which lacks finesse, understanding, nuance and subtlety. Lest this is thought to be too emotive and partisan, we should remind ourselves that Smith's model was quite explicitly founded on self-interest rather than benevolence (Smith, 1785, p. 15), and that our adopted definition of neoliberalism required 'self-interested actors' (Stedman Jones,

2012, p. 2). It is therefore appropriate to conclude our study by considering the ethics and morality of founding a social system on a principle of individual selfishness.

INTERNATIONAL CONTEXT

We have noted that the 40-year transformation of our educational system, which began with marketisation but evolved to encompass aspects of both extremes of the New Right, was not unique to England but has seen parallels around the world, particularly in Europe and North America. The IMF published an analysis of an 'index of competition' which showed what it called a strong and widespread global trend towards neoliberalism since the mid-1980s (Ostry et al., 2016). As in the United Kingdom, even in periods when progressive parties have regained power, they have nonetheless tended to retain neoliberal policies in a 'progressive neoliberalism' (Hursh, 2020). Recent years have seen more global divergence, with England appearing more isolated and perhaps more extreme and harsh in its interpretation of what we might call the standards agenda. This makes it difficult to predict the future direction of policy developments: it will be instructive to consider the wider international context, but probably unwise to assume that England's trajectory will be similar to that of economic neighbours which may have been less affected by neoconservative forces in particular.

The Organisation for Economic Co-operation and Development (OECD) has been a key driver of the marketisation of education globally – Kofold et al. assert that the OECD has become 'one of the most influential transnational organisations in education' (2012, p. 32). Founded in 1961, the OECD aims to promote economic growth of its 38 member states (mainly Europe, Japan and Australasia), and from 1990 onwards developed a global understanding of education systems that promote productivity and growth – though Rizvi and Lingard (2009) identify a tension when education is used to promote both economic prosperity and also democratic equality and social mobility. Greany's review would appear to support the idea that marketisation can undermine social justice:

> International evidence is clear that successful school systems are equitable systems, yet research shows that England's schools have become more socially segregated over time.
>
> (2015, p. 4)

The Programme for International Student Assessment (PISA), introduced by OECD in 2000, provided league tables through which governments could draw comparisons with other states and inevitably consider how to emulate those at the top of the tables. For a decade Finland was the leader of this self-generated race towards perceived excellence; more recently the focus has moved eastwards as practitioners seek to adopt the 'Shanghai method' (PISA tables include a large number of non-OECD states). In doing so, there is a danger that policy borrowing tends to ignore cultural and contextual factors which could have an important bearing on educational outcomes. A further problem with developing policy on the basis of PISA performance is the circular argument that policy developments are driven by the metrics that are used to measure their success. This 'self-perpetuating dynamic' (Sellar and Lingard, 2013) is certainly seen in English policymaking, and tends to generate an inertia which makes it increasingly difficult to escape from a competitive outcomes-driven approach, and which may neglect wider understandings of children's education and development.

There are, however, those who discern signs of change, and we should not subscribe to the heresy that neoliberalism is the only way. Alternative system designs are available, for example Citizen Schools in Brazil (Gandin, 2007) and the 'shady spaces' of New Zealand (McMaster, 2013), and even in the United Kingdom, Rudd and Goodson (2017) suggest we may be witnessing the 'long tail of decline for the neoliberal project'. Shirley and Hargreaves (2021) state that Canada is in a time of transition from an age of individual accountability and tested achievement to one which is characterised by engagement, well-being and identity – though it should be noted that a full decade earlier these same writers had prematurely announced that globally 'we are entering an age of post-standardisation in education' (Hargreaves and Shirley, 2009, p. 1). Such optimism is not common; there are more commentators who would adopt the view of Peters (2018) who agrees that neoliberalism may be on the wane, but suggests that it is being replaced across Europe and the United States by 'right wing authoritarian populism'. The Brexit referendum of 2016 is often cited as a demonstration of this in Britain, but we have seen that England's 21st-century education policies have less of the anti-elitist sentiments of populism, and more of an appeal to traditional (neo)conservative values which may embody elitist overtones. A unifying theme for both of these post-neoliberal stances is the notion of common-sense superseding expert opinion, infamously expressed by Michael Gove who, in a televised 2016 interview, said that the people have had enough of experts. Whether the voices of those who study and research policy are ignored because of a populist perception that they belong to an irrelevant elite, or because of a neoconservative prejudice that they represent an undesirable liberal progressiveness, taking the experts out of the debate leads to an uncomfortable but simple conclusion in which there are merely policymakers and practitioners. Having reached this position, and faced with the question of where to find expert knowledge in order to apply it in improvement strategies, the answer can only be amongst the educators themselves. This results in a situation which ceases to look outwards to see what might be learnt from the rest of the world and instead becomes more inward looking. This has led to a central concept in 21st-century English education policy: the self-improving system.

SELF-IMPROVING SYSTEM

The idea of a self-improving school system first emerged under New Labour, but it was adopted, refined and prioritised by the Coalition government with claims of increased autonomy with less outside influence. The basic principle is that the best schools (or teachers, leaders and practitioners) share their practice with others so that the whole system gets better. The blueprint for a self-improving system was articulated by David Hargreaves in a National College publication in July 2010 – months after the election of the coalition government – and although its language was adopted by the new government the core principles on which it was based were conveniently overlooked. Hargreaves suggested that the building blocks for effective system-wide self-improvement include clusters of schools and a local solutions approach (Hargreaves, 2010, p. 5), both of which are undermined by independent academies and MATs with no geographic basis. Co-construction between schools – the opposite of the competition which league tables deliberately foster – was identified as a third foundational aspect, with the fourth being an understanding of system leadership. This last point links to the moral imperative of educationalists which becomes a recurring theme in this chapter: true system leadership, in which leaders understand the part they play in the wider system and have a concern for others that goes beyond the bounds of their immediate responsibility. Michael Fullan suggested an example in his DfES publication: school heads who are 'almost as concerned about the success of other schools as they are about their own school' (Fullan, 2004, p. 9). Widespread academisation and the emergence of MATs saw a mutation away from the subtlety of system leader as servant, towards acquisitive MATs with ambitious growth targets, redefining system leadership to mean leaders of larger chunks of the system.

This reconceptualisation of system leadership did not, however, sound a death knell to the principles of a self-improving system. Hargreaves identified opportunities presented by potential (neoliberal) decentralisation, and though these were not realised, a more directed, centralised approach enabled an alternative vision of self-improvement within the system. In this new model, centrally accredited and appointed specialists share their wisdom with the wider system: a refinement of the ASTs and lead practitioners that were discussed in Chapter 6. The model goes beyond individual teachers and school leaders (so-called National Leaders of Education): similar evolution of specialist schools saw first Teaching Schools and then Teaching School Hubs (TSHs) take on responsibilities for teacher training and CPD, eroding the part played by universities and commercial providers. Likewise in the early 2020s, the many licences to deliver the NPQ suite of qualifications on a local basis were revoked, with the task being given to a much smaller number of nationally appointed providers. These providers and the TSHs are funded by and directly answerable to central government, and they have to work within very tightly constrained boundaries – an example is in delivering the Early Career Framework for new teachers, which has been criticised for being prescriptive, inflexible and ignorant of local context (Uttley, 2022). The net result of more than 10 years of reinterpreting Hargreaves's vision, for schools at least, is a self-improving system which consists of a feedback loop comprising just the schools, central government and its appointed trainers and developers.

Given the central controlling influence in this model it could be argued that it has evolved beyond the bounds of the original notions of a self-improving system.

To some eyes this new understanding of self-improvement will look neat and tidy. It will not be subject to uncomfortable questioning by well-meaning, well-informed or well-educated outsiders. Government priorities are unlikely to be undermined in a system in which the players are either delivering government contracts or are accountable for achieving centrally prescribed benchmarks. Even when other parties are able to engage – for example universities involved in teacher training – they are barely more than con-tractors implementing the demands of centrally conceived frameworks (in this case the Core Content Framework and the Teacher Standards). This is the opposite of what Christine Gilbert envisaged in 2012 when, writing as HMCI, she proposed a vision of a self-improving system in which accountability is no longer perceived as something that 'is based just on a centralised regime of data and inspection, set by government and invari-ably negative, mechanistic and stressful' (Gilbert, 2012, p. 9). Gilbert's ideal of effective self-evaluation leading to ownership of accountability has been undermined by centralised target-setting and benchmarking which leads to a performative culture where, on a local level, policy is simply driven by the chase for metrics.

If we step away from the way in which performance is measured and put the chosen metrics to one side, there remains a fundamental problem with a recursive self-improving system, which is the danger of an artificial ceiling being established: the system as a whole cannot get any better than its best parts. There is nothing wrong with the idea that where educational providers are perceived to be excelling, they share their practice, nuanced with a contextual understanding, with similar providers. Difficulties arise where other aspects of their practice are not open to challenge because they can be hidden behind a simple single overall measure (such as an Ofsted grade) and where alternative approaches are rejected simply because the organisation carries a leadership label and has been appointed with a mandate to share practice in the name of improvement. When the policy-defined metrics are added back into the mix it becomes apparent that the self-improving system is inev-itably going to be characterised by convergence towards a mean which might demonstrate excellence on some measures, but only at the expense of overall quality. To counteract this, external, independent challenge could act as an aid and stimulant to growth and progress and should not be seen as a threat – and this must surely apply to policy and its enactment just as much as it does to pedagogy and practice.

It is fair to ask that critical friends, whether inside or outside of the system, should be able to justify their propositions and test out questions; in other words it is important to understand the evidence base for decision-making and change management. It might appear self-evident to suggest that interventions and changes should be founded on a strong evidence base, and that the evidence base would be arrived at via thorough, independent research. Indeed, Brown and Zhang (2016) describe evidence informed practice as 'rational behaviour' – though these same authors note that this rational behaviour is proving difficult to achieve in practice, both in England and elsewhere across the world. Their conclusion is that, in regimes with high-stakes accountability, leaders will tend to use common externally mandated approaches to achieve similar goals: an alternative understanding of the limitations of the self-improving system described above. Here in England the situation is further compounded by an implicit canon of evidence that is deemed acceptable: from about 2016 onwards the government began to publish the evidence on which frameworks and other documents were based. In terms of transparency, such openness is laudable, yet it generates an unwritten expectation that only the centrally identified evidence (and research which concurs with it) is valid, and that research which uses alternative methodologies or which comes to different conclusions has little to offer. Given the many complexities of education as a social science, adopting a narrow canon of research literature would seem misguided at best, and at worst potentially harmful. It also conflicts with a core DfE assumption behind the idea of evidence-based teaching, which is that 'the teaching profession will look less to the department and Ofsted for advice, and more towards the evidence and itself' (Coldwell et al., 2017, p. 11).

Those same policymakers that espouse the benefits of evidence informed practice would do well to reflect on their own decision-making processes, which are much more likely to be based on ideology than evidence from research. The Conservative manifesto for the 2017 election stated that rigid dogma and ideology is 'not just needless but dangerous' (Conservatives, 2017, p. 9), echoing the Prime Minister who, 12 months earlier, had tried to resurrect the 11+ selection debate, stating that children's potential was being sacrificed because of dogma and ideology. Yet careful analysis of five years of this particular debate concluded that:

> It would appear there is still a place for moral sidesteps and an avoidance of evidence at the very highest level of education policy making.
>
> (Bainbridge et al., 2022, p. 29)

It would be naïve to imagine that policymaking were not based on political ideology, but it is nonetheless disappointing that evidence is conveniently ignored when it does not support policy decisions. It is not difficult to find examples of this in government policy, but policymakers at all levels, including the new middle tier of MATs, should be aware of the dangers of emulating that practice. It is equally important to remember that context is crucial when it comes to applying research evidence to different situations. As Dylan Wiliam says, 'everything works somewhere and nothing works everywhere' (Wiliam, 2018, p. 2).

FRAGMENTATION

A common criticism of post-1988 education policy in England, and of neoliberal marketisation in particular, is that it has resulted in a fragmented system. There is certainly some truth in this suggestion: the Thatcher government very deliberately sought to break what it saw as the cosy unity of LEA leadership, and marketisation of schools was designed to create competition, thus reducing the likelihood of collaboration. Simkins (2015) notes that within small local areas there is fragmentation as school organisational structures have consequently changed. The term is used in a variety of ways depending on the perspectives and motivations of the commentators: West and Wolfe (2019) appear to equate fragmentation with diversity (again, a specific ambition of 1990s policy), when they discuss varied school governance and financial arrangements. Beauvallet (2014) describes ideological schisms between the major English teaching unions as fragmentation which led to a surrender to policymakers, though confusingly she also states that the unions faced a fragmented landscape which she does not define. Cliffe et al. (2018) illustrate impenetrable barriers for the transfer of CPD access between organisations. The most common understanding of the term (for example Bubb et al., 2019) relates to system fragmentation, in which the support and accountability functions of the so-called middle tier (previously LEAs) have been carved up and distributed amongst numerous operators, some of them private companies, some state-funded, others statutory organisations, leading to 'a muddle' (p. 9), or more charitably, a multi-dimensional middle (Crawford et al., 2020). Even through rose-tinted spectacles the situation looks jumbled at best, and parliament's own Public Account Committee reported that:

> the Department's arrangements for oversight of schools are fragmented and incoherent, leading to inefficiency for government and confusion for schools.
>
> (HC, 2018, Conclusion 5)

This report came a full 30 years after the first destabilising effects of CTCs pioneering new structures, during which time any initial teething problems might have been expected to be resolved.

The education system in England is indeed fragmented, but, as Dickens's Dick Swiveller would have said, ''twas ever thus.' We should not be deluded into thinking that a pure and perfect whole has been shattered into pieces by the 1988 Education Reform Act. In Chapters 2 and 3, we saw how today's system of schooling had its roots in a piecemeal approach that did not yet deserve to be called a system as such. The various approaches to children's education coalesced and amalgamated over 150 years, but the overall whole could always have been described as fragmented. Indeed, Lee (2001) identifies existing fragmentation prior to 1988 as a driver of neoliberal reform. From the beginning of organised schooling there have been different governance and financial arrangements for different kinds of school, largely but not entirely due to continued involvement by the Catholic and Anglican Churches. Even community schools, run by LEAs, exhibited a diversity that was dependent upon geography and which varied considerably from place to place, causing some difficulties for families living near county boundaries. At key moments in history when policy could have been unifying, it was generally fudged so that the system maintained difference and diversity, albeit uncomfortably. Occasionally further division was introduced, such as the tripartite secondary system. The introduction of academies and MATs simply changed the fault lines, redrafting the topography. Nor is this eternal fragmentation limited to schools and compulsory education: we saw in Chapter 11 that Early Years, Further and Higher Education have also been characterised by a multiplicity of providers. In these cases existing in-sector competition has been compounded by increasing marketisation and commodification of education.

Faced with the unarguable fact that the system is in pieces, one might be forgiven for questioning how it continues to function The straightforward answer lies in the fact that policy directives do not create a machine, or even pieces of a machine that require accurate assembly. Whether the fragments we see are broken shards or manufactured component parts, it is impossible to undertake a reductionist analysis in which simple cause and effect apply, because education is a function of society – which is made up of myriad individuals with an almost infinite range of experiences, viewpoints, prejudices and interpretations. Yet it is precisely here, in the messiness of humanity, that we find the solution to the paradox. One of the contributors to Bubb et al.'s 2018 review states that 'there needs to be glue to stick everything together in this disjointed system' (p. 59). That glue is *the people*.

KINTSUGI AS METAPHOR

However the component parts of the educational jigsaw have been defined, they have always been held together by people: individuals and groups who, whether they agree with local and national policy or not, simply do their best for the children and learners in their care. Sometimes this might be in line with policy direction, at others in spite of policy, but in general most of the people working within education are trying their best to make things work. This may come at some personal or professional cost, and it may, as we saw in Chapter 4, prompt some serious soul-searching. The same could also be said for many of the organisations involved in education. Despite dire warnings of unscrupulous companies profiteering from outsourcing or even privatisation of some education functions, this doomsday scenario has not really materialised (that is not to say that there are not questions to be asked about some of the budget surpluses and salary hikes that have been seen since 1998). Of course, there are those that exit education professions because they feel a limit has been reached, but there are more that have remained; as every head teacher and recruiting manager knows, these committed individuals are gold dust. So much so that they could be likened to the tiny specks of pure gold that are mixed with the lacquer that is used to repair fragmented ceramics in the Japanese artform, kintsugi.

Kintsugi (gold join) or kintsukoroi (gold repair) rebuilds broken ceramics using lacquer enhanced with gold so that the form and function of the original pot is recovered, with the addition of beautiful golden scar lines marking the joins between the fragments.

Kintsugi provides an appropriate metaphor to understand educational fragmentation and coherence on a number of levels. Not only does the gold dust of highly committed and skilful individuals contribute to holding the fragmented system together, but it could be said that they add a beauty by their actions. Golden lacquer experiences tension forces, opposing the gravitational inertia that would cause the pot to fall apart: those in the middle of the educational fragments experience tension of a different kind as they struggle to maintain the true purpose of learning. The universe's tendency towards disorder (entropy) appears to apply to social and political constructs as much as it does to physical creations and it requires energy to counterbalance this. Just as shards of crockery on their own cannot hold water in the way that a whole vessel would, the various parts of the educational system cannot operate alone, but need the glue of the people to hold it together and enable it to function. We might argue that the resulting conglomeration does not have the purity and beauty of a single well-designed artefact, yet it nonetheless serves its purpose and has its own unique features.

In today's 21st century, the 400-year-old art form kintsugi has popularly come to represent healing from brokenness, but for our metaphor it is both more and less than this. Kemske (2021) suggests that kintsugi represents a rejection of capitalism – in the sense that profits to be made from throwaway culture are undermined by careful repair – and we have seen that some educationalists might take pleasure at being able to unite what capitalism and neoliberalism are fracturing. There are, of course, those that would approve of the neoliberal approach, but in their work with learners of all ages and levels they play an equal part in holding together some form of wholeness and consistency of direction. Conversely, it is unlikely that many would identify the social glue that holds the system together as healing, when it is very much more a case of make do and mend.

Whether the new fault lines of the last 30 years are intentional or not, there is a perverse sense in which they generate increased coherence. Without the natural geographical bounds and bonds of the LEAs, academies and their staff have had to build new alliances and allegiances; Greany's detailed case study analysis identifies new networks that have been built in the face of system fragmentation, though he is at pains to point out that a more profound level of 'deep partnership' has not yet been achieved (Greany, 2015). In a later work, the same author notes that the decline of Local Authorities can open up opportunities for both new and existing actors to work together and counteract negative effects of fragmentation, though the extent to which they do this is variable (Greany, 2022). The reality on the ground is that individuals and groups re-form new networks in response to policy change, which itself may reshape the system's fragments. They do this both to make the new ideas work, but also to find the support and development that they need.

The need for practitioners to seek ways to build golden repairs into the fragmented system created by policymakers may be lamentable, but it is not unique to England. In an analysis of American policy developments, Tucker notes that while some nations carefully consider new policies and implement them in a way that integrates with existing practice to aid coherence, the United States simply adds new policies and 'hopes for the best' (Tucker, 2011, p. 35). The same might be said of Westminster governments, which generally concur with only half of Tucker's bottom line: that the two key factors for educational success (measured by the usual international performance metrics) are the quality of the teaching force, and coherence of the design of the overall system itself. The reason, he suggests, why the latter factor is so frequently overlooked is that it is no-one's specific responsibility. Educators may, however, be wary of pointing this out to policy-makers who might confuse system coherence for social conformity. The potsherds of educational fragmentation are delicately held together by the fragile gold dust of personal commitment and moral purpose, which centralisation and a drive for compliance have the potential to shatter.

VALUE AND WORTH

There is more to education than the three Rs. Michael Fullan, who has a career based on the study of educational leadership, identifies a spiritual dimension to the work of educators, describing improvements made to literacy and numeracy as only 'skin deep' (2002, p. 2) and noting that education is about making a difference to people's lives. Of course, enabling children to read and write well will open employment and other doors for them, and this can indeed be life-changing, but it is equally apparent that this is only part of the story. Children also learn much from what, in Chapter 7, we called the hidden curriculum, though some of this is difficult to measure or quantify, and we should not forget that, for learners, education is an experience, not an outcome. The very process of educating teaches learners about the society which arranged it: what is important and valued, and conversely what is not.

Biesta (2009) argues that education is more than learning, and that to understand what good education looks like we need to consider issues of value and purpose, which have gradually been forgotten in the quest for higher standards, better metrics and improved measurables – without reflecting on the reasons for these. Biesta's warning that such thinking is likely to perpetuate the status quo and reinforce social stratification echoes the Marxist philosophy of Freire in which oppressors use education to replicate hierarchy. Freire calls for good education to bring emancipation: liberation or freedom from oppression. At the other end of the political spectrum neoliberal advocates would argue that marketisation brings freedom – in this case freedom from state control, though it falls short of the individual liberty valued by Freire. Gray et al. (2018) state that education is important to neoliberals because they see its function as the production of citizen subjects with the knowledge and dispositions to service the economy: use of the terms 'subjects' and 'service' implies inbuilt hierarchy, if not outright oppression.

There is a question of whether societal hierarchy can ever be broken down, by education or otherwise. This is the root of the thorny vocational/academic debate, in which giving real value to vocational and applied learning risks undermining academic elitism, and the fear that if everyone is equal, it will be impossible for employers and others to differentiate between people. Similarly, discussions initiated more than 15 years ago about which curriculum subjects are most valuable would appear to undermine the neoliberal notion of freedom of choice – and in Higher Education where students now pay in full for their courses, should they not therefore be free to choose what to study irrespective of its perceived value? Though neoliberals might respond affirmatively, the increasingly loud voices of neoconservatives remind us that here in England there remains an elite which professes to know what is best and to impose that view on society. If education is to challenge this hegemony it must clearly be from the bottom up, for there are no har-bingers of radical top-down policy direction change on the horizon.

Despite this, the view is not entirely pessimistic. We should never forget that the world of education is populated by well-intentioned individuals who want to see a better world, though their conceptualisations of this might vary. There is a golden irony in the incongruence of a system that was purposefully designed around self-interest becoming totally reliant on altruistic actors to hold it together. This is compounded by the new networks that these participants form: for neoliberals the individual is paramount, yet the edifice they have constructed requires collaboration and collective will to make it work. Commitment to a righteous cause is infectious in a way that conforming to a questionable policy is not; consequently Fullan states that 'the collective motivational well seems bottomless' (2010, p. 72).

Policy direction in England has undoubtedly turned towards the sharp relief of neoconservatism, which hides behind unvalidated arguments based on tradition and common sense, and is made manifest in increasing centralisation and a strong state. In the face of these developments the land of the neoliberals may appear to be relatively benign, for it incorporated a permissiveness that enabled some to flourish even if they felt their principles were challenged. The new landscape feels much harsher and more uncompro-mising, offering a Darwinian future in which only those individuals and organisations that fit the new environment will survive and thrive. There is a danger that this approach will drain the lifeblood of too many educational players, but if history teaches us anything, it is that life will find a way to adapt and survive. The field of education comprises people with necessarily strong character, whose raison d'être is the benefit of others. Such altruism underpins teaching and learning at every level and should be afforded the highest value, for without it education would be reduced to a technical process that could be carried out by automatons. Counterintuitively, perhaps, a coherent system requires free thinkers, reflexive practitioners, maverick leaders, impartial researchers and responsive policy-makers if it is to become genuinely self-improving and world-leading. Such individuals are the nuggets that can survive the sifting and panning of policy enactment and the refining fire of accountability with their elemental identity intact, the gold that serves to highlight rather than hide the cracks created by ideology.

SUMMARY

This chapter rounded off a tour of education policy in England and the system it has created by reflecting on international developments and considering what it means for the system to learn from itself. A discussion of fragmentation caused by marketisation in particular noted the persistently piecemeal nature of education in England over 150 years and more, and considered the way in which countless committed individuals work to fill the gaps and create some coherence. Finally, it turned to value and worth; deeper questions about the purpose of and meaning of education and the importance of those who make it work.

FURTHER READING

About Our Schools: Improving on Previous Best (Brighouse & Waters, 2022) is a comprehensive review of neoliberal education in England, as experienced by two outstanding practitioners and leaders, and including the views of more than 100 of the key players in the 21st century. The book examines the complexity of policy enactment since Callaghan's Ruskin speech and optimistically looks to a 'new age' beyond markets, centralisation and managerialism.

REFERENCES

Abbott, D., Broadfoot, P., Croll, P., Osborn, M., & Pollard, A. (1994). Some sink, some float: National curriculum assessment and accountability. *British Educational Research Journal, 20*(2), 155–174.

Abbott, I., Rathbone, M., & Whitehead, P. (2013). *Education policy*. London: SAGE.

Abbott, I., Rathbone, M., & Whitehead, P. (2019). *The transformation of initial teacher education*. Abingdon: Routledge.

Acland, A. H. D. (1908). *Report on the school attendance of children below the age of 5*. London: HMSO.

Adams, P. (2006). Exploring social constructivism: Theories and practicalities. *Education, 34*(3), 243–257.

Adhami, M. (2003). From lesson objectives to lesson agenda: Flexibility in whole-class lesson structure. In I. Thompson (Ed.), *Enhancing primary mathematics teaching*. London: McGraw-Hill.

Ahtiainen, R. (2017). Shades of change in Fullan's and Hargreaves's models: Theoretical change perspectives regarding Finnish special education reform. *Helsinki Studies in Education, 13*, 1–170.

Ainscow, M. (2016). Diversity and equity: A global education challenge. *New Zealand Journal of Educational Studies, 51*(2), 143–155.

Alexander, C., & Weekes-Bernard, D. (2017). History lessons: Inequality, diversity and the national curriculum. *Race Ethnicity and Education, 20*(4), 478–494.

Alexander, R., Rose, J., & Woodhead, C. (1992). *Classroom organisation and classroom practice in primary schools: A discussion paper*. London: HMSO.

Alexander, R., Willcocks, J., & Nelson, N. (1996). Discourse, pedagogy and the national curriculum: Change and continuity in primary schools. *Research Papers in Education, 11*(1), 81–120.

Alexander, R. J. (2008). *Essays on pedagogy*. London: Routledge.

Allen, L. (2011). *Young people and sexuality education*. Cham: Springer.

Allen, R. (2008). *Choice-based secondary school admissions in England: Social stratification and the distribution of educational outcomes*. Online Ph.D. Thesis. Retrieved 8 January 2021, from http://eprints.ioe.ac.uk/632/1/Allen_2008_thesis_with_corrections.pdf

Allen, R., Burgess, S., Rasul, I., & McKenna, L. (2010). *Understanding school financial decisions*. DfE research report RR183. London: DfE.

Allen, R., & West, A. (2011). Why do faith secondary schools have advantaged intakes? The relative importance of neighbourhood characteristics, social background and religious identification amongst parents. *British Educational Research Journal, 37*(4), 691–712.

Ameen, R., & Hassan, N. (2013). Are faith schools educationally defensible? *Research in Teacher Education, 3*(1), 11–17.

Anderson, R. (2013). The history of Scottish education, pre-1980. In T. G. K.Bryce, W. M.Humes, D.Gillies, & A.Kennedy (Eds.), *Scottish education 4th edition: Referendum* (pp. 241–250). Edinburgh: Edinburgh University Press.

Andrews, J. (2018). *Does the claim of '1.9 million more children in good or outstanding schools' stack up?* London: Education Policy Institute.

Andrews, J., Hutchinson, J., & Johnes, R. (2016). *Grammar schools and social mobility.* London: Education Policy Institute.

Andrews, J., & Perera, N. (2017). *The impact of academies on educational outcomes.* London: Education Policy Institute.

Androne, M. (2014). Notes on John Locke's views on education. *Procedia-Social and Behavioral Sciences, 137,* 74–79.

Apple, M. W. (2006). Understanding and interrupting neoliberalism and neoconservatism in education. *Pedagogies, 1*(1), 21–26.

Arendt, H. (1961). The crisis in education. In H. Arendt (Ed.), *Between past and future: Eight exercises in political thought.* New York, NY: Viking Press.

Arnold, M. (1869). *Culture and anarchy: An essay in political and social criticism.* London: Smith, Elder & Co.

Ashbee, R. (2021). *Curriculum: theory, culture and the subject specialisms.* Abingdon: Routledge.

Augar, P. (2019). *Review of post-18 education and funding.* London: OGL.

Bainbridge, A., Troppe, T., & Bartley, J. (January 2022). Responding to research evidence in parliament: A case study on selective education policy. *Review of Education, 10*(1), 1–38.

Baird, J. A., Cresswell, M., & Newton, P. (2000). Would the real gold standard please step forward? *Research Papers in Education, 15*(2), 213–229.

Bajwa-Patel, M., & Devecchi, C. (2014). 'Nowhere that fits': The dilemmas of school choice for parents of children with statements of special educational needs (SEN) in England. *Support for Learning, 29*(2), 117–135.

Baker, K. (1993). *The turbulent years. My life in politics.* London. Faber and Faber.

Baker, K. (2013). *14-18-A new vision for secondary education.* London: Bloomsbury.

Ball, S. J. (1993a). What is policy? Texts, trajectories and toolboxes. *The Australian Journal of Education Studies, 13*(2), 10–17.

Ball, S. J. (1993b). Education, Majorism and 'the curriculum of the dead'. *Curriculum Studies, 1*(2), 195–214.

Ball, S. J. (2003). The teacher's soul and the terrors of performativity. *Journal of Education Policy, 18*(2), 215–228.

Ball, S. J. (2007). *Education plc: Understanding private sector participation in public sector education.* Abingdon: Routledge.

Ball, S. J. (2012). *The micro-politics of the school: Towards a theory of school organization.* London: Routledge.

Ball, S. J. (2017). *The education debate* (3rd ed.). Bristol: Policy Press.

Ball, S. J., Maguire, M., & Braun, A. (2012). *How schools do policy. Policy enactments in secondary schools.* London: Routledge.

Ball, S. J., & Nikita, D. P. (2014). The global middle class and school choice: A cosmopolitan sociology. *Zeitschrift für Erziehungswissenschaft, 17*(3), 81–93.

Barber, M. (1994). *The making of the 1944 education act.* London: Cassell.

Barber, M. (2002). The dark side of the moon: Imagining an end to failure in urban education. In L. Stoll & K. Myers (Eds.), *No quick fixes* (pp. 27–43). Abingdon: Routledge.

Barber, M. (2010). How government, professions and citizens combine to drive successful educational change. In A. Hargreaves, A. Lieberman, M. Fullan, & D. Hopkins (Eds.), *Second international handbook of educational change* (pp. 261–278). Cham, Switzerland: Springer.

Barker, I. (18 February 2011). Clint and me: Mossbourne head says school leaders are 'lone heroes'. *TES.* Retrieved from https://www.tes.com/news/clint-and-me-mossbourne-head-says-school-leaders-are-lone-heroes

Barker, I. (28 September 2012). RE doesn't have a prayer after EBac omission. *TES.* Retrieved 16 July 2021, from https://www.tes.com/news/re-doesnt-have-prayer-after-ebac-omission

Barlow, A. (1946). *Scientific man-power.* Government report. Retrieved 7 December 2020, from http://filestore.nationalarchives.gov.uk/pdfs/small/cab-129-9-cp-46-185-35.pdf

Barros, R. (2012). From lifelong education to lifelong learning. Discussion of some effects of today's neoliberal policies. *European Journal for Research on the Education and Learning of Adults, 3*(2), 119–134.

Bartlett, S. (2000). The development of teacher appraisal: A recent history. *British Journal of Educational Studies, 48*(1), 24–37.

Barton, C. (2019). *The ResearchED guide to education myths.* Woodbridge: John Catt.

Barton, G. (8 February 2018). Ofsted doesn't sack headteachers – But it is part of an unforgiving accountability system. *TES.* Retrieved 29 January 2021, from https://www.tes.com/news/ofsted-doesnt-sack-headteachers-it-part-unforgiving-accountability-system

Bates, A. (2015). *Transforming education: Meanings, myths and complexity.* London: Routledge.

Bates, B., & Bailey, A. (2018). *Educational leadership simplified: A guide for existing and aspiring leaders.* London: SAGE.

Bauckham, I. (2021). *Initial teacher training (ITT) market review report.* London: OGL.

Baxter, J. A. (2014). An independent inspectorate? Addressing the paradoxes of educational inspection in 2013. *School Leadership & Management, 34*(1), 21–38.

Baxter, J. A., & Cornforth, C. (2021). Governing collaborations: How boards engage with their communities in multi-academy trusts in England. *Public Management Review, 23*(4), 567–589.

Baxter, J., & Floyd, A. (2019). Strategic narrative in multi-academy trusts in England: Principal drivers for expansion. *British Educational Research Journal, 45*(5), 1050–1071.

Beare, H., Caldwell, B., & Millikan, R. H. (2018). *Creating an excellent school. Some new management techniques.* London: Routledge.

Beauvallet, A. (2014). English teachers unions in the early 21st century: What role in a fragmented world? *Revue LISA/LISA e-journal. Littératures, Histoire des Idées, Images, Sociétés du Monde Anglophone, 12*(8). Retrieved 19 May 2022, from https://journals.openedition.org/lisa/7108

Beck, J. (2012). Reinstating knowledge: Diagnoses and prescriptions for England's curriculum ills. *International Studies in Sociology of Education, 22*(1), 1–18.

Belfield, C., Britton, J., Dearden, L., & van der Erve, L. (2017). *Higher education funding in England: Past, present and options for the future.* London: IFS.

Bell, A. (1797). *An experiment in education, made at the male asylum of Madras. Suggesting a system by which a school or family may teach itself under the superintendence of the master or parent.* London: Cadell and Davies.

Bell, L., & Stevenson, H. (2006). *Education policy: Process, themes and impact.* Abingdon: Routledge.

Benn, C. (1980). Comprehensive school reform and the 1945 labour Government. *History Workshop, 10*, 197–204.

Bennett, S., Maton, K., & Kervin, L. (2008). The 'digital natives' debate: A critical review of the evidence. *British Journal of Educational Technology, 39*(5), 775–786.

Bennett, N. C., Newton, W., Wise, C., Woods, P., & Economou, A. (2003). *The role and purpose of middle leaders in schools.* Nottingham: NCSL.

Bentham, J. (1791). *Panopticon: Or, the inspection-house.* Dublin: Thomas Byrne.

Berlinski, C. (2008). *"There is no alternative" Why Margaret Thatcher matters.* New York, NY: Basic Books.

Bernardinelli, D., Rutt, S., Greany, T., & Higham, R. (2018). *Multi-academy trusts: Do they make a difference?* London: UCL Institute of Education Press.

Biesta, G. (2009). Good education in an age of measurement: On the need to reconnect with the question of purpose in education. *Educational Assessment, Evaluation and Accountability, 21*(1), 33–46.

Billett, S. (2018). Distinguishing lifelong learning from lifelong education. *Journal of Adult Learning, Knowledge and Innovation*, *2*(1), 1–7.

BIS. (2010). *Skills for sustainable growth* (Government Strategy Report). London: OGL.

Black, A. (2019). A picture of special educational needs in England: An overview. *Frontiers in Education*, *4*, 79.

Blackmore*, J., & Thomson, P. (2004). Just 'good and bad news'? Disciplinary imaginaries of head teachers in Australian and English print media. *Journal of Education Policy*, *19*(3), 301–320.

Blake, D., Hanley, V., Jennings, M., & Lloyd, M. (2000). 'Superteachers' the views of teachers and head teachers on the advanced skills teacher grade. *Research in Education*, *63*(1), 48–59.

Blatchford, P., Bassett, P., Brown, P., Martin, C., Russell, A., & Webster, R. (2009). *Deployment and impact of support staff project*. DCSF Research Brief. London: DCSF.

Blundell, C., Lee, K.-T., & Nykvist, S. (2016). Digital learning in schools: Conceptualizing the challenges and influences on teacher practice. *Journal of Information Technology Education: Research*, *15*, 535–560.

BoE. (1943). *Educational reconstruction* (Government White Paper). London: HMSO.

Bolam, R. (2004). Reflections on the NCSL from a historical perspective. *Educational Management Administration & Leadership*, *32*(3), 251–267.

Boli, J., Ramirez, F. O., & Meyer, J. W. (1985). Explaining the origins and expansion of mass education. *Comparative Education Review*, *29*(2), 145–170.

Bolton, P. (2010) *National challenge schools: Statistics*. London: House of Commons Library.

Bolton, P. (2012). *Education: Historical statistics*. London: House of Commons Library.

Bolton, P., & Hubble, S. (2019). *Who should pay for tertiary education?* London: House of Commons Library. Retrieved 18 February 2022, from https://commonslibrary.parliament.uk/who-should-pay-for-tertiary-education/

van Bommel, J., Randahl, A. C., Liljekvist, Y., & Ruthven, K. (2020). Tracing teachers' transformation of knowledge in social media. *Teaching and Teacher Education*, *87*, 102958.

Bowers, T., & Wilkinson, D. (1998). The SEN code of practice: Is it user-friendly? *British Journal of Special Education*, *25*(3), 119–125.

Braun, A., Ball, S. J., Maguire, M., & Hoskins, K. (2011). Taking context seriously: Towards explaining policy enactments in the secondary school. *Discourse: Studies in the Cultural Politics of Education*, *32*(4), 585–596.

Brehony, K. J. (2001). From the particular to the general, the continuous to the discontinuous: Progressive education revisited. *History of Education*, *30*(5), 413–432.

Brewer, R., & Movahedazarhouligh, S. (2018). Successful stories and conflicts: A literature review on the effectiveness of flipped learning in higher education. *Journal of Computer Assisted Learning*, *34*, 309–416.

Bridges, D., Smeyers, P., & Smith, R. (Eds.). (2009). *Evidence-based education policy. What evidence? What basis? Whose policy?* Chichester: Wiley-Blackwell.

Brighouse, T., & Waters, M. (2022). *About our schools: Improving on previous best.* Bancyfelin: Crown House Publishing.

Brockmann, M., & Laurie, I. (2016). Apprenticeship in England–the continued role of the academic–vocational divide in shaping learner identities. *Journal of Vocational Education & Training, 68*(2), 229–244.

Brown, M., & Rutherford, D. (1998). Changing roles and raising standards: New challenges for heads of department. *School Leadership & Management, 18*(1), 75–88.

Brown, M., & Rutherford, D. (1999). A re-appraisal of the role of the head of department in UK secondary schools. *Journal of Educational Administration, 37*(3), 229–242.

Brown, C., & Zhang, D. (2016). Is engaging in evidence-informed practice in education rational? What accounts for discrepancies in teachers' attitudes towards evidence use and actual instances of evidence use in schools? *British Educational Research Journal, 42*(5), 780–801.

Bruce, T. (2018). The importance of play. In C. Trevarthen, J. Delafield-butt, & A.-W. Dunlop (Eds.), *The child's curriculum: Working with the natural values of young children.* Oxford: Oxford University Press.

Bryce, T., & Humes, W. (2013). Scottish secondary education: Philosophy and practice. In T. G. K. Bryce, W. M. Humes, D. Gillies, & A. Kennedy (Eds.), *Scottish education fourth edition: Referendum.* Edinburgh: Edinburgh University Press.

Bubb, S., Crossley-Holland, J., Cordiner, J., Cousin, S., & Earley, P. (2019). *Understanding the middle tier: Comparative costs of academy and LA-maintained school systems.* Bromley: Sara Bubb Associates.

Burgess, S., Greaves, E., Vignoles, A., & Wilson, D. (2015). What parents want: School preferences and school choice. *The Economic Journal, 125*(587), 1262–1289.

Burkard, T. (2007). *Inside the secret garden: The progressive decay of liberal education.* Buckingham: UBP.

Burnard, B., & White, J. (2008). Creativity and performativity: Counterpoints in British and Australian education, *British Educational Research Journal, 34*(5), 667–682.

Bush, T. (1998). The national professional qualification for headship: The key to effective school leadership? *School Leadership & Management, 18*(3), 321–333.

Bush, T. (2006). The national college for school leadership: A successful English innovation? *Phi Delta Kappan, 87*(7), 508–511.

Butler, C. (2021). When are governing parties more likely to respond to public opinion? The strange case of the liberal democrats and tuition fees. *British Politics, 16*(3), 336–354.

Butt, G. (2008). *Lesson planning* (3rd ed.). London: Continuum.

Bynner, J. (2017). Whatever happened to lifelong learning? And does it matter? *Journal of the British Academy, 5*, 61–89.

CACE (England). (1963). *Half our future*. London: HMSO.

Callaghan, J. (1976). Towards a national debate: The Prime Minister's Ruskin speech. *Education, 148*(17), 332–333.

Calvert, M. (2009). From 'pastoral care' to 'care': Meanings and practices. *Pastoral Care in Education, 27*(4), 267–277.

Campbell, L. (2019). Pedagogical bricolage and teacher agency: Towards a culture of creative professionalism. *Educational Philosophy and Theory, 51*(1), 31–40.

Carpenter, M. (1851). *Reformatory schools, for the children of the perishing and dangerous classes, and for juvenile offenders*. London: Gilpin.

Carpentier, V. (2018). *Expansion and differentiation on higher education: The historical trajectories of the UK, the USA and France*. London: Centre for Global Higher Education.

Carter, L. (2016). 'Experimental' secondary modern education in Britain, 1948–1958. *Cultural and Social History, 13*(1), 23–41.

Case, P., Case, S., & Catling, S. (2000). Please show you're working: A critical assessment of the impact of ofsted inspection on primary teachers, *British Journal of Sociology of Education, 21*(4), 605–621.

Caslin, M. (2017). The SEN/D child. In A. Owen (Ed.), *Childhood today*. London: SAGE.

Cedefop. (2018). *The changing nature and role of vocational education and training in Europe. Volume 4: Changing patterns of enrolment in upper secondary initial vocational education and training (IVET) 1995–2015*. Luxembourg: Publications Office of the European Union.

Charles, M. (2017). Venus, mars, and math: Gender, societal affluence, and eighth graders' aspirations for STEM. *Socius, 3*, 1–16.

Chitty, C. (1989). *Towards a new education system: The victory of the new right?* Lewes: Falmer Press.

Chitty, C. (1991). *The great debate: The politics of the secondary school curriculum, 1976–1988*. Doctoral thesis, London: Institute of Education, University of London.

Chitty, C. (2014). *Education policy in Britain* (3rd ed.). London: MacMillan.

Christodoulu, D. (2014). *Seven myths about education*. Abingdon: Routledge.

Churchill, W. S. (1942). *The unrelenting struggle, 1942*. London: Cassell.

Cigman, R. (Ed.). (2007). *Included or excluded? The challenge of the mainstream for some SEN children*. Abingdon: Routledge.

Cingolani, P. (2019). Neoliberalism, outsourcing, and domination. In A. Scribano, F. T. Lopez, & M. E. Korstanie (Eds.), *Neoliberalism in multi-disciplinary perspective* (pp. 171–184). Cham, Switzerland: Palgrave Macmillan.

CIPD. (2017). *From 'inadequate' to 'outstanding': Making the UK's skills system world class*. Policy Report. London: CIPD.

Clapham, A. (2015). Post-fabrication and putting on a show: Examining the impact of short notice inspections. *British Educational Research Journal, 41*(4), 613–628.

Clark, M. (2018). The phonics screening check: Intended and unintended effects on early years classrooms in England. *Education Journal, 349*, 29–33.

Clark, M., & Glazzard, J. (Eds.). (2018). *The phonics screening check 2012–2017: An independent enquiry into the views of head teachers, teachers and parents.* Birmingham: Newman University.

Clegg, N., Allen, R., Fernandez, S., Freedman, S., & Kinnock, S. (2016). *Commission on inequality in education.* London: Social Market Foundation.

Cliffe, J., Fuller, K., & Moorosi, P. (2018). Secondary school leadership preparation and development: Experiences and aspirations of members of senior leadership teams. *Management in Education, 32*(2), 85–91.

Clotfelter, C. T., Ladd, H. F., & Vigdor, J. L. (2007). Teacher credentials and student achievement: Longitudinal analysis with student fixed effects. *Economics of Education Review, 26*(6), 673–682.

Cochrane, H., & Soni, A. (2020). Education, health and care plans: What do we know so far? *Support for Learning, 35*(3), 372–388.

Coldwell, M., Greany, T., Higgins, S., Brown, C., Maxwell, B., Stiell, B., & Burns, H. (2017). *Evidence-informed teaching: An evaluation of progress in England.* Research Report. London: DfE.

Collarbone, D. P. (2005). Touching tomorrow: Remodelling in English schools. *Australian Economic Review, 38*(1), 75–82.

Collins, J. (2001). *Good to great.* London: Random House.

Collinson, V. (2001). Intellectual, social, and moral development: Why technology cannot replace teachers. *The High School Journal, 85*(1), 35–44.

Connell, R. (2013). Why do market 'reforms' persistently increase inequality? *Discourse: Studies in the Cultural Politics of Education, 34*(2), 279–285.

Connor, L. (2016). Reflections on inclusion: How far have we come since Warnock and Salamanca? *Research in Teacher Education, 6*(1), 18–23.

Conservative Party. (1979). *Election manifesto.* Retrieved 15 December 2020, from https://www.margaretthatcher.org/document/110858

Conservative Party. (2006). *Commission on special educational needs in education.* The second report. London: The Conservatives.

Conservative Party. (2017). *Election manifesto.* Retrieved 13 May 2022, from https://ucrel.lancs.ac.uk/wmatrix/ukmanifestos2017/localpdf/Conservatives.pdf

Cooper, P. A. (1993). Paradigm shifts in designed instruction: From behaviorism to cognitivism to constructivism. *Educational Technology, 33*(5), 12–19.

Copeland, J. (2019). A critical reflection on the reasoning behind, and effectiveness of, the application of the pupil premium grant within primary schools. *Management in Education, 33*(2), 70–76.

Corry, D., & Stoker, G. (2002). *New localism: Refashioning the centre-local relationship.* London: The New Local Government Network.

Courtney, S. J. (2015). Corporatised leadership in English schools. *Journal of Educational Administration and History, 47*(3), 214–231.

Courtney, S. J. (2016). Post-panopticism and school inspection in England. *British Journal of Sociology of Education*, *37*(4), 623–642.

Courtney, S. J., & Gunter, H. M. (2015). Get off my bus! School leaders, vision work and the elimination of teachers. *International Journal of Leadership in Education*, *18*(4), 395–417.

Craske, J. (2018). 'You can't show impact with a new pair of shoes': Negotiating disadvantage through pupil premium. *Journal of Education Policy*, *33*(4), 526–557.

Crawford, M., Maxwell, B., Coldron, J., & Simkins, T. (2020). Local authorities as actors in the emerging 'school-led' system in England. *Educational Review*, 1–17. Retrieved 19 May 2022, from https://doi.org/10.1080/00131911.2020.1739625

Crouch, C. (2015). The paradoxes of privatisation and public service outsourcing. *The Political Quarterly*, *86*, 156–171.

Cuff, B. M. P., Meadows, M., & Black, B. (2019). And investigation into the sawtooth effect in secondary school assessments in England. *Assessment in Education: Principles, Policy & Practice*, *26*(3), 321–339.

Cullinane, A., Erduran, S., & Wooding, S. J. (2019). Investigating the diversity of scientific methods in high-stakes chemistry examinations in England. *International Journal of Science Education*, *41*(16), 2201–2217.

Curran, H., & Boddison, A. (2021). 'It's the best job in the world, but one of the hardest, loneliest, most misunderstood roles in a school.' Understanding the complexity of the SENCO role post-SEND reform. *Journal of Research in Special Educational Needs*, *21*(1), 39–48.

Curran, H., Moloney, H., Heavey, A., & Boddison, A. (2018). *It's about time: The impact of SENCO workload on the professional and the school*. Bath: Bath Spa University/NASEN/NEU.

Cushing, I. (2021). Grammar tests, de facto policy and pedagogical coercion in England's primary schools. *Language Policy*, *20*, 1–24.

Davis, V. (1996). The early experience of Ofsted. In J. Ousten, P. Earley, & B. Fidler (Eds.), *Ofsted inspections: The early experience*. Oxford: Routledge.

Davy, Z., & Cordoba, S. (2020). School cultures and trans and gender-diverse children: Parents' perspectives. *Journal of GLBT Family Studies*, *16*(4), 349–367.

Day, C., & Sammons, P. (2016). *Successful school leadership*. Reading: Education Development Trust.

De Lissovoy, N. (2013). Pedagogy of the impossible: Neoliberalism and the ideology of accountability. *Policy Futures in Education*, *11*(4), 423–435.

De Vries, M. S. (2010). Performance measurement and the search for best practices. *International Review of Administrative Sciences*, *76*(2), 313–330.

Dean, D. W. (1992). Consensus or conflict? The Churchill government and educational policy 1951–55. *History of Education*, *21*(1), 15–35.

Dean, J. (1995). What teachers and headteachers think about inspection. *Cambridge Journal of Education, 25*(1), 45–52.

Deem, R. (1988). The great education reform bill 1988 – Some issues and implications. *Journal of Education Policy, 3*(2), 181–189.

Deem, R., & Baird, J. A. (2020). The English teaching excellence (and student outcomes) framework: Intelligent accountability in higher education? *Journal of Educational Change, 21*(1), 215–243.

Dekker, S., Lee, N. C., Howard-Jones, P., & Jolles, J. (2012). Neuromyths in education: Prevalence and predictors of misconceptions among teachers. *Frontiers in Psychology, 3*, 429.

Delors, J. (Ed.). (1996). *Learning: The treasure within*. Paris: UNESCO.

Demie, F. (2021). The experience of black Caribbean pupils in school exclusion in England. *Educational Review, 73*(1), 55–70.

Denman, J., & McDonald, P. (1996). Unemployment statistics from 1881 to the present day. *Labour Market Trends, 104*(1), 5–18.

DES. (1976). *School education in England – problems and initiatives*. London: HMSO.

DES. (1985). *Better schools* (Government White Paper). London: HMSO.

DES. (1987). *The National Curriculum 5–16* (Government Consultation Document). London: HMSO.

Dewey, J. (1938). *Experience and education*. New York, NY: Touchstone.

de Waal, A. (2009). *School improvement – or the 'equivalent'*. London: Civitas.

DfE. (1994). *Local Management of Schools*. DfE Circular 2/94. London: HMSO.

DfE. (2010). *The importance of teaching* (Government White Paper). London: HMSO.

DfE. (2011a). *The national Strategies 1997–2011*. London: OGL.

DfE. (2011b). *Support and aspiration: A new approach to special educational needs and disability* (Government Green Paper). London: OGL.

DfE. (2014a). *The national curriculum in England*. Framework document. London: OGL.

DfE. (2014b). Michael Gove speaks about computing and education technology. Retrieved 28 June 2021, from https://www.gov.uk/government/speeches/michael-gove-speaks-about-computing-and-education-technology

DfE. (2015a). *Academies annual report academic year 2013–14*. London: OGL.

DfE. (2015b). *Reading: The next steps*. London: OGL.

DfE. (2015c). *Special educational needs and disability code of practice: 0 to 25 years*. London: OGL.

DfE. (2016). *Coasting schools: Provisional data*. London: OGL.

DfE. (2017a). *Unlocking talent, fulfilling potential: A plan for social mobility through education*. London: OGL.

DfE. (2017b). Amanda spielman's speech at the festival of education. Retrieved 22 June 2021, from https://www.gov.uk/government/speeches/amanda-spielmans-speech-at-the-festival-of-education

DfE. (2018). *Statement of intent on the diversity of the teaching workforce – Setting the case for a diverse teaching workforce.* Explain or Change factsheet. London: DfE.

DfE. (2019a). *Functional skills reform.* FSQ reform factsheet. London: DfE.

DfE. (2019b). *Timpson review of school inclusion.* London: OGL.

DfE. (2019c). *Outcomes of pupils at the end of key Stage 4 by geography.* London: OGL.

DfE. (2020a). *Headteachers' standards 2020.* Retrieved 19 February 2021, from https://www. gov.uk/government/publications/national-standards-of-excellence-for-headteachers/head-teachers-standards-2020

DfE. (2020b). *Maintained school governance: Structures and role descriptors.* London: OGL.

DfE. (2020c). *School workforce in England.* Retrieved 23 April 2021, from https://explore-education-statistics.service.gov.uk/find-statistics/school-workforce-in-england

DfE. (2021a). *Induction for early career teachers (England).* London: OGL.

DfE. (2021b). *Understanding progress in the 2020/21 academic year.* London: OGL.

DfE. (2021c). *Early years foundation stage profile.* London: OGL.

DfE. (2021d). *Skills for jobs: Lifelong learning for opportunity and growth* (Government White Paper). London: OGL.

DfE. (2022a). *Levelling up* (Government White Paper). London: OGL.

DfE. (2022b). *Fairer higher education system for students and taxpayers.* Press release. Retrieved 22 March 2022, from https://www.gov.uk/government/news/fairer-higher-education-system-for-students-and-taxpayers

DfE. (2022c). *School workforce in England.* Retrieved 2 August 2022, from https://explore-education-statistics.service.gov.uk/find-statistics/school-workforce-in-england

DfE. (n.d.). *'Evidence check' memorandum: Raising the participation age.* DfE memorandum. Retrieved 18 February 2022, from https://www.parliament.uk/globalassets/documents/commons-committees/Education/evidence-check-forum/Raising-participation-age.pdf

DfEE. (1997). *Excellence in schools* (Government White Paper). London: HMSO.

DfEE. (1999). *The national numeracy strategy.* Cambridge: Cambridge University Press.

DfES. (2002). *Time for standards: Reforming the school workforce.* London: HMSO.

DfES. (2003). *Excellence and enjoyment: A strategy for primary schools.* London: HMSO.

DfES. (2004). *Pedagogy and practice: Teaching and learning in secondary schools.* London: HMSO.

Dickens, C. (1846). *Crime and education.* London: British Library. Letter to the Daily. Retrieved 15 December 2020, from https://www.bl.uk/collection-items/letter-from-charles-dickens-on-ragged-schools-from-the-daily-news

Dinham, A., & Shaw, M. (2017). Religious literacy through religious education: The future of teaching and learning about religion and belief. *Religions, 8*(7), 119–138.

Dix, P. (2017). *When the adults change, everything changes.* Bancyfelin: Crown House.

Doak, L. (2020). Realising the 'right to play' in the special school playground. *International Journal of Play, 9*(4), 414–438.

Dobson, G. J. (2019). Understanding the SENCo workforce: Re-examination of selected studies through the lens of an accurate national dataset. *British Journal of Special Education, 46*(4), 445–464.

Doherty, B. (1966). Compulsory day continuation education: An examination of the 1918 experiment. *The vocational aspect of secondary and further education, 18*(39), 41–56.

Dominguez-Reig, G., & Robinson, D. (2019). *16–19 education funding. Trends and implications*. London: EPI.

Done, E. J., & Knowler, H. (2020). A tension between rationalities: 'Off-rolling' as gaming and the implications for head teachers and the inclusion agenda. *Educational Review*, 1–20. doi:10.1080/00131911.2020.1806785

Donnelly, M., Brown, C., Batlle, I. C., & Sandoval-Hernandez, A. (2020). *Social and emotional skills. Education policy and practice in the UK home nations*. London: NESTA.

Doyle, A. C. (2000). *The memoirs of Sherlock Holmes* (Oxford Classics Edition). Oxford: Oxford University Press.

Drew, H., & Banerjee, R. (2019). Supporting the education and well-being of children who are looked-after: What is the role of the virtual school? *European Journal of Psychology of Education, 34*(1), 101–121.

Durbin, B., Wespieser, K., Bernardinelli, D., & Gee, G. (2015). *A guide to regional schools commissioners September 2015*. Slough: NFER.

Duschinsky, R. (2012). Tabula rasa and human nature. *Philosophy, 87*(4), 509–529.

Duxbury, P., & Bradwell, P. (2012). *Review of special school and mainstream unit provision*. Lincoln: Lincolnshire County Council.

Dwyer, C., & Parutis, V. (2013). 'Faith in the system?' State-funded faith schools in England and the contested parameters of community cohesion. *Transactions of the Institute of British Geographers, 38*(2), 267–284.

Earley, P., & Greany, T. (Eds.). (2017). *School leadership and education system reform*. London: Bloomsbury.

Eddo-Lodge, R. (2017). *Why I'm no longer talking to white people about race*. London: Bloomsbury Circus.

Edmond, N., & Price, M. (2009). Workforce re-modelling and pastoral care in schools: A diversification of roles or a de-professionalisation of functions? *Pastoral Care in Education, 27*(4), 301–311.

EEF. (2019). *Improving social and emotional learning in primary schools*. London: EEF.

EEF. (2021a). *Teaching and learning toolkit*. London: EEF.

EEF. (2021b). *Cognitive science approaches in the classroom: A review of the evidence*. London: EEF.

Eggleston, J. (1977). Making decisions in the classroom. *Cambridge Journal of Education, 7*(1), 5–11.

Egglestone, C., Stevens, C., Jones, E., & Aldridge, F. (2018). *Adult participation in learning survey 2017*. London: DfE.

Ehren, M., & Perryman, J. (2017). Accountability of school networks: Who is accountable to whom and for what? *Educational Management Administration & Leadership*, *46*(6), 942–959.

Elliott, A. (November 2012). Twenty years inspecting English schools—ofsted 1992–2012. *RISE Review*, 1–4.

Elton-Chalcraft, S., Lander, V., Revell, L., Warner, D., & Whitworth, L. (2017). To promote, or not to promote fundamental British values? Teachers' standards, diversity and teacher education. *British Educational Research Journal*, *43*(1), 29–48.

Ertmer, P. A., & Newby, T. J. (2013). Behaviorism, cognitivism, constructivism: Comparing critical features from an instructional design perspective. *Performance Improvement Quarterly*, *26*(2), 43–71.

Evans, P. (2004). A comparison of inclusion practice in OECD countries. *Education Canada*, *44*(1), 32–35.

Evans, L. (2011). The 'shape' of teacher professionalism in England: Professional standards, performance management, professional development and the changes proposed in the 2010 white paper. *British Educational Research Journal*, *37*(5), 851–870.

Evans, L. (2018). Re-shaping the EHEA after the demise of neoliberalism: A UK-informed perspective. In A. Curaj, L. Deca, & R. Pricopie (Eds.), *European higher education area: The impact of past and future policies*. Cham, Switzerland: Springer.

Exley, S. (2014). Are quasi-markets in education what the British public wants? *Social Policy & Administration*, *48*(1), 24–43.

Eynon, R., & Malmberg, L. E. (2021). Lifelong learning and the internet: Who benefits most from learning online? *British Journal of Educational Technology*, *52*(2), 569–583.

Faas, S., Wu, S. C., & Geiger, S. (2017). The importance of play in early childhood education: A critical perspective on current policies and practices in Germany and Hong Kong. *Global Education Review*, *4*(2), 75–91.

Farrell, P., Alborz, A., Howes, A., & Pearson, D. (2010). The impact of teaching assistants on improving pupils' academic achievement in mainstream schools: A review of the literature. *Educational Review*, *62*(4), 435–448.

Farrell, C., & Morris, J. (2004). Resigned compliance. Teacher attitudes towards performance related pay in schools. *Educational Management Administration & Leadership*, *32*(1), 81–104.

Feinstein, L. (2015). *Social and emotional learning: Skills for life and work*. London: Early Intervention Foundation.

Ferguson, D. (28 April 2019). 'I cook, clean and fix': How cuts are forcing headteachers to take on extra roles. *The Observer*. Retrieved 14 May 2021, from https://www.the-guardian.com/education/2019/apr/28/school-budget-cuts-headteachers-cook-clean-fix-naht-conference

Fleming, P. (2019). *Successful middle leadership in secondary schools: A practical guide to subject and team effectiveness*. London: Routledge.

Flintham, A. (2003). *When reservoirs run dry: Why some headteachers leave headship early.* Nottingham: National College for School Leadership.

Foote, K., Knaub, A., Henderson, C., Dancy, M., & Beichner, R. J. (2016). Enabling and challenging factors in institutional reform: The case of SCALE-UP. *Physical Review Physics Education Research, 12*(1), 010103.

Forde, C., McMahon, M., McPhee, A. D., & Patrick, F. (2006). *Professional development, reflection and enquiry.* London: Paul Chapman Publishing.

Foskett, N. (2012). Marketisation and education marketing: The evolution of a discipline and a research field. In I. Oplatka & J. Hemsley-Brown (Eds.), *The management and leadership of educational marketing: Research, practice and applications.* Bingley: Emerald Group Publishing Limited.

Fosnot, C. T. (Ed.). (2005). *Constructivism: Theory, perspectives and practice* (2nd ed.). New York, NY: Teachers College Press.

Foster, D. (2019). *Initial teacher training in England* (HC Briefing Paper 6710). London: House of Commons Library.

Foster, D., & Long, R. (2016). *Regional schools commissioners* (HC Briefing Paper 7308). London: House of Commons Library.

Foster, D., & Long, R. (2020). *The pupil premium* (HC Briefing Paper 6700). London: House of Commons Library.

Foster, D., & Powell, A. (2019). *T levels: Reforms to technical education* (HC Briefing Paper 7951). London: House of Commons Library.

Foucault, M. (1977). *Discipline and punish: The birth of the prison* (1995 ed.). New York, NY: Vintage.

Francis, B. (2000). The gendered subject: Students' subject preferences and discussions of gender and subject ability. *Oxford Review of Education, 26*(1), 35–48.

Francis, A. (2021). *Rethinking social mobility for the levelling up era.* London: Policy Exchange.

Francis, B., Mills, M., & Lupton, R. (2017). Towards social justice in education: Contradictions and dilemmas. *Journal of Education Policy, 32*(4), 414–431.

Francis, B., & Wong, B. (2013). *What is preventing social mobility? A review of the evidence.* Leicester: ASCL.

Freire, P. (2018). *Pedagogy of the oppressed* (50th Anniversary Edition). New York, NY: Bloomsbury.

Frick, T. W. (1991). *Restructuring education through technology.* Bloomington: Phi Delta Kappa.

Froebel, F. (1826). *The education of man* (Translated Hailmann, W.N., 1887). New York, NY: D. Appleton & Company.

Frost, D., & Harris, A. (2003). Teacher leadership: Towards a research agenda. *Cambridge Journal of Education, 33*(3), 479–498.

Fryer, R. (1997). *Learning for the 21st century: First report of the national advisory group for continuing education and lifelong learning.* London: National Advisory Group for Continuing Education and Lifelong Learning.

Fullan, M. (1998). Leadership for the 21st century: Breaking the bonds of dependency. *Educational Leadership, 55*(7), 6–11.

Fullan, M. (2002). Moral purpose writ large. *School Administrator, 59*(8), 14–17.

Fullan, M. (2004). *Systems thinkers in action: Moving beyond the standards plateau.* London: DfES.

Fullan, M. (2010). *All systems go: The change imperative for whole system reform.* Thousand Oaks, CA: Corwin Press.

Fullan, M. (2013). *Stratosphere. Integrating technology, pedagogy and change knowledge.* Toronto: Pearson.

Fuller, K. (2019). 'That would be my red line': An analysis of headteachers' resistance of neoliberal education reforms. *Educational Review, 71*(1), 31–50.

Furlong, J. (2013). Globalisation, neoliberalism, and the reform of teacher education in England. *The Educational Forum, 77*(1), 28–50.

Gandin, L. A. (2007). Construction of the Citizen School Project as an alternative to neoliberal educational policies. *Policy Futures in Education, 5*(2), 179–193.

Gane, N. (2012). The governmentalities of neoliberalism: Panopticism, post-panopticism and beyond. *The Sociological Review, 60*(4), 611–634.

Garrison, M. J. (2016). Resurgent behaviourism and the rise of neoliberal schooling. In K. J.Salman & A. J.Means (Eds.), *The Wiley handbook of global educational reform.* London: John Wiley & Sons.

GB. (1988). *The education reform act 1988.* London: HMSO.

Gewirtz, S. (1998). Conceptualizing social justice in education: Mapping the territory. *Journal of Education Policy, 13*(4), 469–484.

Gewirtz, S., Ball, S. J., & Bowe, R. (1993). Values and ethics in the education market place: The case of northwark park. *International Studies in Sociology of Education, 3*(2), 233–254.

Gewirtz, S., Maguire, M., Neumann, E., & Towers, E. (2019). What's wrong with 'deliver-ology'? Performance measurement, accountability and quality improvement in English secondary education. *Journal of Education Policy, 36*(4), 504–529.

Gibb, K., Tunbridge, D., Chua, A., & Frederickson, N. (2007). Pathways to inclusion: Moving from special school to mainstream. *Educational Psychology in Practice, 23*(2), 109–127.

Gibb, N. (2021). Education after Covid. We must not let the pandemic lead us astray from our mission to raise school standards. *Conservativehome.* Retrieved 18 June 2021, from https://www.conservativehome.com/platform/2021/03/nick-gibb-education-we-must-not-let-the-pandemic-lead-us-astray-from-our-mission-of-raising-school-standards.html

Gibbons, A. (2021). DfE criticised for promoting debunked learning styles. TES. Retrieved 5 October 2021, from https://www.tes.com/news/dfe-criticised-promoting-debunked-learning-styles

Gibbons, S. (2012). Big ideas: Valuing schooling through house prices. *Centrepiece, 17*(2), 2–5.

Gibbons, S. (2017). *English and its teachers. A history of policy, pedagogy and practice.* London: Routledge.

Gibson, A., & Asthana, S. (2000). Local markets and the polarization of public-sector schools in England and Wales. *Transactions of the Institute of British Geographers, 25*(3), 303–319.

Gilbert, C. (2012). *Towards a self-improving school system: The role of school accountability.* Nottingham: NCSL.

Gill, T. (2017). *The impact of the introduction of Progress 8 on the uptake and provision of qualifications in English schools.* Cambridge Assessment Research Report. Cambridge, UK: Cambridge Assessment.

Gillard, D. (2018). *Education in England: A history.* Retrieved 15 December 2020, from www.educationengland.org.uk/history

Gillborn, D., Demack, S., Rollock, N., & Warmington, P. (2017). Moving the goalposts: Education policy and 25 years of the Black/White achievement gap. *British Educational Research Journal, 43*(5), 848–874.

Gillies, D. (2013). The history of Scottish education, 1980 to the present day. In T. G. K. Bryce, W. M. Humes, D. Gillies, & A. Kennedy (Eds.), *Scottish education fourth edition: Referendum.* Edinburgh: Edinburgh University Press.

Glazzard, J. (2017). Assessing reading development through systematic synthetic phonics. *English in Education, 51*(1), 44–57.

Goepel, J. (2012). Upholding public trust: An examination of teacher professionalism and the use of teachers' standards in England. *Teacher Development, 16*(4), 489–505.

Gorard, S. (2001). International comparisons of school effectiveness: The second component of the 'crisis account' in England? *Comparative Education, 37*(3), 279–296.

Gorard, S. (2008). A re-consideration of rates of 'social mobility' in Britain: Or why research impact is not always a good thing. *British Journal of Sociology of Education, 29*(3), 317–324.

Gorard, S. (2009). What are academies the answer to? *Journal of Education Policy, 24*(1), 101–113.

Gorard, S. (2016). A cautionary note on measuring the pupil premium attainment gap in England. *Journal of Education, Society and Behavioural Science, 14*(2), 1–8.

Gorard, S., Siddiqui, N., & See, B. H. (2021). The difficulties of judging what difference the pupil premium has made to school intakes and outcomes in England. *Research Papers in Education, 36*(3), 355–379.

Gordon, P. (1988). UK commentary: The new right, race and education-or how the black papers became a white paper. *Race & Class*, *29*(3), 95–103.

Gordon, P., Aldrich, R., & Dean, D. (2013). *Education and policy in England in the twentieth century*. London: Taylor & Francis.

Gorski, P. (April 2019). Avoiding racial equity detours. *Educational Leadership*, 56–61. Retrieved from https://www.fairforall.org/content/pdfs/haakmat-consulting/avoiding-racial-equity-detours.pdf

Gove, M. (2011). The scale of our education challenge is so great that we need urgent freorm. On every front. *Conservativehome*. Retrieved 28 June 2021, from https://www.conservativehome.com/platform/2011/01/michael-gove-the-scale-of-our-educa-tion-challenge-is-so-great-that-we-need-urgent-reform-on-every-fr.html

Gove, M. (2013). The civil rights struggle of our time. City Hall speech published by DfE, retrieved from https://www.gov.uk/government/speeches/the-civil-rights-struggle-of-our-time

Graham, L. J. (2018). Student compliance will not mean 'all teachers can teach': A critical analysis of the rationale for 'no excuses' discipline. *International Journal of Inclusive Education*, *22*(11), 1242–1256.

Graham, B., White, C., Edwards, A., Potter, S., & Street, C. (2019). *School exclusion: A literature review on the continued disproportionate exclusion of certain children*. London: DfE.

Granoulhac, F. (2021). Twenty years on: The impact and legacy of the private finance initiative in UK schools. *The Political Quarterly*. DOI: 10.1111/1467-923X.12990

Graves, S., & Williams, K. (2017). Investigating the role of the HLTA in supporting learning in English schools. *Cambridge Journal of Education*, *47*(2), 265–276.

Gray, J. (1992). *Men are from Mars, women are from Venus*. London: Thorsons.

Gray, J., O'Regan, J. P., & Wallace, C. (2018). Education and the discourse of global neoliberalism. *Language and Intercultural Communication*, *18*(5), 471–477.

Greany, T. (2015). More fragmented, and yet more networked: Analysing the responses of two local authorities in England to the coalition's 'self-improving school-led system' reforms. *London Review of Education*, *13*(2), 125–143.

Greany, T. (2022). Place-based governance and leadership in decentralised school systems: Evidence from England. *Journal of Education Policy*, *37*(2), 247–268.

Greatbatch, D., & Teate, S. (2018) *Teaching, leadership and governance in further education*. London: DfE.

Gunn, A. (2018). The UK teaching excellence framework (TEF): The development of a new transparency tool. In A. Curaj, L. Deca, & R. Pricopie (Eds.), *European higher education area: The impact of past and future policies*. Cham, Switzerland: Springer.

Gunter, H. (2007). Remodelling the school workforce in England: A study in tyranny. *Journal for Critical Education Policy Studies*, *5*(1), 1–11.

Gu, Q., Sammons, P., & Chen, J. (2018). How principals of successful schools enact education policy: Perceptions and accounts from senior and middle leaders. *Leadership and Policy in Schools, 17*(3), 373–390.

Hager, P. E. (1959). Nineteenth century experiments with monitorial teaching. *The Phi Delta Kappan, 40*(4), 164–167.

Hager, P., & Beckett, D. (2019). *The emergence of complexity: Rethinking education as a social science*. Cham, Switzerland: Springer.

Halfon, R. (2021). *The forgotten: How white working-class pupils have been let down, and how to change it. House of commons education committee: First report of session 2021–22*. London: House of Commons.

Hall, C., & Noyes, A. (2009). School self-evaluation and its impact on teachers' work in England. *Research Papers in Education, 24*(3), 311–334.

Hall, S. (2003). New labour's double-shuffle. *Soundings, 24*(1), 10–24.

Hamblin, D. (1978). *The teacher and pastoral care*. Oxford: Blackwell.

Hargreaves, A. P., & Shirley, D. L. (Eds.). (2009). *The fourth way: The inspiring future for educational change*. Thousand Oaks, CA: Corwin Press.

Hargreaves, D. H. (2010). *Creating a self-improving school system*. Nottingham: NCSL.

Harris, A., Brown, D., & Abbott, I. (2006). Executive leadership: Another lever in the system? *School Leadership and Management, 26*(4), 397–409.

Harris, A., & Jones, M. (2017). Middle leaders matter: Reflections, recognition, and renaissance. *School Leadership & Management, 37*(3), 213–216.

Harris, A., Jones, M., Ismail, N., & Nguyen, D. (2019). Middle leaders and middle leadership in schools: Exploring the knowledge base (2003–2017). *School Leadership & Management, 39*(3–4), 255–277.

Harris, N. S. (1991). Progressive introduction of the Education Reform Act 1988 in the schools sector – The story so far. *Education and the Law, 3*(4), 165–177.

Harrison, A. (29 September 2013). Michael Gove acts to block 'damaging' early GCSE entry. *BBC News*. Retrieved 21 January 2021, from https://www.bbc.co.uk/news/uk-24326087

Hart, R. A., Moro, M., & Roberts, J. E. (2017). Who gained from the introduction of free universal secondary education in England and Wales? *Oxford Economic Papers, 69*(3), 707–733.

Hatcher, R. (2011). The conservative-liberal democrat coalition Government's 'free schools' in England. *Educational Review, 63*(4), 485–503.

Hattie, J. (2012). *Visible learning for teachers*. London: Routledge.

HC. (11 July 2018). Converting schools to academies. *Public Accounts Committee report*. Retrieved 19 May 2022, from https://publications.parliament.uk/pa/cm201719/cmselect/cmpubacc/697/69702.htm

HC. (2006). *Special educational needs. Third report of session 2005–06*. Vol.*I*. HC Report 478-1. London: The Stationery Office Ltd.

HC. (2009). *House of commons children, schools and families committee*. National Curriculum. HC Report 344-1. London: The Stationery Office Ltd.

HC. (2015). *House of commons education committee life lessons: PSHE and SRE in schools*. HC Report 145. London: The Stationery Office Ltd.

HC Deb. (4 February 1988). Vol 126 cc1174-97. Retrieved from https://api.parliament.uk/historic-hansard/commons/1988/feb/04/inner-london-education-authority

HC Deb. (15 June 1874). Vol 219 cc1589-623. Retrieved from https://api.parliament.uk/historic-hansard/commons/1874/jun/15/motion-for-a-select-committee#S3V0219P0_18740615_HOC_43

HC Deb. (16 February 1927). Vol 202 cc1026-72. Retrieved from https://api.parliament.uk/historic-hansard/commons/1927/feb/16/secondary-education].

Heath, A., Sullivan, A., Boliver, V., & Zimdars, A. (2013). Education under new labour, 1997–2010. *Oxford Review of Economic Policy*, 29(1), 227–247.

Heath, D. (2 November 2018). British Empire is still being whitewashed by the school curriculum – historian on why this must change. *The Conversation*. Retrieved 28 June 2021, from https://theconversation.com/british-empire-is-still-being-whitewashed-by-the-school-curriculum-historian-on-why-this-must-change-105250

Hebson, G., Earnshaw, J., & Marchington, L. (2007). Too emotional to be capable? The changing nature of emotion work in definitions of 'capable teaching'. *Journal of Education Policy*, 22(6), 675–694.

Hennessy, J., & Mannix McNamara, P. (2013). At the altar of educational efficiency: Performativity and the role of the teacher. *English Teaching: Practice and Critique*, 12(1), 6–22.

Hextall, I., & Mahoney, P. (2000). Consultation and the management of consent: Standards for qualified teacher status. *British Educational Research Journal*, 26(3), 323–342.

Higgins, S. (2020). *Teachers' media habits report*. London: Edge Foundation.

Hill, D. (2005). Globalisation and its educational discontents: Neoliberalisation and its impacts on education workers' rights, pay and conditions. *International Studies in Sociology of Education*, 15(3), 257–288.

Hill, R. (1997). Pupil Referral Units: 'Are they effective in helping schools work with children who have emotional and behavioural difficulties?' *Emotional and Behavioural Difficulties*, 2(1), 28–36.

Hillier, Y. (1990). Is vocationalism a conspiracy? (Book review). *Higher Education Review*, 22(2), 70–77.

Hirsch, E. D. (1967). *Validity in interpretation*. New Haven: Yale University Press.

Hirsch, E. D. (1988). *Cultural literacy: What every American needs to know*. New York, NY: Houghton Mifflin.

Hodgson, A., & Spours, K. (2019). Further education in England: At the crossroads between a national, competitive sector and a locally collaborative system? *Journal of Education and Work*, 32(3), 224–237.

Holloway, J., & Brass, J. (2018). Making accountable teachers: The terrors and pleasures of performativity, *Journal of Education Policy, 33*(3), 361–382.

Holt, M. (2017). More than a score. In D. Price (Ed.), *Education forward: Moving schools into the future.* London: Crux.

Hubble, S., & Bolton, P. (2018). *Higher education tuition fees in England* (HC Briefing Paper 8151). London: House of Commons Library.

Hursh, D. (2020). Editor's introduction: The end of neoliberalism. *Policy Futures in Education, 18*(1), 1–8.

Hustler, D. (1999). The ofsted lay inspector: To what purpose? In C. Cullingford (Ed.), *An inspector calls: Ofsted and its effect on school standards.* London: Kogan Page Ltd.

Ingrey, J. (2018). Problematizing the cisgendering of school washroom space: Interrogating the politics of recognition of transgender and gender non-conforming youth. *Gender and Education, 30*(6), 774–789.

Institute for Government. (2012). *The development of quasi-markets in secondary education.* London: Institute for Government.

Irby, D., & Clough, C. (2015). Consistency rules: A critical exploration of a universal principle of school discipline. *Pedagogy, Culture & Society, 23*(2), 153–173.

Isaacs, T. (2013). The diploma qualification in England: An avoidable failure? *Journal of Vocational Education & Training, 65*(2), 277–290.

Isaacs, T. (2014). Curriculum and assessment reform gone wrong: The perfect storm of GCSE English. *The Curriculum Journal, 25*(1), 130–147.

Jackson, C. (2002). Can single-sex classes in co-educational schools enhance the learning experiences of girls and/or boys? An exploration of pupils' perceptions. *British Educational Research Journal, 28*(1), 37–48.

Jackson, P. M. (2011). Governance by numbers: What have we learned over the past 30 years? *Public Money & Management, 31*(1), 13–26.

Jackson, P. W. (1990, orig. 1968). *Life in classrooms.* New York, NY: Teachers College Press.

Jacobson, M. J., Kapur, M., & Reimann, P. (2016). Conceptualizing debates in learning and educational research: Toward a complex systems conceptual framework of learning. *Educational Psychologist, 51*(2), 210–218.

James, C., & Phillips, P. (1995). The practice of educational marketing in schools. *Educational Management & Administration, 23*(2), 75–88.

James, D. (2020). Is lifelong learning still useful? Disappointments and prospects for rediscovery. *Journal of Education and Work, 33*(7–8), 522–532.

James, E. (1949). *An essay on the content of education.* London: George Harrap.

James, L. (2017). *The question of knowledge.* London: ASCL/PTE.

Jasman, A. (2007). Big change question. *Journal of Educational Change, 8*(1), 85–90.

Jeffrey, B., & Woods, P. (1996). Feeling deprofessionalised: The social construction of emotions during an ofsted inspection. *Cambridge Journal of Education, 26*(3), 325–343.

Jenkins, E. W. (2000). Constructivism in school science education: Powerful model or the most dangerous intellectual tendency? *Science & Education*, *9*(6), 599–610.

Johnston, R. S., & Watson, J. E. (2004). Accelerating the development of reading, spelling and phonemic awareness skills in initial readers. *Reading and Writing*, *17*, 327–357.

Jones, K. (2004). A balanced school accountability model: An alternative to high-stakes testing. *Phi Delta Kappan*, *85*(8), 584–590.

Jones, K. (2016). *Education in Britain: 1944 to the present* (2nd ed.). London: John Wiley & Sons.

Jones, K., & Tymms, P. (2014). Ofsted's role in promoting school improvement: The mechanisms of the school inspection system in England. *Oxford Review of Education*, *40*(3), 315–330.

Judd, J. (22 October 2011). Education: Blunkett says 'naming and shaming' bad schools works. *The Independent*. Retrieved 21 January 2021, from https://www.independent.co.uk /news/education-blunkett-says-naming-and-shaming-bad-schools-works-1293402.html

Kanuka, H., & Anderson, T. (1999). Using constructivism in technology-mediated learning: Constructing order out of the chaos in the literature. *Radical Pedagogy*, *1*(2). https:// radicalpedagogy.icaap.org/content/issue1_2/02kanuka1_2.html

Kaser, L., & Halbert, J. (2009). *Leadership mindsets: Innovation and learning in the transformation of schools*. London: Routledge.

Kay, L. (2021). 'What works' and for whom? Bold beginnings and the construction of the school ready child. *Journal of Early Childhood Research*. Retrieved from https://doi.org/ 10.1177/1476718X211052791

Keddie, A. (2017). Primary school leadership in England: Performativity and matters of professionalism. *British Journal of Sociology of Education*, *38*(8), 1245–1257.

Kelly, E., Lee, T., Sibieta, L., & Waters, T. (2018). *Public spending on children in England: 2000 to 2020*. London: Institute for Fiscal Studies.

Kelly, S. (2017). *Reforming BTECs: Applied general qualifications as a route to higher education*. Oxford: HEPI.

Kemske, B. (2021). *Kintsugi: The poetic mend*. London: Herbert Press.

Kennedy, M. (2014). To kill a mockingbird and of mice and men axed as Gove orders more brit lit. *The Guardian*. Retrieved 28 June 2021, from https://www.theguardian.com/ education/2014/may/25/mockingbird-mice-and-men-axed-michael-gove-gcse

Khan, O. (2016). Colourblindness fails to deliver race equality. *Runnymede Trust Race Matters blog*. Retrieved 21 December 2021, from https://www.runnymedetrust.org/blog/ cerd-reflections

Kidson, M., & Norris, E. (2014). *Implementing the London challenge*. London: Joseph Rowntree Foundation.

Kofod, K., Louis, K. S., Moos, L., & Velzen, B. V. (2012). Historical perspectives on educational policy and political cultures. In K. Seashore Louis & B. van Velzen (Eds.), *Educational policy in an international context* (pp. 29–47). New York, NY: Palgrave Macmillan.

Kulz, C. (2021). Everyday erosions: Neoliberal political rationality, democratic decline and the multi-academy trust. *British Journal of Sociology of Education, 42*(1), 95–110.

Lancaster, J. (1806). *Improvements in education, as it respects the industrious classes of the community: Containing among other important particulars, an account of the institution for the education of one thousand poor children, borough road, southwark; and of the new system of education on which it is conducted.* London: Darton and Harvey.

Lander, V. (2016). Introduction to fundamental British values. *Journal of Education for Teaching, 42*(3), 274–279.

Lauchlan, F., & Greig, S. (2015). Educational inclusion in England: Origins, perspectives and current directions. *Support for Learning, 30*(1), 69–82.

Lawson, J., & Silver, H. (1973). *A social history of education in England.* London: Routledge.

Leask, M., & Terrell, I. (2013). *Development planning and school improvement for middle managers.* London: Routledge.

Leckie, G., & Goldstein, H. (2009). The limitations of using school league tables to inform school choice. *Journal of the Royal Statistical Society. Series A (Statistics in Society), 172*(4), 835–851.

Leckie, G., & Goldstein, H. (2017). The evolution of school league tables in England 1992–2016: 'Contextual value-added', 'expected progress' and 'progress 8'. *British Educational Research Journal, 43*(2), 193–212.

Lee, C. (2020). *Courage in the classroom: LGBT teachers share their stories.* Suffolk: John Catt Publications.

Lee, J. (2001). Policy variation among Japan, Korea, England and the United States. *Education Policy Analysis Archives, 9*(13), 13.

Lee, M., & Friedrich, T. (2011). Continuously reaffirmed, subtly accommodated, obviously missing and fallaciously critiqued: Ideologies in UNESCO's lifelong learning policy. *International Journal of Lifelong Education, 30*(2), 151–169.

Lees, M. (2016). *Estonian education system 1990–2016: Reforms and their impact.* Tallinn: Estonian Ministry of Education and Research.

Lemov, D. (2010). *Teach like a champion.* San Francisco: Jossey-Bass.

Le Métais, J. (1994). *Legislating for change. School reforms in England and Wales 1979–1994.* Slough: NfER.

Le Métais, J. (1995). *Legislating for change: School reforms in England and Wales 1079–1994.* Slough: NFER.

Levačić, R. (1998). Local management of schools in England: Results after 6 years. *Journal of Education Policy, 13*(3), 331–350.

Levačić, R., & Jenkins, A. (2006). Evaluating the effectiveness of specialist schools in England. *School Effectiveness and School Improvement, 17*(3), 229–254.

Lévi-Strauss, C. (1962). *The savage mind.* Chicago: University of Chicago Press.

Lightman, B. (16 March 2017). School leaders aren't to blame for 'gaming' the system. *Schoolsweek*. Retrieved 28 June 2021, from https://schoolsweek.co.uk/school-leaders-arent-to-blame-for-gaming-the-system/

Littlecott, H. J., Long, S., Hawkins, J., Murphy, S., Hewitt, G., Eccles, G., & Moore, G. F. (2018). Health improvement and educational attainment in secondary schools: Complementary or competing priorities? Exploratory analyses from the school health research network in Wales. *Health Education & Behavior, 45*(4), 635–644.

Lloyd, C. (2008). Removing barriers to achievement: A strategy for inclusion or exclusion? *International Journal of Inclusive Education, 12*(2), 221–236.

Locke, K. (2015). Performativity, performance and education. *Educational Philosophy and Theory, 47*(3), 247–259.

Long, R. (2017). *GCSE, A level and AS reform (England)* (HC Briefing Paper 06962). London: House of Commons Library.

Long, R., & Danechi, S. (2019). *Faith schools in England: FAQs* (HC Briefing Paper 06972). London: House of Commons Library.

Long, R., Loft, P., & Danechi, S. (2019). *Religious education in schools (England)* (HC Briefing Paper 07167). London: House of Commons Library.

Lord, P., Wespieser, K., Harland, J., Fellows, T., & Theobald, K. (2016). *Executive headteachers: What's in a name? A full report of the findings*. Slough, Birmingham and London: NFER, NGA and TFLT.

Louden, L. (2012). *Distinctive and inclusive: The national society and church of England schools 1811–2011*. London: The National Society.

Loxley, A., & Thomas, G. (2001). Neo-conservatives, neo-liberals, the new left and inclusion: Stirring the pot. *Cambridge Journal of Education, 31*(3), 291–301.

Lyotard, J.-F. (1979). *The postmodern condition: A report on knowledge* (Tr. B. Bennington, & B. Massumi, 1984). Manchester: Manchester University Press.

Machin, S., & McNally, S. (2008). The literacy hour. *Journal of Public Economics, 92*(5–6), 1441–1462.

MacLure, S. (8 November 1987). A radical proposal for English schools. *New York Times*, 57.

Mahoney, J. L., Durlak, J. A., & Weissberg, R. P. (2018). An update on social and emotional learning outcome research. *Phi Delta Kappan, 100*(4), 18–23.

Mahoney, P., & Hextall, I. (2013). 'Building schools for the future': 'transformation' for social justice or expensive blunder? *British Educational Research Journal, 39*(5), 853–871.

Maisuria, A., & Cole, M. (2017). The neoliberalization of higher education in England: An alternative is possible. *Policy Futures in Education, 15*(6), 602–619.

Major, J. (1991). Speech to the windsor fellowship, 25 September 1991. Retrieved 8 January 2021, from http://www.johnmajorarchive.org.uk/1991/mr-majors-speech-to-the-windsor-fellowship-25-september-1991/.

Malcolm, A. (2018). Exclusions and alternative provision: Piecing together the picture. *Emotional and Behavioural Difficulties, 23*(1), 69–80.

Male, T. (2018). School leadership in England: Reflections on research activity between 1997 and 2017. *Educational Futures, 9*(1), 4–17.

Male, T. (2019). Governance in multi-academy trusts (MATs)-Evidence from the field. *EERA Proceedings of ECER*, 1–22.

Mandler, G. (2002). Origins of the cognitive (r)evolution. *Journal of the History of the Behavioral Sciences, 38*, 339–353.

Maringe, F. (2012). Integrating marketing into the leadership and management of schools: A curriculum-focused approach. In I. Oplatka & J. Hemsley-brown (Eds.), *The management and leadership of educational marketing: Research, practice and applications*. Bingley: Emerald Group Publishing Limited.

Marquand, D. (1988). *The unprincipled society. New demands and old politics*. London: Fontana Press.

Marsh, H. F. (1811). *The national religion the foundation of national education*. London: SPCK.

Martin, S., & Cloke, C. (2000). Standards for the award of qualified teacher status: Reflections on assessment implications. *Assessment & Evaluation in Higher Education, 25*(2), 183–190.

Martindale, N. (2019). Does outsourcing school systems degrade education workforces? Evidence from 18,000 English state schools. *British Journal of Sociology of Education, 40*(8), 1015–1036.

Martinez, C., & Pritchard, J. (2019). *Proceed with caution. What makes personal budgets work?* London: ReformUK.

Mateos, P., Singleton, A., & Longley, P. (2009). Uncertainty in the analysis of ethnicity classifications: Issues of extent and aggregation of ethnic groups. *Journal of Ethnic and Migration Studies, 35*(9), 1437–1460.

Mathou, C., Sarazin, M. A., & Dumay, X. (2022). Whither employment protections? Deregulation and the flexibilisation of the teaching workforce in the state-funded sector. *Journal of Education Policy, 37*(2), 285–307.

McCall, A. (26 November 2017). 25 year of empowering parents. *The Times*. Retrieved 31 December 2020, from https://www.thetimes.co.uk/article/25-years-of-empowering-parents-best-uk-schools-guide-t6wkp37js

McCulloch, G. (1994). *Educational reconstruction: The 1944 education act and the 21st century*. London: Woburn.

McCulloch, G. (2002). Local education authorities and the organisation of secondary education, 1943–1950. *Oxford Review of Education, 28*(2), 235–246.

McCulloch, G., & Sobell, E. (1994). Towards a social history of the secondary modern schools. *History of Education, 23*(3), 275–286.

McGill, R. M. (2016). War boards. *@TeacherToolkit*. Retrieved 21 January 2021, from https://www.teachertoolkit.co.uk/2016/03/14/classcharts-2/

McLaren, P. (1988). Culture or canon? Critical pedagogy and the politics of literacy. *Harvard Educational Review, 58*(2), 213–234.

McMaster, C. (2013). Working the 'shady spaces': Resisting neoliberal hegemony in New Zealand education. *Policy Futures in Education*, *11*(5), 523–531.

McQueen, H. (2014). *Performativity and accountability in the UK education system: A case for humanness*. New York, NY: Palgrave MacMillan.

McShane, J. (2020). We know off-rolling happens. Why are we still doing nothing? *Support for Learning*, *35*(3), 259–275.

Meo, A., & Parker, A. (2004). Teachers, teaching and educational exclusion: Pupil referral units and pedagogic practice. *International Journal of Inclusive Education*, *8*(1), 103–120.

Millard, W., Bowen-Viner, K., Baars, S., Tretheway, A., & Menzies, L. (2018). *Boys on track. Improving support for black Caribbean and free school meal-eligible while boys in London*. London: LKMco.

Miller, P. (2011). Free choice, free schools and the academisation of education in England. *Research in Comparative and International Education*, *6*(2), 170–182.

Miller, C., & Evans, S. (2019). England's worst schools REVEALED – Is YOUR child's school on the 2019 list? *Mirror*. Retrieved 10 January 2021, from https://www.mirror.co.uk/news/uk-news/breaking-englands-worst-schools-revealed-13899939

Mills, M., & Thompson, P. (2018). *Investigative research into alternative provision*. London: DfE.

MoE. (1956). *Technical education* (Government White Paper). London: HMSO.

Moore, D., Benham-Clarke, S., Kenchington, R., Boyle, C., Ford, T., Hayes, R., & Rogers, M. (2019). *Improving behaviour in schools: Evidence review*. London: Education Endowment Foundation.

Moore, A., George, R., & Halpin, D. (2002). The developing role of the headteacher in English schools: Management, leadership and pragmatism. *Educational Management & Administration*, *30*(2), 175–188.

Morris, R., & Dobson, G. (2021). Spending the pupil premium: What influences leaders' decision-making? *Educational Management Administration & Leadership*, *49*(2), 284–302.

Moyles, J. (2001). Passion, paradox and professionalism in early years education. *Early Years: An International Journal of Research and Development*, *21*(2), 81–95.

Mroz, M., Smith, F., & Hardman, F. (2000). The discourse of the literacy hour. *Cambridge Journal of Education*, *30*(3), 379–390.

Mukoro, J. (2021). The representation of gender in England's sexuality education policy. *Sexuality, Gender & Policy*, *4*(2), 130–141.

Myhill, D. (2021). Parents, don't worry if your child knows more about grammar than you do. *The Guardian*. Retrieved 28 June 2021, from https://www.theguardian.com/commentisfree/2021/feb/08/parents-child-grammar-home-schooling

NAO. (2002). *Individual learning accounts (Report)*. London: The Stationery Office.

Nash, C. J., & Browne, K. (2021). Resisting the mainstreaming of LGBT equalities in Canadian and British schools: Sex education and trans school friends. *Environment and Planning C: Politics and Space*, *39*(1), 74–93.

National Archives. (n.d.). Voluntary and comprehensive schools. *The Cabinet Papers*. Retrieved 25 November 2020, from https://www.nationalarchives.gov.uk/cabinet-papers/themes/voluntary-comprehensive-schools.htm

NATRE. (2019). *An analysis of a survey of teachers on the impact of government policy on student opportunity to study GCSE RS. An Eighth survey – July 2019*. Birmingham: NATRE.

NCTL. (2014). *Governance in multi-academy trusts*. Nottingham: NCTL.

Neumann, E., Gewirtz, S., Maguire, M., & Towers, E. (2020). Neoconservative education policy and the case of the English baccalaureate. *Journal of Curriculum Studies, 52*(5), 702–719.

Norwich, B. (2017). The future of inclusive education in England: Some lessons from current experiences of special educational needs. *REACH: Journal of Inclusive Education in Ireland, 30*(1), 4–21.

Norwich, B., & Kelly, N. (2004). Pupils' views on inclusion: Moderate learning difficulties and bullying in mainstream and special schools. *British Educational Research Journal, 30*(1), 43–65.

NRP. (2000). *Teaching children to read. An evidence-based assessment of the scientific research literature on reading and its implications for reading instruction*. Bethesda: NIH.

Nutt, J. (22 April 2018). Teachers shouldn't have to do the parents' job too. *TES*. Retrieved 16 July 2021, from https://www.tes.com/news/teachers-shouldnt-have-do-parents-job-too

Nylund, M., Rosvall, P. Å., Eiríksdóttir, E., Holm, A. S., Isopahkala-Bouret, U., Niemi, A. M., & Ragnarsdóttir, G. (2018). The academic–vocational divide in three Nordic countries: Implications for social class and gender. *Education Inquiry, 9*(1), 97–121.

O'Connor, K. (2022). Constructivism, curriculum and the knowledge question: Tensions and challenges for higher education. *Studies in Higher Education, 47*(2), 412–422.

OECD. (2002). *Understanding the brain: Towards a new learning science*. Paris: OECD.

OECD. (2017a). *Pedagocal knowledge and the changing nature of the teaching profession*. Paris: OECD.

OECD. (2017b). *Starting strong V: Transitions from early childhood education and care to primary education*. Paris: OECD.

Ofqual. (2019). *Entries for GCSE, AS and A level summer 2019 exam series*. London: OGL.

Ofsted. (1995a). *Annual report of her majesty's inspector of schools. 1993/4*. London: HMSO.

Ofsted. (1995b). *Annual report of her majesty's inspector of schools part 2: Quality and service in inspection 1993/4*. London: HMSO.

Ofsted. (2008). *The deployment, training and development of the wider school workforce*. London: HMSO.

Ofsted. (2010). *Workforce reform in schools: Has it made a difference?* London: HMSO.

Ofsted. (2013a). *Not yet good enough: Personal, social, health and economic education in schools*. London: OGL.

Ofsted. (2013b). *Religious education: Realising the potential*. London: OGL.

Ofsted. (2015). *Annual report of HMCI 2014/15*. London: OGL.

Ofsted. (2016). *Alternative provision.* London: Ofsted.

Ofsted. (2017). *Bold beginnings: The reception curriculum in a sample of good and outstanding primary schools.* London: OGL.

Ofsted. (2019a). *Multi-academy trusts: Benefits, challenges and functions.* London: OGL.

Ofsted. (2019b). *Annual report of HMCI 2018/19.* London: OGL.

Ofsted. (2019c). *Education inspection framework: Overview of evidence.* London: OGL.

Ofsted. (2021). *Research review series: Science.* Retrieved 18 June 2021, from https://www.gov.uk/government/publications/research-review-series-science/research-review-series-science

Osler, A. (2009). Patriotism, multiculturalism and belonging: Political discourse and the teaching of history. *Educational Review, 61*(1), 85–100.

Ostry, J. D., Loungani, P., & Furceri, D. (2016). Neoliberalism: Oversold? *IMF Finance and Development, 53*(2), 38–41.

Ouston, J., Fidler, B., & Earley, P. (1997). What do schools do after OFSTED school inspections – or before? *School Leadership & Management, 17*(1), 95–104.

Ozga, J., Segerholm, C., & Lawn, M. (2015). The history and development of the inspectorates in England, Sweden and Scotland. In S. Grek & J. Lindgren (Eds.), *Governing by inspection.* London: Routledge.

Pajo, B., & Cohen, D. (2012). The problem with ADHD: Researchers' constructions and parents' accounts. *International Journal of Early Childhood, 45*(1), 11–33.

Palikara, O., Castro, S., Gaona, C., & Eirinaki, V. (2019). Professionals' views on the new policy for special educational needs in England: Ideology versus implementation. *European Journal of Special Needs Education, 34*(1), 83–97.

Papacharissi, Z. (2015). *Affective publics: Sentiment, technology, and politics.* Oxford: Oxford University Press.

Parfitt, A. (2021). Turning around coast-based schools: An interpretive narrative analysis of a report on school reform in English coastal communities. *Improving Schools, 24*(3), 245–260.

Parish, N., Baxter, A., & Sandals, L. (2012). *Action research into the evolving role of the local authority in education.* London: DfE/ISOS.

Parish, N., & Bryant, B. (2015). *Research on funding for young people with special educational needs.* London: DfE/ISOS.

Parton, N. (2006). 'Every child matters': The shift to prevention whilst strengthening protection in children's services in England. *Children and Youth Services Review, 28*(8), 976–992.

Pashler, H., McDaniel, M., Rohrer, D., & Bjork, R. (2008). Learning styles: Concepts and evidence. *Psychological Science in the Public Interest, 9*(3), 105–119.

Perry, P. (2019). 'Phantom' compositional effects in English school value added measures: The consequences of random baseline measurement error. *Research Papers in Education, 34*(2), 239–262.

Perryman, J. (2002). Surviving special measures: A case study of a 'fresh start' school. *Improving Schools, 5*(3), 46–59.

Perryman, J. (2007). Inspection and emotion. *Cambridge Journal of Education, 37*(2), 173–190.

Perryman, J., & Calvert, G. (2020). What motivates people to teach, and why do they leave? Accountability, performativity and teacher retention. *British Journal of Educational Studies, 68*(1), 3–23.

Perryman, J., Maguire, M., Braun, A., & Ball, S. (2018). Surveillance, governmentality and moving the goalposts: The influence of Ofsted on the work of schools in a post-panoptic era, *British Journal of Educational Studies, 66*(2), 145–163.

Peters, M. A. (2004). 'Performative', 'performativity' and the culture of performance: Knowledge management in the new economy (Part 2). *Management in Education, 18*(2), 20–24.

Peters, M. A. (2018). The end of neoliberal globalisation and the rise of authoritarian populism. *Educational Philosophy and Theory, 50*(4), 323–325.

Pinto, L. E. (2015). Fear and loathing in neoliberalism: School leader responses to policy layers. *Journal of Educational Administration and History, 47*(2), 140–154.

Pirrie, A., Macleod, G., Cullen, M. A., & McCluskey, G. (2011). What happens to pupils permanently excluded from special schools and pupil referral units in England? *British Educational Research Journal, 37*(3), 519–538.

Plowden, B. (Ed.). (1967). *Children and their primary schools: A report of the control advisory council for education (England)* (Vol. 1: Report). London: HMSO.

Plutarch. (1927). *Moralia, volume I: The education of children. How the young man should study poetry. On listening to lectures. How to tell a flatterer from a friend. How a man may become aware of his progress in virtue.* Translated by F. C. Babbitt, Loeb Classical Library 197. Cambridge, MA: Harvard University Press.

Pollard, A., Collins, J., Maddock, M., Simco, N., Swaffield, S., Warin, J., & Warwick, P. (2005). *Reflective teaching* (2nd ed.). London: Continuum.

Pound, P., Denford, S., Shucksmith, J., Tanton, C., Johnson, A. M., Owen, J., & Campbell, R. (2017). What is best practice in sex and relationship education? A synthesis of evidence, including stakeholders' views. *BMJ Open, 7*(5), e014791. Retrieved 16 July 2021, from https://bmjopen.bmj.com/content/bmjopen/7/5/e014791.full.pdf

Pring, R. (2018). *The future of publicly funded faith schools. A critical perspective.* Abingdon: Routledge.

Priyadharshini, E., & Robinson-Pant, A. (2003). The attractions of teaching: An investigation into why people change careers to teach. *Journal of Education for Teaching, 29*(2), 95–112.

Propper, C., & Wilson, D. (2003). The use and usefulness of performance measures in the public sector. *Oxford Review of Economic Policy, 19*(2), 250–267.

Rasheed-Karim, W. (2020). The influence of policy on emotional labour and burnout among further and adult education teachers in the UK. *International Journal of Emerging Technologies in Learning, 15*(24), 232–241.

Rawls, J. (1971). *A theory of justice.* London: Belknap Press.

Reay, D. (2004). Exclusivity, exclusion, and social class in urban education markets in the United Kingdom. *Urban Education, 39*(5), 537–560.

Reese, W. J. (2001). The origins of progressive education. *History of Education Quarterly, 41*(1), 1–24.

Reilly, M. (2009). Opening spaces of possibility: The teacher as bricoleur. *Journal of Adolescent & Adult Literacy, 52*(5), 376–384.

Rezai-Rashti, G., Segeren, A., & Martino, W. (2017). The new articulation of equity education in neoliberal times: The changing conception of social justice in ontario. *Globalisation, Societies and Education, 15*(2), 160–174.

Rhodes, C., Brundrett, M., & Nevill, A. (2008). Leadership talend identification and development: Perceptions of heads, middle leaders and classroom teachers in 70 contextually different primary and secondary schools in England. *Educational Management Administration and Leadership, 36*(3), 311–335.

Richards, H. (2021). EHCP implementation in the early years: Constrictions and possibilities. *Support for Learning, 36*(2), 204–221.

Riordan, S., Jopling, M., & Starr, S. (2021). *Against the odds. Achieving greater progress for secondary students facing socio-economic advantage.* London: SMC.

Rippon, G. (2019). *The gendered brain: The new neuroscience that shatters the myth of the female brain.* London: Vintage.

Rizvi, F., & Lingard, B. (2009). The OECD and global shifts in education policy. In R. Cowen & A. M. Kazamias (Eds.), *International handbook of comparative education* (pp. 437–453). London: Springer.

Roach, J. (1991). *Secondary education in England 1870–1902: Public activity and private enterprise.* London: Routledge.

Robbins, L. C. (1963). *Higher education.* Report. London: HMSO.

Roberts, N. (2017). *'SATs' and primary school assessment in England* (HC Briefing Paper 07980). London: House of Commons Library.

Roberts, N. (2021). *The school curriculum in England* (HC Briefing Paper 06798). London: House of Commons Library.

Roberts, N., Foster, D., & Long, R. (2021). *The pupil premium* (HC Briefing Paper 6700). London: House of Commons Library.

Roberts, P. (2019). Performativity, big data and higher education: The death of the professor? *Beijing International Review of Education, 1*(1), 73–91.

Roberts-Holmes, G., & Bradbury, A. (2016). The datafication of early years education and its impact upon pedagogy. *Improving Schools, 19*(2), 119–128.

Robinson, K. H., Smith, E., & Davies, C. (2017). Responsibilities, tensions and ways forward: Parents' perspectives on children's sexuality education. *Sex Education, 17*(3), 333–347.

Roffey-Barentsen, J., & Watt, M. (2014). The voices of teaching assistants (are we value for money?) *Research in Education, 92*(1), 18–31.

Rogers, A. (1959). Churches and children—A study in the controversy over the 1902 education Act. *British Journal of Educational Studies, 8*(1), 29–51.

Rolph, C. D. (2004). The paradoxes of distributed leadership in schools. Focus paper iNET online international conference.

Rose, J. (2006). *Independent review of the teaching of early reading.* Nottingham: DfES.

Ross, A. (2021). *Educational research for social justice.* Cham, Switzerland: Springer.

Rousseau, J.-J. (1762). *Emile, or on education* (Translated Bloom, A., 1979). New York, NY: Perseus.

Rüber, I. E., Rees, S. L., & Schmidt-Hertha, B. (2018). Lifelong learning–Lifelong returns? A new theoretical framework for the analysis of civic returns on adult learning. *International Review of Education, 64*(5), 543–562.

Rudd, T., & Goodson, I. F. (Eds.). (2017). *Negotiating neoliberalism: Developing alternative educational visions.* Rotterdam: Sense Publishers.

Ruth, K., & Grollmann, P. (2009). *Monitoring VET systems of major EU competitor countries. The cases of Australia, Canada, USA and Japan.* Bremen: ITB Forschungsberichte 38/2009.

Sainsbury, D. (2016). *Report of the independent panel on technical education.* London: OGL.

Sammons, P. (2008). Zero tolerance of failure and New Labour approaches to school improvement in England. *Oxford Review of Education, 34*(6), 651–664.

Savadia, S., da Costa, C. P. G., & Jackson, H. (2021). Is the national curriculum inclusive? The perspectives of three undergraduates students regarding the current UK education system. In M. Moncrieffe (Ed.), *Decolonising the curriculum. Teaching and learning about race equality* (Issue 4). Brighton: University of Brighton.

Scanlon, M. (1999). *The impact of Ofsted inspections.* London: NFER and NTU.

Schupf, H. W. (1972). Education for the neglected: Ragged schools in nineteenth-century England. *History of Education Quarterly, 12*(2), 162–183.

Scullion, R., Moleworth, M., & Nixon, E. (2011). Arguments, responsibility and what is to be done about marketisation. In M. Moleworth, R. Scullion, & E. Nixon (Eds.), *The marketisation of higher education and the student as consumer.* Abingdon: Routledge.

Sellar, S., & Lingard, B. (2013). The OECD and global governance in education. *Journal of Education Policy, 28*(5), 710–725.

Selleck, R. J. W. (1972). The hadow report: A study in ambiguity. *Critical Studies in Education, 14*(1), 143–184.

Selwyn, N. (2011). *Schools and schooling in the digital age: A critical analysis.* Abingdon: Routledge.

Séville, A. (2017). From 'one right way' to 'one ruinous way'? Discursive shifts in 'there is no alternative'. *European Political Science Review, 9*(3), 449–470.

Sharp, J. G., Hopkin, R., & Lewthwaite, B. (2011). Teacher perceptions of science in the National Curriculum: Findings from an application of the science curriculum implementation questionnaire in English primary schools. *International Journal of Science Education, 33*(17), 2407–2436.

Sharpe, R. (2005). New approaches: The national numeracy project, the 'numeracy hour' and the teaching of mathematics. In K. Ashcroft & J. Lee (Eds.), *Improving teaching and learning in the core curriculum*. London: Routledge.

Shaw, A. (2017). Inclusion: The role of special and mainstream schools. *British Journal of Special Education, 44*(3), 292–312.

Shaw, I. L., Newton, D. P., Aitken, M., & Darnell, R. (2003). Do Ofsted inspections of secondary schools make a difference to GCSE results? *British Educational Research Journal, 29*(1), 63–75.

Sherington, G. E. (1976). The 1918 education act: Origins, aims and development. *British Journal of Educational Studies, 24*(1), 66–85.

Sherrington, T. (2018). What is a knowledge-rich curriculum? *Journal of the Chartered College of Teaching, 4*, 229–250.

Shirley, D., & Hargreaves, A. (2021). *Five paths of student engagement: Blazing the trail to learning and success*. Bloomington, IN: Solution Tree Press.

Silva, M. V. (2020). The privatization of secondary education in England through sponsored academies and multi-academy trusts. *Educação & Sociedade*. Retrieved 12 March 2021, from https://www.scielo.br/scielo.php?pid=S0101-73302020000100956&script=sci_arttext

Simkins, T. (2012). Understanding school leadership and management development in England: Retrospect and prospect. *Educational Management Administration and Leadership, 40*(5), 621–640.

Simkins, T. (2015). School restructuring in England: New school configurations and new challenges. *Management in Education, 29*(1), 4–8.

Simkins, T., Maxwell, B., & Aspinwall, K. (2009). Developing the whole-school workforce in England: Building cultures of engagement. *Professional Development in Education, 35*(3), 433–450.

Simon, B. (1991). *Education and the social order 1940–1990*. London: Lawrence and Wishart.

Simon, C. A., James, C., & Simon, A. (2021). The growth of multi-academy trusts in England: Emergent structures and the sponsorship of underperforming schools. *Educational Management Administration & Leadership, 49*(1), 112–127.

Slater, H., Davies, N. M., & Burgess, S. (2012). Do teachers matter? Measuring the variation in teacher effectiveness in England. *Oxford Bulletin of Economics and Statistics, 74*(5), 629–645.

SMC. (2019). *State of the nation 2018–19: Social mobility in great Britain*. London: OGL.

SMC. (2021). *Socio-economic diversity and inclusion. Employers' toolkit: Cross-industry edition*. London: SMC.

Smelser, N. J. (1991). *Social paralysis and social change. British working-class education in the nineteenth century*. Oxford: University of California Press Ltd.

Smith, A. (1785). *An inquiry into the nature and causes of the wealth of nations*. (4th ed.). Dublin: Colles, Moncrieffe, Burnet, Wilson, Jenkin, White, Whitestone, Byrne, Cash and M'Kenzie.

Smith, A. (2021). Special educational needs/disabilities and the evolution of the primary school Special educational needs co-ordinator (SENCo) in England. *Journal of Exceptional People*, *10*(18), 23–42.

Smith, E. (2011). Women into science and engineering? Gendered participation in higher education STEM subjects. *British Educational Research Journal*, *37*(6), 993–1014.

Smith, J. (2017). Discursive dancing: Traditionalism and social realism in the 2013 English history curriculum wars. *British Journal of Educational Studies*, *65*(3), 307–329.

Smith, P. (2009). New labour and the commonsense of neoliberalism: Trade unionism, collective bargaining and workers' rights. *Industrial Relations Journal*, *40*(4), 337–355.

Smith, S. (1810). Remarks on the system of education in public schools. *Edinburgh Review*, *16*, 326–333.

Southworth, G. (2004). A response from the national college for school leadership. *Educational Management Administration & Leadership*, *32*(3), 339–354.

Spens, W. (1938). *Secondary education*. Report to the Board of Education. London: HMSO.

Spielman, A. (2019). *HMCI commentary: Managing behaviour research*. Retrieved 4 October 2021, from https://www.gov.uk/government/speeches/research-commentary-managing-behaviour?hootPostID=8d37363331fbb6774948d3eaa449eb7b

Stainthorp, R. (2020). A national intervention in teaching phonics: A case study from England. *The Educational and Developmental Psychologist*, *37*(2), 114–122.

Starkey, H. (2018). Fundamental British values and citizenship education: Tensions between national and global perspectives. *Geografiska Annaler: Series B, Human Geography*, *100*(2), 149–162.

Staudt Willet, K. B., Greenhow, C., & Lewin, C. (2021). Tweeting across the pond: COVID-19 emergency learning networks in the United Kingdom and the United States through twitter #edchat. In E. Langran & L. Archambault (Eds.), *Proceedings of society for information technology & teacher education international conference* (pp. 1769–1778). Retrieved 6 September 2021 from online, United States: Association for the Advancement of Computing in Education (AACE). https://www.learntechlib.org/primary/p/219343/

Staufenberg, J. (3 July 2017). Academy boss: 20 schools is 'too small' for a multi-academy trust. *Schoolsweek*. Retrieved 12 March 2021, from https://schoolsweek.co.uk/academy-boss-20-schools-is-too-small-for-a-multi-academy-trust/

Stedman Jones, D. (2012). *Masters of the universe: Hayek, Friedman, and the birth of neoliberal politics*. Princeton: Princeton University Press.

Steinberg, S. R., & Down, B. (Eds.). (2020). *The SAGE handbook of critical pedagogies*. London: SAGE.

Stevens, D. (2010). A Freirean critique of the competence model of teacher education, focusing on the standards for qualified teacher status in England. *Journal of Education for Teaching*, *36*(2), 187–196.

Street, M. (2021). Theorising child well-being: Towards a framework for analysing early childhood education policy in England. *Journal of Early Childhood Research*, *19*(2), 211–224.

Sugrue, C. (2010). Plowden: Progressive education – a 4-decade odyssey? *Curriculum Inquiry*, *40*(1), 105–124.

Sullivan, A., Joshi, H., & Leonard, D. (2012). Single-sex and co-educational secondary schooling: What are the social and family outcomes in the short and longer term? *Longitudinal and Life Course Studies*, *3*(1), 137–156.

Supovitz, J. (2014). *Building a lattice for school leadership: The top-to-bottom rethinking of leadership development in England and what it might mean for American education*. Philadelphia: CPRE.

Sutcliffe, J. (23 December 1994). Long march to the middle ground. *TES*. Retrieved 31 December 2020, from https://www.tes.com/news/long-march-middle-ground

Sutherland, M. B. (1985). Whatever happened about coeducation? *British Journal of Educational Studies*, *33*(2), 155–163.

Sutton, A., Wortley, A., Harrison, J., & Wise, C. (2000). Superteachers: From policy towards practice. *British Journal of Educational Studies*, *48*(4), 413–428.

Swanson, E., McCulley, L. V., Osman, D. J., Scammacca Lewis, N., & Solis, M. (2019). The effect of team-based learning on content knowledge: A meta-analysis. *Active Learning in Higher Education*, *20*(1), 39–50.

Tardif, E., Doudin, P. A., & Meylan, N. (2015). Neuromyths among teachers and student teachers. *Mind, Brain, and Education*, *9*(1), 50–59.

Tawney, R. H. (1922). *Secondary education for all: A policy for labour*. London: Hambledon Press.

Taylor, T. (1994). Arthur Balfour and educational change: The myth revisited. *British Journal of Educational Studies*, *42*(2), 133–149.

Taylor, L. M., Hume, I. R., & Welsh, N. (2010). Labelling and self-esteem: The impact of using specific vs. generic labels. *Educational Psychology*, *30*(2), 191–202.

TDA. (2007). *Professional standards for teachers in England from September 2007*. London: TDA.

TEM. (2009). A short history of technical education. *Technical Education Matters*. Retrieved 15 December 2020, from https://technicaleducationmatters.org/2009/08/20/chapter-12-developments-in-the-1950s-and-1960s/

Tereshchenko, A., Mills, M., & Bradbury, A. (2020). *Making progress? Employment and retention of BAME teachers in England*. London: UCL Institute of Education.

Thane, P. (2011). The making of national insurance, 1911. *The Journal of Poverty and Social Justice*, *19*(3), 211–219.

Thatcher, M. (1976). The historic choice. Speech to conservative central council. *Margaret Thatcher Foundation*. Retrieved 7 April 2022, from https://www.margaretthatcher.org/document/102990

Thompson, M. (2006). Re-modelling as de-professionalisation. *FORUM: For Promoting 3-19 Comprehensive Education*, *48*(2), 189–200.

Thompson, P. (2010). Headteacher autonomy: A sketch of a Bourdieuian field analysis of position and practice. *Critical Studies in Education*, *51*(1), 5–20.

Thorpe, A., & Bennett-Powell, G. (2014). The perceptions of secondary school middle leaders regarding their needs following a middle leadership development programme. *Management in Education, 28*(2), 52–57.

Thrupp, M. (2005). The national college for school leadership: A critique. *Management in Education, 19*(2), 13–19.

Thrupp, M., & Willmott, R. (2003). *Educational management in managerialist times.* Maidenhead: Oxford University Press.

Tickle, L. (2000). Teacher probation resurrected: England 1999–2000. *Journal of Education Policy, 15*(6), 701–713.

Tidd, M. (2016). Science is so often forgotten at primary—many assume computing is the third core subject instead. *TES.* Retrieved 18 June 2021, from https://www.tes.com/news/science-so-often-forgotten-primary-many-assume-computing-third-core-subject-instead

Torgerson, C., Brooks, G., Gascoine, L., & Higgins, S. (2019). Phonics: Reading policy and the evidence of effectiveness from a systematic 'tertiary' review. *Research Papers in Education, 34*(2), 208–238.

Torgerson, C., Brooks, G., & Hall, J. (2006). *A systematic review of the research literature on the use of phonics in the teaching of reading and spelling.* Nottingham: DfES.

Tress, D. M. (1997). Aristotle's child: Development through genesis, oikos, and polis. *Ancient Philosophy, 17*(1), 63–84.

Tucker, M. S. (2011). *Standing on the shoulders of giants: An American agenda for education reform.* Washington, DC: NCEE.

Tuckett, A. (2017). The rise and fall of life-wide learning for adults in England. *International Journal of Lifelong Education, 36*(1–2), 230–249.

Turan, S. (2011). Plato's concept of education in 'republic' and aristotle's concept of education in 'politics'. *Education and Science, 36*(162), 31–38.

UNESCO. (1994). *The Salamanca statement and framework for action on special needs education.* Paris: UNESCO.

UNESCO. (2020). *Towards inclusion in education: Status, trends and challenges.* Paris: UNESCO.

UNICEF. (2012). *School readiness: A conceptual framework.* New York, NY: UNICEF.

Uttley, S. (2022). *Early career framework—school leaders' early experiences of the new model.* Research Paper 1/22. Portsmouth: Koinonia Group.

van Poortvliet, M., Clarke, A., & Gross, J. (2019). *Improving social and emotional learning in primary schools.* EEF Guidance report. London: EEF.

Vidal Rodeiro, C., & Vitello, S. (2021). Progression to post-16 education in England: The role of vocational qualifications. *Research Papers in Education,* 1–23. doi:10.1080/02671522.2021.1961295

Vieler-Porter, C. G. (2021). *The under-representation of black and minority ethnic educators in education.* Abingdon: Routledge.

Volante, L. (2004). Teaching to the test: What every educator and policy-maker should know. *Canadian Journal of Educational Administration and Policy, 35*, 1–6.

Vygotsky, L. (1934). *Thought and language* (Translated E. Hanfmann, G. Vakar, & A. Kozulin, 2012). Cambridge, MA: MIT Press.

Walker, J. L. (2001). A qualitative study of parents' experiences of providing sex education for their children: The implications for health education. *Health Education Journal*, *60*(2), 132–146.

Wallace, D., & Joseph-Salisbury, R. (2021). How, still, is the Black Caribbean child made educationally subnormal in the English school system? *Ethnic and Racial Studies*. DOI: 10.1080/01419870.2021.1981969

Wallace, M. (2003). Managing the unmanageable?: Coping with complex educational change. *Educational Management & Administration*, *31*(1), 9–29.

Warmington, P. (2009). Taking race out of scare quotes: Race-conscious social analysis in an ostensibly post-racial world. *Race Ethnicity and Education*, *12*(3), 281–296.

Warmington, P., Gillborn, D., Rollock, N., & Demack, S. (2018). 'They can't handle the race agenda': Stakeholders' reflections on race and education policy, 1993–2013. *Educational Review*, *70*(4), 409–426.

Warnock, M. (1978). *Report of the Committee of Enquiry into the education of handicapped children and young people*. London: HMSO.

Warnock, M. (2005). Special schools or not? *Education Review*, *19*(1), 13–17.

Warnock, M., & Norwich, B. (2010). *Special educational needs: A new look*. London: Continuum.

Warrington, M., & Younger, M. (2003). 'We decided to give it a twirl': Single-sex teaching in English comprehensive schools. *Gender and Education*, *15*(4), 339–350.

Waters, M. (2015). The Gove legacy: Where policy meets the pupil. In M. Finn (Ed.), *The Gove legacy: Education in Britain after the coalition* (pp. 63–74). Basingstoke: Palgrave MacMillan.

Watson, S. (2021). New right 2.0: Teacher populism on social media in England. *British Educational Research Journal*, *47*(2), 299–315.

Webb, R., Vulliamy, G., Häkkinen, K., & Hämäläinen, S. (1998). External inspection or school self-evaluation? A comparative analysis of policy and practice in primary schools in England and Finland. *British Educational Research Journal*, *24*(5), 539–556.

Webb, R., Vulliamy, G., Sarja, A., Hämäläinen, S., & Poikonen, P. L. (2012). Rewards, changes and challenges in the role of primary headteachers/principals in England and Finland. *Education 3–13*, *40*(2), 145–158.

Webster, R., & Blatchford, P. (2015). Worlds apart? The nature and quality of the educational experiences of pupils with a statement for special educational needs in mainstream primary schools. *British Educational Research Journal*, *41*(2), 324–342.

Webster, R., & Blatchford, P. (2017). *The special educational needs in secondary education (SENSE) study: Final report: A study of the teaching and support experienced by pupils with statements and education, health and care plans in mainstream and special schools*. London: UCL/Nuffield.

Webster, R., Bosanquet, P., Franklin, S., & Parker, M. (2021). *Maximising the impact of teaching assistants in primary schools*. London: Routledge.

West, A. (2020). Legislation, ideas and pre-school education policy in the twentieth century: From targeted nursery education to universal early childhood education and care. *British Journal of Educational Studies, 68*(5), 567–587.

West, A., & Bailey, E. (2013). The development of the academies programme: 'privatising' school-based education in England 1986–2013. *British Journal of Educational Studies, 61*(2), 137–159.

West, A., & Noden, P. (2019). 'Nationalising' and transforming the public funding of early years education (and care) in England 1996–2017. *British Journal of Educational Studies, 67*(2), 145–167.

West, A., & Wolfe, D. (2019) Academies, autonomy, equality and democratic accountability: Reforming the fragmented publicly funded school system in England. *London Review of Education, 17*(1), 70–86.

Wheelahan, L. (2015). Not just skills: What a focus on knowledge means for vocational education. *Journal of Curriculum Studies, 47*(6), 750–762.

Wheeler, S. (2018). The (re)production of (dis)advantage: Class-based variations in parental aspirations, strategies and practices in relation to children's primary education. *Education 3–13, 46*(7), 755–769.

Whetton, C. (2009). A brief history of a testing time: National curriculum assessment in England 1989–2008. *Educational Research, 51*(2), 137–159.

Whitebread, D. (2012). *The importance of play*. Brussels: Toy Industries of Europe.

Whitty, G. (1997). Creating quasi-markets in education: A review of recent research on parental choice and school autonomy in three countries. *Review of Research in Education, 22*, 3–47.

Whitty, G., & Menter, I. (1988). Lessons of Thatcherism: Education policy in England and Wales 1979–88. *Journal of Law and Society, 16*(1), 42–64.

Whitty, G., & Power, S. A. (2015). Selective, comprehensive and diversified secondary schooling in England: A brief history. In de Waal, A. (Ed.). *The ins and outs of selective secondary schools: A debate*. London: Civitas.

Wiborg, S., Green, F., Taylor-Gooby, P., & Wilde, R. J. (2018). Free schools in England: 'Not unlike other schools?' *Journal of Social Policy, 47*(1), 119–137.

Wigelsworth, M., Humphrey, N., & Lendrum, A. (2012). A national evaluation of the impact of the secondary social and emotional aspects of learning (SEAL) programme. *Educational Psychology, 32*(2), 213–238.

Wilby, P. (26 February 2018). Ofsted head: 'The last thing a chief inspector should be is a crusader'. Oh really? *The Guardian*. Retrieved 29 January 2021, from https://www.theguardian.com/education/2018/feb/06/ofsted-chief-inspector-amanda-spielman-q`2hijab

Wiliam, D. (2018). *Creating the schools our children need*. West Palm Beach, FL: Learning Sciences International.

Wilkins, A. (2017). Rescaling the local: Multi-academy trusts, private monopoly and statecraft in England. *Journal of Educational Administration and History*, *49*(2), 171–185.

Wilkins, C. (2015). Education reform in England: Quality and equity in the performative school. *International Journal of Inclusive Education*, *19*(11), 1143–1160.

Wilkinson, G. (2005). Workforce remodelling and formal knowledge: The erosion of teachers' professional jurisdiction in English schools. *School Leadership and Management*, *25*(5), 421–439.

Wilkinson, L. C., & Wilkinson, M. D. (2020). Value for money and the commodification of higher education: Front-line narratives. *Teaching in Higher Education*, 1–17. doi:10.1080/13562517.2020.1819226

Williams, P. (1965). The ascertainment of educationally subnormal children. *Educational Research*, *7*(2), pp. 136–146.

Williams, R. (17 May 2010). New minister Nick Gibb upsets teachers—already. *The Guardian*. Retrieved 8 April 2021, from https://www.theguardian.com/education/mortarboard/2010/may/17/nick-gibb-upsets-teachers

Williams, M., & Gersch, I. (2004). Teaching in mainstream and special schools: Are the stresses similar or different? *British Journal of Special Education*, *31*(3), 157–162.

Williams, M., & Grayson, H. (2018). *School funding in England since 2010 – what the key evidence tells us*. Slough: NFER.

Williams, T., Lamb, B., Norwich, B., & Peterson, L. (2009). Special educational needs has outlived its usefulness: A debate: Policy paper 4, 6th series, March 2009. *Journal of Research in Special Educational Needs*, *9*(3), 199–217.

Williams-Brown, Z., & Hodkinson, A. (2020). Development of inclusive education in England: Impact on children with special educational needs and disabilities. In R. Papa (Ed.), *Handbook on promoting social justice in education* (pp. 1561–1583). Cham, Switzerland: Springer.

Williamson, G. (2021). Learning from the crisis. Speech to the HEPI Conference 24 June 2021. Retrieved 28 June 2021, from https://www.gov.uk/government/speeches/education-secretary-at-hepi-conference-learning-from-the-crisis

Wilson, D., Croxson, B., & Atkinson, A. (2006). What gets measured gets done. *Policy Studies*, *27*(2), 153–171.

Wolf, A. (2011). *Review of vocational education: The Wolf report*. London: DfE.

Woodhead, C. (2002). *The standards of today and how to raise them to the standards of tomorrow*. London: Adam Smith Institute.

Woods, P., & Jeffrey, B. (1998). Choosing positions: Living the contradictions of Ofsted. *British Journal of Sociology of Education*, *19*(4), 547–570.

Woods, P., & Jeffrey, B. (2002). The reconstruction of primary teachers' identities. *British Journal of Sociology of Education*, *23*(1), 89–106.

Woods, P., & Simkins, T. (2014). Understanding the local: Themes and issues in the experience of structural reform in England. *Educational Management Administration & Leadership*, *42*(3), 324–340.

Woodward, W. H. (2000). Single sex lessons plan to counter laddish culture. *The Guardian*. Retrieved 21 December 2021, from https://www.theguardian.com/uk/2000/aug/21/alevels2000.educationnews

Wrigley, T. (2018). For the many: A curriculum for social justice. In S. Gannon, R. Hattam, & W. Sawyer (Eds.), *Resisting educational inequality*. London: Routledge.

Wyse, D., McCreery, E., & Torrance, H. (2008). *The trajectory and impact of national reform: Curriculum and assessment in English primary schools*. Primary Review Interim Report. Cambridge: University of Cambridge.

Wyse, D., & Styles, M. (2007). Synthetic phonics and the teaching of reading: The debate surrounding England's 'rose report'. *Literacy, 41*(1), 35–42.

Yeomans, E., & Sylvester, R. (2021). We have to teach new staff basic maths, says John Lewis boss. *The Times*, Wednesday 16 June 2021.

Young, I. M. (2006). Responsibility and global justice: A social connection model. *Social Philosophy and Policy, 23*(1), 102–130.

Young, M. (2011). The return to subjects: A sociological perspective on the UK coalition government's approach to the 14–19 curriculum. *Curriculum Journal, 22*(2), 265–278.

Zhao, Y. (2020). COVID-19 as a catalyst for educational change. *Prospects, 49*(1), 29–33.

Zierer, K. (2019). *Putting learning before technology: The possibilities and limits of digitalization*. Abingdon: Routledge.

GLOSSARY OF ACRONYMS

A level	GCE Advanced level examination (taken at 18+)
AP	Alternative Provision
AST	Advanced Skills Teacher
BoE	Board of Education (1899–1944)
BSF	Building Schools for the Future
CPD	Continuing Professional Development
CSE	Certificate of Secondary Education
CTC	City Technology College
DCSF	Department for Children, Schools and Families (2007–10)
DES	Department of Education and Science (1964–92)
DfE	Department for Education (1992–5, 2010–)
DfEE	Department for Education and Employment (1995–2001)
DfES	Department for Education and Skills (2001–07)
EBacc	English Baccalaureate
EEF	Education Endowment Foundation
EHCP	Education, Health and Care Plan
EMA	Education Maintenance Allowance
ERA	Education Reform Act (1988)
EYFS	Early Years Foundation Stage
EYFSP	Early Years Foundation Stage Profile
FE	Further Education (16+)
FSQ	Functional Skills Qualification
GCE	General Certificate of Education
GCSE	General Certificate of Secondary Education
GM	Grant Maintained
GNVQ	General National Vocational Qualification
HE	Higher Education (18+)
HLTA	Higher Level Teaching Assistant
HMCI	Her Majesty's Chief Inspector
HMI	Her Majesty's Inspector
ITT	Initial Teacher Training
KS	Key Stage

LA	Local Authority (renamed from LEA in 2004)
LEA	Local Education Authority (established 1902)
LMS	Local Management of Schools
MAT	Multi-Academy Trust
MFL	Modern Foreign Language
MoE	Ministry of Education (1944–64)
MTL	Masters in Teaching and Learning
NCSL	National College of School Leadership
NPQ	National Professional Qualification
NPQEH	National Professional Qualification for Executive Headship
NPQH	National Professional Qualification for Headship
NPQML	National Professional Qualification for Middle Leadership
NQT	Newly Qualified Teacher
O level	GCE Ordinary level examination (taken at 16+)
OfS	Office for Students
Ofsted	Office for Standards in Education
PFI	Private Finance Initiative
PPA	Planning, Preparation and Assessment
PRP	Performance Related Pay
PRU	Pupil Referral Unit
PSHE	Personal, Social and Health Education
QTS	Qualified Teacher Status
RSC	Regional Schools Commissioner
RSE	Relationships and Sex Education
SEAL	Social and Emotional Aspects of Learning
SEN	Special Educational Needs
SENCo	Special Educational Needs Co-ordinator
SEND	Special Educational Needs and Disabilities
SMC	Social Mobility Commission
SMSC	Spiritual, Moral, Social and Cultural (education)
STPCD	School Teachers' Pay and Conditions Document
TA	Teaching Assistant
TDA	Training and Development Agency
TEF	Teaching Excellence and Student Outcomes Framework
T level	Technical qualification taken at 18+
TLR	Teaching and Learning Responsibility
TSH	Teaching School Hub
TVEI	Technical and Vocational Education Initiative

INDEX